OPENING CREDIT

Every owner of a physical copy of

Opening Credit

can download the eBook for free direct from us at Harriman House, in a DRM-free format that can be read on any eReader, tablet or smartphone.

Simply head to:

ebooks.harriman-house.com/openingcredit

to get your copy now.

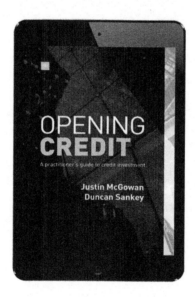

OPENING CREDIT

A practitioner's guide to credit investment

Justin McGowan & Duncan Sankey

Hh

HARRIMAN HOUSE LTD

18 College Street

Petersfield

Hampshire

GU31 4AD

GREAT BRITAIN

Tel: +44 (0)1730 233870

Email: contact@harriman-house.com

Website: www.harriman-house.com

First published in Great Britain in 2015. This special edition printed in 2017.

Copyright © Harriman House Ltd

The right of Justin McGowan and Duncan Sankey to be identified as the Authors has been asserted in accordance with the Copyright, Designs and Patents Act 1988.

Hardcover ISBN: 9780857192424

eBook ISBN: 9780857194688

British Library Cataloguing in Publication Data

A CIP catalogue record for this book can be obtained from the British Library.

Foreword
by Stuart C. Fiertz & Andrea Gentilini

ASSET MANAGEMENT IS AT AN UNQUESTIONABLY CRITICAL JUNCTURE, ONE THAT IS posing a serious threat to its long-term existence and historical role in allocator portfolios. To put this into perspective, several industry studies[1] indicate that 2016 was the most disappointing year for the average active asset manager since 2008 in terms of performance, inflows and profitability.

There is a number of diverse factors at play, including technical ones like central-bank-driven distortions as well as more structural aspects, such as increased regulatory burdens. Perhaps the most significant of these is the rise of passive investments – including smart-beta or risk-premia products – that are increasingly capturing the structural inefficiencies traditionally exploited by active asset managers but at a fraction of their cost. Given the lack of outperformance by active managers and the pressure on allocators to reduce fees in a low-expected-return environment, it does not come as a surprise that passive investments have steadily captured market share at the expense of the active management industry.

On top of all this, technological developments make it increasingly difficult to sustain the historical information advantages associated with traditional security research. Information advantages, which underpin sustainable, long-term outperformance, are crucial to active asset managers, and are the basic tenet upon which the USD 40 trillion industry rests.

Astonishingly, about 90% of the world's data has been produced in the past two years[2], and the time for any new information – on a security or a company – to hit all market participants empowered with a Bloomberg screen has shrunk from a few days back in the 1980s to a few milliseconds today. So much, then, for a sustainable information advantage. It would be naïve to postulate that such a significant, technology-driven trend will ever be reversed. Continuing to do things as we used to while expecting different results (i.e., suddenly all active managers outperforming again thanks to traditional security research) is the very definition of insanity – to paraphrase Einstein.

---

1 BCG, Global Asset Management Study 2016, "Doubling Down on Data"; Moody's Investor Services, 2017, "Asset Managers – Global: Passive Market Share to Overtake Active in the US No Later than 2024"
2 IBM, "Bringing big data to the enterprise".

As traditional analytical methodologies come under intensified scrutiny, new ones present themselves for examination. One about which we are particularly excited is Portfolio Intelligence, a technology-driven approach to transforming the growing abundance of data into insights for making better investment decisions.

Before elaborating further, we should emphasise that, among these contemporary challenges to performance, there is some good news. Industry data, academic research[3] and Cheyne's own track record over the years suggest that sustainable outperformance – despite all the challenges mentioned above – is still achievable, although it is increasingly concentrated among a dwindling (and often less visible) number of managers. Quietly, but with confidence, Cheyne has established a place in this exclusive group over the past 16 years. What will it take to retain that place? In essence, it is in striking the right balance between sticking to investment disciplines that have served us well historically and remaining open-minded to new paradigms and new approaches. Portfolio Intelligence is our latest example of such a new approach – one which, we believe, will generate benefits for all participants in the investment ecosystem and for asset allocators and investment managers alike.

We believe Portfolio Intelligence will transform investment management like Business Intelligence (BI) changed the common enterprise a few decades ago, and that analysing large amounts of data will help investors make more informed investment decisions.

Investment allocators and managers, especially those running institutional portfolios, reliant on a superabundance of data to make investment decisions, have mostly used what we call 'security data', e.g., a stock's liquidity, financial statements, ownership structure, price charts to achieve their goals.

Many of them are now turning to a new data set, one generated by their own investment processes. This is done to gain insight into their own behaviours, quantify their strengths and weaknesses, as well as to monitor the investment managers to whom they outsource mandates and ensure that aggregate exposures across the whole portfolio are aligned with their desired targets. Portfolio Intelligence today is much more than understanding where risks lie. It enables allocators to develop sophisticated investment skillsets and maximise performance potential.

For institutional allocators, Portfolio Intelligence facilitates a better understanding of traditional and factor exposures through the collection, validation, enrichment and aggregation of portfolio data coming from the external managers with whom they invest, as well as from internally managed portfolios.

Sophisticated data management technology and data aggregation techniques improve the understanding of asset allocation targets across geographies, sectors and asset classes, even where data is either hard to collect or hard to integrate. Portfolio Intelligence brings actionable transparency to decision making, allowing allocators to calibrate managers' investment skills and verify their adherence to their investment mandates. For example,

---

3 Kosowski R, Naik NY, Teo M, 2007, "Do hedge funds deliver alpha? A Bayesian and bootstrap analysis", JOURNAL OF FINANCIAL ECONOMICS, Vol: 84, Pages: 229-264, ISSN: 0304-405X.

the Novus platform can calculate all exposures on a daily basis to provide independent, real-time confirmation that guidelines are being adhered to by the portfolio manager.

With transparency and accountability now priorities for Trustees and Board Members, instantaneous investment decision data analytics are being used to report more incisively and to understand more fully the skills of appointed asset managers. A further step will be to fully analyse the effectiveness of the decisions taken at investment committee meetings.

As investment managers, Portfolio Intelligence allows us to quantify our skill sets and value-added, break them down by the degrees of freedom we are using to generate returns, and use those insights to sustain and deliberately improve performance over time. We can ask how enduring are those skill-sets and how do they differ, depending on the various markets in which a manager is deploying them? For example, in more / less liquid securities, higher / lower conviction positions, sectors, market caps, geographies, value / growth stocks.) We can also understand how effective the manager is at buying, sizing, and selling positions.

Striving to outperform relies on deliberate practice[4], which itself depends on clear feedback, which in turn hinges upon having access to the right data and the right analytics to measure what managers do well and areas in which they need to raise their game. Without such transparency (and feedback) deliberate practice is impossible. Managers will be good at what they practise, but will not practice what they need to be good at. Portfolio Intelligence furnishes such transparency.

Portfolio Intelligence is also key to applying the insights unearthed by behavioural and emotional finance, two disciplines which have gained traction in recent years. Assume, for example, that an investor would like to understand whether endowment bias – a phenomenon which makes managers hold on to winning positions beyond their productive life – hinders performance. Is this a statistically significant bias, based on a historical track record, or just conjecture? If it is significant, what potential improvement could be captured by seeking to eliminate this bias? What are the elements to focus on in order to achieve this goal? And finally, how does the investor practise without destroying the things he/she is getting right? This is made possible through Portfolio Intelligence, where data and analytics can quickly validate or disprove such hypotheses. Without such analysis remain only speculation and is liable to be flawed by even stronger behavioural biases. Finally, it allows us to communicate more openly and more concretely with allocators on how we add value, validating our claims of superior skill through numbers.

In this respect, we are delighted to announce that Cheyne and Novus have joined forces to further accelerate the development and integration of Portfolio Intelligence in our industry and share its benefits. Our firms started working together in November 2015 to deploy Portfolio Intelligence in the context of Cheyne's equity business, an asset-class where Novus is established as a world-class leader.

---

4 Matthew Syed, "Bounce".

Cheyne is excited to work with Novus to translate their unrivalled expertise in the domain of listed equities into the world of fixed income which, so far, has not benefited from such attempts to apply advanced skill-set analytics.

Cheyne intends to contribute its credit expertise to Novus, helping extend its capabilities into credit and the broader fixed income arena. In that context, Cheyne will work with Novus to garner input from trustees, asset allocators, portfolio managers and investment consultants. We are also looking forward to contributing to the growing understanding of credit factors, an area which has received much less attention from academia than equity market factors.

Opening Credit was written by Cheyne's Duncan Sankey and Justin McGowan to give allocators, portfolio managers and research analysts practical insights into how to use a holistic range of analytical approaches to consistently outperform in the credit markets. The central premise – to focus on a more human-centric approach to corporate governance – is cardinal, as the financial profile and the division of risk and reward can pivot from credit investors to shareholders by no more than a stroke of management's pen and a nod from an acquiescent board.

At Novus, we have been impressed by Cheyne's world-class expertise in fixed-income investing, built over more than a decade of foundational work and constant refinement. With thorough and robust market data operations and sophisticated portfolio analytics, Cheyne has created a track record and an analytical ecosystem to which many fixed income investors may only aspire. We are delighted to give this expertise a new digital home, one that the investor community will be able to access through the Novus platform.

Novus intends to devote its new-generation technology platform and engineering team to create a fully deployable fixed income analytical platform for the investment community.

Novus' platform innovation will revolve around three main functionalities. First, users will be able to disaggregate investment skill (whether their own or their managers') into its underlying composites, unearthing skills to hone and weaknesses to improve on.

As practitioners in this industry, we have tried to assess skill before through monthly return streams. Running these numbers alone lacks predictive power. Novus works with a more granular data set – daily position-level data – and the most robust data to distinguish the signal from the background noise.

Lastly, all this will happen in a fluid, responsive, and simple way, facilitated by the significant improvement in modern data-processing-technology and responsive interfaces, rather than using quantitative frameworks through locally-installed computing power, which has never been as responsive or as rapid).

In the meantime, we hope that you enjoy reading this special edition of *Opening Credit*. Cheyne has had the privilege and pleasure of working with the authors, Duncan and Justin, through three severe credit cycles and we can happily attest to the effectiveness of their approach to credit research, so eloquently explained within these pages. What's more – a clear example to illustrate the power Novus' analytics to quantify skill-set – consider Figure (a), where the authors' investment recommendations (as measured by their overweight and underweight ratings on individual corporate credits) have correlated strongly with future performance, a testament to their investment foresight.

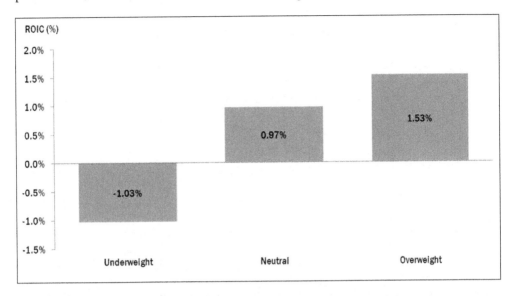

FIGURE (A) - AVERAGE RETURN ON INVESTED CAPITAL (ROIC) FOR SECURITIES MARKED 'UNDERWEIGHT', 'NEUTRAL', 'OVERWEIGHT' WITHIN CHEYNE'S CAPITAL CREDIT RESEARCH PORTFOLIOS, FROM MARCH 2006 - OCTOBER 2016.

Enjoy reading.

Stuart C. Fiertz CFA, CAIA
Co-Founder and Director of Research
Cheyne Capital Management (UK) LLP

Andrea Gentilini, Ph.D.
Managing Director, Head of Europe
Novus Partners, Inc.

Contents

About the Authors

Justin McGowan's career in finance spans 25 years. His analytical experience covers the full range of the capital structure, in both equity and credit instruments and he has worked on the sell- and buy-sides in disciplines ranging from bank loans, corporate bonds, emerging market equities, long/short equity and credit hedge funds, long-only funds and synthetic credit products. After an early apprenticeship in corporate finance, spent largely in Southern European markets, he moved on to work at a major credit ratings agency in New York and London, where he focused on the energy sector and subsequently on Germany's Mittelstand issuers across a wide range of industries.

Thereafter, he became an I.I.-rated emerging markets equity analyst and director of research, working principally out of New York, Mexico City and Rio de Janeiro. Returning to England in 2001, he re-entered the world of credit, where he has worked ever since. He has advised on investments in corporations and parastatal entities in the financial, manufacturing, energy, natural resources, retailing, consumer, healthcare and media sectors globally.

Justin has an MA in Medieval and Modern Languages from St Edmund Hall, Oxford. He is a holder of the Investment Management Certificate. He lives in Surrey with his wife and two daughters.

Duncan Sankey has 27 years' experience in credit investment and lending in a career spanning commercial and investment banking, a leading ratings agency, the origination and management of sell-side research teams and, most recently, fund management, including investment in alternative strategies and structured corporate credit. His analytical experience has covered the full gamut from financials and corporates (utilities, autos and suppliers, industrials, leisure, consumer products, transportation and real estate) to sovereigns, supra-sovereigns and parastatals. His experience of credit analysis and investment encompasses both established and emerging markets (particularly those of Asia and Eastern Europe) and he has worked in London, New York and Atlanta.

As a practitioner of credit in the wake of the corporate scandals during the first few years of the millennium, he became increasingly interested in the role played by corporate governance. This led him to pursue studies in the topic in the academic arena, where he has written on such matters as the bond market's failure to adopt standardised comprehensive bond covenants and contributed to published academic research on governance, regulation and financial market instability and its impact on policy. Duncan has written on credit issues for trade journals, discussed them on financial TV and often presents on credit matters to industry conferences. He is an associate of the London Centre for Corporate Governance and Ethics and a member of the Examinations and Education Committee of the Chartered Financial Analyst Society UK.

Duncan has an MSc in Corporate Governance and Ethics from the University of London and an MA in Medieval and Modern Languages from St. Edmund Hall, Oxford. He lives in London with his wife and daughter.

The authors have worked together for over 20 years. Since 2005 and 2003, respectively, Justin and Duncan have both worked in the award-winning corporate credit team of Cheyne Capital Management, one of Europe's leading alternative credit managers, participating in the management of both long-biased and long/short credit strategies specialising in global investment-grade and crossover corporate credit. Cheyne's long-only corporate credit funds have compounded at approximately 17% per annum since 2002 and have recorded cumulative default losses of only 0.34% over that period, despite navigating some of the worst market conditions ever experienced.

Preface

What is this book about?

THIS BOOK HAS ITS GENESIS IN THREE IMPORTANT PROBLEMS IN THE WORLD OF investing in credit. It is written to help solve them, and to that end brings to bear our experience in investment in general, and in the credit markets in particular.

The first problem is that much of the work available on investment in both credit and equity is quantitative in its focus. Without in any way seeking to diminish the importance of quantitative analysis, it strikes us that success in selecting investments that yield above-market returns and in avoiding investments that materially underperform and possibly default, depends on understanding the strategies that led to the quantitative output. Those strategies do not emerge from the ether but are the product of individual decisions. The focus of the investor should therefore be on identifying the persons responsible for the decisions and understanding their motives and the factors underlying their decision-making. Our goal, then, is to return the analysis of human factors to the centre stage of investment evaluation.

The second problem is that any analysis that focuses on the human elements of the corporation must also evaluate the rules that regulate how those humans interact and relate to their investors (i.e. corporate governance). However, for most investors this has been reduced to a box-ticking exercise. We champion a more holistic approach to finding the holes in the corporate structure, something we believe is of paramount importance for credit investors, since – while they may rarely use it – shareholders at least have the nuclear trigger of being able to fire the managers that steward their assets. Credit investors can only fall back on the contractual rights that they have been able to negotiate; they are stuck with the management and, hence, need to understand at the most fundamental level how management's actions are regulated.

The third and final problem is that much work on credit analysis seems to treat it as simply an adjunct to equity analysis. This is both misleading and simplistic. Often the desires of equity and credit investors and the strategies they pursue are in conflict. Whereas the equity market is, we would argue, more or less efficient and most equities of an individual corporation are fungible, the same is simply not true of credit. The credit market is far from efficient in the generally accepted sense of the term – it has increasingly patchy liquidity, multiple traded asset classes with widely differing claims on the assets of the corporation in the event of a bankruptcy and highly idiosyncratic characteristics affecting their relative pricing. In addition to differences in claims, differences in maturity also ensure that credit instruments of the same entity are rarely fungible. These variances affect the valuation of the underlying securities to a profound degree and must be clearly identified in order to determine where, if anywhere, value exists. Thus, while investors might have a solid grasp of fundamental corporate analysis, they will be unlikely to succeed in credit investing without an equally robust understanding of the technical issues pertaining to credit. We will attempt to outline some of the factors that matter.

The ratings agencies have published their own methodologies for assessing credit risk, and publications of an academic nature detail the more quantitative side of the discipline, along with the mathematical aspects of portfolio risk. However, there are few options available when setting out into a field which remains, relative to other investment options, somewhat obscure. We hope to address this in the coming chapters, tying the thematic and theoretical elements of the book into a selection of factual case studies from the recent past.

This book, then, is intended for readers who already have some awareness of corporate credit as an asset class but are not themselves seasoned credit practitioners. In our view, this group is fairly wide-ranging and diverse, and includes:

- independent financial advisors who are seeking to direct clients towards asset classes besides equities

- business school, undergraduate and graduate students of finance

- graduate trainees at financial institutions – banks, asset managers and insurance companies

- financial journalists and equity or fixed income fund managers who are seeking to broaden their understanding of an adjacent investment discipline that is little followed and less understood among these groups.

What this book covers

This book examines seven broad areas:

1. **Management and Governance:** In this section, we first give our perspective on the nature of corporations and how, behind the veil of corporate identity, the actions and decisions of a corporate entity are determined by the individuals in the management suite. We then discuss the influence of differing models of corporate ownership on underlying credit, and move on to examine the success or failure of regulators' response to governance failures so far. We address the ways in which regulators have sought to impose controls over boards of directors, executive directors, non-executive directors, remuneration, reporting and controls.

2. **Management and Governance Case Studies:** In the following section, we seek to illustrate some of these themes with the real-life examples of Chesapeake Energy, the Royal Bank of Scotland, Smithfield Foods and Sallie Mae. We summarise by drawing conclusions from these cases from the perspective of a credit investor.

3. **Traditional Credit Analysis:** In this section, we cover the key numerical techniques applied by financial analysts in the assessment of corporate credit risk. This begins with a general economic overview of a corporation in the context of its industry, through the threats from competition, obsolescence and substitution that it faces, to the core, accountancy-driven assessment of its financial metrics. We consider scale and cyclicality. We then incorporate liquidity and seasonality analysis as further filters to these metrics and go on to discuss the implications of off-balance-sheet obligations and risks for the true 'adjusted' financial status of the corporation. We further demonstrate some of these adjustments and the implications of significant concentrations of shareholders. Finally, we attempt to illustrate these concepts by placing corporate risk on a scale of relative creditworthiness as an example of how to put the foregoing into practice.

4. **How Managements Present Reality:** In this section of the book we discuss some of the ways in which management's discretion in the way it presents accounting data can influence the outcome of a numbers-driven credit analysis. We go through the profit-and-loss, balance sheet and cash flow statements and illustrate a range of ways in which management can flatter the accounting data reported in the public disclosures on which credit analysis depends, accompanied by a range of illustrative case studies from recent corporate history.

5. **Behind the Numbers:** Here we go in-depth to illustrate the kind of adjustments that have to be made in order to interpret the published financial statements of a corporation in a way that reflects their economic realities. We present each major theme in the context of a real-life case study from recent history. We examine the credit implications of pension and other off-balance-sheet liabilities, adjustments for operating leases, work through an exercise in assessing event risk, run a full liquidity analysis, and offer an examination of the definition of what are often blithely described as 'cash' and 'committed' bank lines. We examine the concept of liquidity in some depth, illustrating many of its key aspects in two recent case studies.

6. **How Non-Credit Factors Drive Credit:** In this section of the book, we seek to illustrate how it is important to look for factors outside the field of credit as potential determinants of credit quality. We examine equity performance and valuation, especially in the context of comparable peer companies, and the viability of individual credits as leveraged buyouts (LBOs). We walk the reader though a basic LBO analysis and the steps that might influence potential buyers in assessing the risk/reward of such a transaction. We frame individual credits in the context of merger and acquisition trends within their sectors and go in-depth to examine two further real-life LBOs.

7. **How Market Considerations Affect Credit:** In the concluding section of this book, we discuss some of the pitfalls we have encountered in trying to generate super-normal

investment returns based on the findings of our fundamental credit analysis. We cover some of the other risks that affect credit performance – sovereign, interest rate and market technicals – and look into the vital but still controversial role played in the credit market by the major ratings agencies. We debate the validity of indexation as an investment strategy in light of the credit market's technicalities, and briefly cover some of the main strategies and instruments available to investors seeking credit exposure.

Introduction

The case for corporate credit

I N JUNE 2010, STRATEGISTS AT US INVESTMENT BANK J.P. MORGAN CONTENDED IN A research document that investment-grade corporate credit was the asset class that our "great-grandfathers should have bought".[1] Investment-grade credit, it turned out, had outperformed all other asset classes over the long run (and not in the Keynesian sense of the period over which we are all dead,[2] but during the specific period 1919–2010).

Nonetheless, it is fair to say that credit investments receive only a fraction of the market and media attention devoted to their more volatile but readily accessible alternatives in the equity markets. There is no equivalent to CNBC's *Mad Money* devoted to the movements of the credit markets. Yet these markets are substantially greater in both scale and scope than the world's stock markets and, with the growth of exchange-traded funds, are increasingly accessible to retail investors. The US Federal Reserve measured the size of the US credit market at $59.4 trillion in Q1 2014, at which point the market capitalisation of the S&P 500 was $17.2 trillion.[3]

So why is the usually voluble Mr Cramer (and others like him) so reticent about credit?

The data, it turns out, is pretty stark:

---

1 Doctor, Saul; Elizalde, Abel; Singh, Harpreet (2010), *What Your Great-Grandfather Should Have Bought*. J.P. Morgan. Europe Credit Research.
2 Keynes, J. M. (1923), *A Tract on Monetary Reform*. London: Macmillan and Co.
3 Federal Reserve Statistical Release (2014). *Financial Accounts of the United States*. [Online]. Available at: **www.federalreserve.gov/releases/z1/current/accessible/l1.htm** [Accessed 21 November 2014].

TABLE 1: COMPOUNDED ANNUAL RETURNS, 1919-2010

Asset	BBB credit	US Tsy 10yr	US equity	Gold	CPI
Return	7.0%	5.3%	9.8%	4.5%	2.7%
Volatility	7.4%	5.6%	18.6%	14.2%	
Information ratio	0.95	0.94	0.53	0.32	

Source: J.P. Morgan

J.P. Morgan defines the *information ratio* as a means of ascertaining annualised returns on a risk-adjusted basis, i.e. the nominal return divided by the volatility of this return. Thus the data in table 1 demonstrates that returns from credit have been among the most attractive *risk-weighted* investments in the major asset classes that have been available to investors over the past 90 years.

TABLE 2: REAL RETURNS 1919-2010

Asset	IG credit	US Tsy 10y	US equity	Gold
Return	4.2%	2.5%	6.9%	1.7%
Volatility	7.8%	6.2%	18.7%	14.2%
Information ratio	0.54	0.41	0.37	0.12

Source: J.P. Morgan

The real returns afforded by credit are even more striking once all asset classes have been discounted for annual compound inflation of 2.7% over the study period. Credit is the only asset class with an information ratio over 0.5 once volatility and inflation have been taken into account. Nonetheless, it should be pointed out that credit does not outperform other asset classes in all economic environments.

An asset class that has arrived

To be fair, pension funds and other institutional investors have increasingly recognised the returns and information ratio provided by credit, shifting their allocation towards fixed income and credit products in recent years – partly to hedge the discount rate risk at which their funds are deemed to be under- or over-funded, partly driven by the growth of this pension under-funding, which derives somewhat from the relative weakness of equity markets over the period 1999–2012.

In 2007, US pension funds typically had a 60% allocation to equities, with 30% in bonds (both government and corporate). As of April 2012, according to the Milliman survey, these proportions had shifted to 41% in fixed income (i.e. a mixture of government bonds and corporate credit) for the top 100 US pension funds.[4] Financial research firm Preqin published statistics in October 2012, showing that US public pension funds have also been increasing their exposure to non-traditional forms of credit investment (mainly hedge fund products), with 21% of funds stating they have exposure to such products vs. 6% in 2009.

The performance of credit relative to other asset classes can be a function of the highly technical and, especially in the bond market, increasingly illiquid secondary market for credit products. One of the unintended consequences of well-intentioned initiatives such as the Volcker rule on proprietary trading and increased capital requirements under Basel III for assets on bank balance sheets has been effectively to penalise investment banks for holding inventories of bonds with which to make markets.

Thus, while the US corporate bond market has grown 42% since 2008, dealer inventories of corporate bonds and other non-US Treasuries have declined by 78% since 2007,[5] such that average daily trading volumes in US corporate bonds now represent only 0.2% of the outstanding market. The consequence of such depleted inventories is for the reaction to macro or idiosyncratic events – for instance, rising rates or an unexpected downgrade of an individual credit – to turn from an exit into a rout, as the channels for trading out of corporate bond mutual funds and ETFs are bottlenecked; the introduction of 'hot' money into a market that has historically been dominated by 'sticky' investors such as insurers and pension funds has exacerbated this phenomenon. The reaction in Summer 2013 to the first hints of the Fed's 'tapering' its easy-money asset purchase scheme illustrates this point. Credit spreads widened 53% in response over the course of a month.[6]

As the debt-like nature of pension liabilities has been brought to the fore by the poor performance of global equity markets since the dotcom bubble burst in 2000, attitudes to risk management in the pension industry have also grown more conservative, seeking to match liabilities to more reliable sources of funding.

---

4 [Online] Available at **us.milliman.com/pfi** [Accessed 19 January 2015].

5 Alloway, T. (2013). 'The big read. Markets: the debt penalty'. *Financial Times*, 10 September 2013 [Online]. Available at: **www.ft.com/cms/s/0/0d1c9b38-195a-11e3-83b9-00144feab7de.html#axzz3JyK4PFiT** [Accessed 21 November 2014].

6 The iTraxx generic index of investment-grade European corporate credits widened from 86 basis points (bps) to 132bps from 22 May to 24 June 2013. (Bloomberg, 2013)

Credit analysis – a gulf between theory and practice

Somewhere between the strong returns of corporate credit as an investment class and the lacklustre reality of many credit funds' performance lies a telling inconsistency. High-profile casualties of corporate bankruptcy are mercifully few, yet returns on investment-grade funds are inconsistent with the underlying statistics relating to the returns that are theoretically available, despite the high degree of 'expert' support available to investors.

Between the ratings agencies, with their privileged access to corporate management and internal accounts, the sell-side bankers who bring new deals to market and the seasoned professionals at fund management companies, schooled in the disciplines of credit analysis and savvy to the sharp practices of these market professionals, it should be possible to bridge this gap, at least partially.

Yet few credit fund managers achieve this.

Figure 1 illustrates the performance of the CDX Investment Grade Index from 2004–2012, eight years that include the greatest financial crisis in living memory.

FIGURE 1: ILLUSTRATIVE INDEX OF RETURNS - INVESTMENT-GRADE

Source: Barclays Capital

It can be seen from this that an investment of $100 in an unmanaged investment-grade credit index fund in 2004 would have risen to $104 in 2012. Hardly a stellar return. Yet were the same investment to have been made using perfect market timing at the low on 29 September 2008, two weeks after Lehman Brothers filed for bankruptcy, it would have risen by 13% in the subsequent period. Of course, the chances of timing the market to perfection are very slight, but they can be enhanced by a greater awareness of the factors affecting credit valuation. Nonetheless, we offer this statistic more in the spirit of emphasising the market opportunity that can arise within this asset class.

For the corresponding high yield index over the same periods, shown in figure 2, the figures are more compelling. The investment's value would be $152 and $165 in these two cases. In cash bonds, the impact of interest rates on credit returns is substantial. Yet when we turn to examine the actual performance of managed funds over this time, the range of outcomes is almost infinitely variable.

FIGURE 2: ILLUSTRATIVE INDEX OF RETURNS - HIGH-YIELD

Source: Barclays Capital

In our own experience, far higher returns can be achieved on levered investment-grade products than these data series suggest. What, then, differentiates index-type returns from those that are potentially available to the skilled practitioner? The answer, especially for investors in leveraged products, is surprisingly straightforward: avoid taking long-term positions in the debt of companies that fail to pay coupons or default on or restructure debt.

If this can be achieved, then, over time, the bonds in a portfolio will pay coupons and revert to their par value. In order to take advantage of the 'pull to par', the investor must avoid defaults.

However, there is a big difference between ability to pay, which can be analysed quantitatively, and willingness to pay, which requires an understanding of the human factors at play. The analytical techniques we set out in this book are a methodology for avoiding this critical error, and can be enhanced in ways that this book will seek to demonstrate.

What is the matter with traditional credit analysis as a means of making money?

We do not argue against the necessary role of traditional credit analysis in the investment decision-making process, and indeed, we go to some lengths to illustrate its usefulness later in this book. However, we do strongly advocate that it should not be used in isolation. Credit analysis differs from equity analysis in many regards, but most fundamentally in that it is not based on the assumption that the underlying market is itself a model of efficiency. We discuss this in more detail in chapter 7.

The numbers are not enough

The focus of corporate credit analysis has traditionally been on the numbers published in quarterly and annual reports, rather than on the individuals that drive them. This is as unsurprising as it is, frankly speaking, daft. The phalanxes of credit analysts hail mostly from – and subsequently hire mostly from – business schools, which seem to us to place an overwhelming emphasis on quantitative analysis. But this approach, in our view, is fundamentally lacking.

In the first instance, it requires reliance on the use of accounting-based data: a retrospective scorecard. It gives the investor a very necessary but imperfect reduction of the impact of foregone management initiatives; it tells nothing of the future. (Tyco and WorldCom, two of the most egregious examples of senior management predation, reported numbers giving little or no indication of an underlying problem, until their crises broke. Accounting-based analysis has a poor track record of identifying corporate fraud before other factors, such as a lack of cash, bring it to light.)

To avoid such investment pitfalls, the investor needs to use more than just the numbers. Indeed, quantitative projections in corporate finance have much in common with those of meteorology.

Prediction is very difficult, especially about the future

It appears self-evident to us that, just as a TV weatherman can make a reasonable call as to whether it will rain in the next 24 hours, so an analyst can take a look at a company's access to cash, committed bank lines, saleable assets and forthcoming maturing obligations and cash requirements and make a reasonable call, assuming no fraud, on whether or not a company will fail to pay coupons, breach covenants or default over 6–12 months.

However, longer-term projections are much more problematic. Just as the meteorologist cannot begin to model with any meaningful accuracy the plethora of independent yet interacting variables that determine the weather, so the credit practitioner cannot hope to synthesise the vast range of political, economic and social externalities – the economic situation, regulatory changes, input prices, potential substitution threats, changes in consumer taste, to name but a few – into a quantitative model.

Large numbers of shifting and inter-dependent variables effectively make longer-term numerical projections no more reliable than a very long-term weather forecast.

The secret lies with management

However, it *is* possible to evaluate the way in which senior corporate management – the C-suite – react to these externalities and how they will treat creditors and other stakeholders in the process.

We would contend that a corporation is a legal fiction, which has no agency in its own right. The collective action of its workforce is guided by the individuals at the top, as are its financial policy decisions. When we talk of the agency of 'corporations' and 'companies', we are really using the terms to refer to that of its executive management. And it *is* possible to probability-weight, with a degree of subjectivity, the motivations of these individuals by looking for potential areas of conflict between their fiduciary duty and, among other factors, their self-interest, enlightened or otherwise.

Objectives of this book

Investors who are suitably informed about the credit market's idiosyncrasies are able to participate in an investment universe of perhaps unparalleled and growing variety and scale, as the global banking industry seeks increasingly to disintermediate its own credit exposure.

We therefore encourage you to read on as we:

- develop a methodology of credit analysis rooted in an evaluation of management, testing its performance against its stated objectives

- overlay this approach to traditional analytical measures

- illustrate, through case studies, investors' options for generating attractive, risk-adjusted returns from credit investing.

1

Management and Governance: A Qualitative Overlay to Investment Decisions

Introduction

Why does all this matter?

I N THIS CHAPTER WE HOPE TO ADDRESS THE MORE QUALITATIVE AREA OF OUR APPROACH to analysis, corporate governance, and the examination of overlapping groups within corporate executive and non-executive teams. We give examples of how this approach can be a valuable tool in assessing the likely actions of management teams – actions which can, in our view, be *the* deciding factor in the long-term credit standing of the corporation concerned. We explore the nature of a corporation and the blurring of its identity with that of those who run it. We argue that the actions of these individuals can be more important in determining the trajectory of a corporation's credit standing than those of its owners.

We also examine a range of ownership structures with the aim of ascertaining whether one form or another is better aligned to the interests of the credit investor. We look at the response of regulators to the more egregious abuses of agency that have come to light in the past two decades and examine their effectiveness to date. We then tie these themes together from a credit perspective and give four case studies from corporate life that illustrate some of the more important aspects.

From the outset our perspective is that a grasp of these interconnected factors is the key to understanding credit transition early – which is where the investor will make or avoid losing money – yet this more narrative-based, qualitative side of credit assessment is often demoted to a distant second place by mathematical modelling and number-crunching, methods far better at inspiring confidence in investment committees. This is a serious omission. How meaningful can a numerical projection be if it is not viewed from a perspective that is also informed by management's motivations?

1. The nature of the corporation

"Neither bodies to be punished nor souls to be condemned"[7]

Consider the following headlines:

'Adidas seeks criminal probe into Reebok India irregularities'

'J.P. Morgan and taking responsibility'

'Centrica warns of higher gas costs'

'Eurostar eyes expansion across Europe'

'3i set to appoint ex-City banker as chief'

Do you notice anything? In each of these headlines, one could substitute the company's name with that of a human being without compromising meaning:

'Inspector Morse seeks criminal probe into Reebok India irregularities'

'William Murdoch warns of higher gas costs'

'George Osborne set to appoint ex-City banker as chief'

We are accustomed to talking and thinking of corporations as people. For example, beverages multinational Diageo, in the 'Sustainability and Responsibility' section of its website, states that it is "[a]cting with integrity in everything we do"[8]– something to which most individuals would aspire. US auto behemoth Ford "has supported thousands of programs that strengthen communities and improve quality of life" and in 2012/13 gave $30m to US-based nonprofit organisations.[9] Just like an individual giving money to United Way or working for his or her local Rotary Club; indeed, "Ford believe commitment to community is an important part of who and what we are."[10] (Note the use of the pronoun "we".)

But who or what *are* they? Do these corporations have a right to make assertions that could plausibly come from a human individual?

A fundamental ambiguity

Companies do bear some similarities to people in the manner in which they operate in the legal and economic sphere. Individuals pay taxes; so (for the most part) do corporations.

---

7 Attributed to Edward Thurlow (1731–1806), lord chancellor of Great Britain.
8 Diageo (2014). *Sustainability and responsibility.* [Online]. Available at: **www.diageo.com/en-row/CSR/Pages/default.aspx** [Accessed 21 November 2014].
9 Ford Motor Company (2013). *Drive Community. Ford Motor Company Fund and Community Services 2012/2013 report.* [Online]. Available at: **corporate.ford.com/doc/FFAR_2013_Pages_FINAL.pdf** [Accessed 24 November 2014].
10 Ford Motor Company (2011). *Drive Community. Ford Motor Company Fund and Community Services 2011 report.* [Online]. Available at: **corporate.ford.com/doc/fmcfcs_ffar_2011-2012.pdf** [Accessed 24 November 2014].

Individuals can enter into contracts (including credit contracts) and end up before the court if they renege on them; so can corporations. Individuals can own and trade in property; so can corporations. Individuals may commit manslaughter and murder; so, in some jurisdictions, may corporations be charged with crimes of corporate manslaughter or homicide although, in reality, convictions under such legislation are few and far between.[11] Individuals in most liberal democracies can express political views through campaign contributions to political parties; indeed, in many societies, such a right is held inalienable and enshrined in constitutional law. And, in the US at least, following the US Supreme Court's ruling in 2010 in the case of *Citizens United vs. Federal Election Commission*, corporations can do the same through contributions to "electioneering communications".[12]

Can it be right to think of corporations as persons? In a word, no. The *sine qua non* of personhood is sentience and, with a few basic tests, we can dismiss the idea that a corporation is a sentient agent. Can a corporation feel? No. Can it perceive? No. Is it conscious? No. Does it experience subjective conscious experiences? Again, no. To cite Ben Cohen and Jerry Greenfield of the eponymous ice cream: "I'm Ben, I'm a person. I'm Jerry, I'm a person. Ben & Jerry's Ice Cream? Not a person."[13]

The relationship between senior management and corporate identity

But go back to the beginning of this chapter. If, as a corporation, J.P. Morgan lacks intentionality, how can it take responsibility? How can 3i make any appointments? How can Adidas seek a criminal probe or Centrica warn about anything?

Herein lies the true nature of corporate personhood. The corporation itself has no intentionality but the individuals who run it – the senior-most executives frequently identified as the 'C-suite' (chief executive officer, chief financial officer, chief operating officer) and, to a limited extent, the corporation's board of directors (more about them later) most definitely do.

It is these individuals who steer the company's strategic direction. They commit resources to expand in some areas, while withdrawing them to contract in others they deem less profitable. They decide what markets to be active in and where to locate facilities. They hire their immediate reports, determine their remuneration and establish their performance criteria; in so doing, they determine the working environment and set the ethical tone of the organisation, since their appointees will, most likely, share some of the values of management (which presumably attracted them to this employer as opposed to another)

---

11   By the authors' calculations, convictions under the UK's 2007 Corporate Manslaughter and Corporate Homicide Act are still in single digits.

12   Liptak, A. (2010). Justices, 5–4, Reject Corporate Spending Limit, *New York Times*, 21 January 2010. Available at: **www.nytimes.com** [Accessed 24 November 2014]. Authors' note: Corporations in the US still may not fund campaigns or parties directly.

13   *Eitner, C.* (2011). *Montpelier citizens united forum draws standing-room crowd.* [Online]. Available at: **vtdigger.org/2011/11/30/montpelier-citizens-united-forum-draws-standing-room-crowd**. [Accessed 24 November 2014].

and will, in turn, hire and set performance criteria which enable them to meet the goals set for them by the C-suite, and so on down the chain. The C-suite will also hire lobbyists to persuade politicians (or, as we have seen in some cases, do a bit of persuasion themselves). They forge, or at least approve, the company's standard operating practices. Of particular interest to credit investors, they decide the company's policies on capital allocation and funding, its appetite for leverage, its willingness to engage in mergers and acquisitions, and its generosity towards shareholders.

Good credit analysis examines the C-suite

These individuals make or approve all the decisions that affect a corporation and its interaction with all other stakeholders. Thus, when we analyse corporations as credit investors, we cannot emphasise enough the importance of evaluating senior management. They, after all, are driving the corporate machine, whoever it may be that owns it.

The corporation? It is a legal fiction. Moreover, it is a fiction that under US law, at least, was ushered in by judicial fiat under rather questionable circumstances,[14] has never been subject to democratically enacted legislation and does not enjoy universal support.[15] Examining the individuals who run the corporation can yield telling indications of its likely future actions. Unfortunately, it is a technique which we freely admit does not lend itself to modelling; more propitiously, it is a skill that at its unrefined level most human beings – not just investment professionals – possess. Indeed, those not afflicted by the social dystrophy that accompanies spending all one's hours in the markets might actually be better placed to practise it.

2. Ownership ≠ control

But even if the corporation is a legal fiction and much power does reside with its senior managers, what about the shareholders who own companies and the boards that putatively represent their interests? What of their ability to replace executives with other teams that they feel could do a better job?

This question goes to the very heart of one of the key issues of governance for a modern, investor-owned corporation, viz. the conflicts of interest arising from corporate stewardship by its senior management team.

---

14 Authors' note: In the case of Santa Clara County vs. Southern Pacific Railroad in 1886, the Supreme Court noted in a court reporter's headnote (not part of the binding opinion in the case) that corporations were persons for the purposes of the Fourteenth Amendment – the original intention and purpose of which was to protect freed slaves. The chief justice began oral argument thus: "The court does not wish to hear argument on the question of whether the provision in the Fourteenth Amendment to the Constitution, which forbids a State to deny any person within its jurisdiction the equal protection of the laws, applies to these corporations. We are all of the opinion that it does." Reported in: Justia.com (2014). *Santa Clara County v. Southern Pacific R. Co. 1118 U.S. 394* (1886). [Online]. Available at: **supreme.justia.com/cases/federal/us/118/394/case.html#396** [Accessed 24 November 2014].
15 Reclaim Democracy (2010). *Proposed constitutional amendments.* [Online]. Available at: **reclaimdemocracy.org/?s=proposed+constitutional+amendments** [Accessed 24 November 2014].

The legal legerdemain that conjured the corporate person into existence also undermined the nature of ownership by separating the owners from their assets and necessitating the creation of a steward class (the C-suite again) to manage them. This was a function of the break-neck speed with which corporations developed in the late 19th and early 20th centuries, necessitating the creation of a professional managerial tier, rather than traditional family participation. In what sense, then, can shareholders really be said to 'own' the companies in which they have shares?

Consider the following example: I own the freehold on my house and I also own stock in the Royal Bank of Scotland. At any time of the day or night, I can enter my house; if I attempted to cross the threshold of RBS's HQ in the wee small hours, the chances are I would be escorted swiftly out of the door by a burly security guard. At any time of the day or night, I can use the amenities that my house has to offer and regulate their use by others. Neither I, nor any other shareholders, have such authority over RBS's assets. I only 'own' RBS in the most attenuated sense of the word.

What I actually lay claim to is merely the right to vote at AGMs, a share of the spoils if the bank is wound up and my share of the residual cash flows generated by the company once it has satisfied its obligations to all those other parties that have contracted with it – employees, suppliers, creditors, customers and arguably even society at large.

Alternative ownership models – nothing is perfect

Ownership ≠ control is a sweeping claim and it is not without exceptions. In much of Germany, Italy and France, it is not uncommon for relatively large corporations with publicly traded debt securities to be family-owned or at least family-controlled. Various scions of the Quandt family maintain about 47% collectively in German global car giant BMW;[16] Peugeot is still roughly 14% held by the eponymous family;[17] the Bettencourts maintain about 31% of L'Oréal; the Agnelli family still maintains control of Fiat Chrysler Automobiles through various holding company structures. The so-called *Mittelstand* of mid-cap corporates that form the backbone of the German and Italian economies are largely owned by their founders or founding families, or in the possession of foundations created by the controlling family. Even in the USA, the Ford family maintains control of the Blue Oval through the use of a dual shareholding structure.

Conflicts of interest attendant upon stewardship are much less of a complication for closely held corporations. Understand where the owners want to go and you will get a good idea of the corporation's strategic direction. Unfortunately this can present its own set of problems. In closely held corporations with limited disclosure, the intentions and strategic direction of the owners might be hard to ascertain beyond scanning business newspaper columns for corporate gossip. In Europe, in particular, such companies have not been precluded

---

16 Bloomberg (2014). Authors' note: Bloomberg uses its proprietary system to deliver data, news and analytics to participants in the financial services sector and beyond. References to Bloomberg in this book relate to material sourced from that service. More information on Bloomberg can be found at **www. bloomberg/company/#menu**.

17 Bloomberg (2014).

from issuing public bonds by an unwillingness to disclose detailed historical financials. In addition, as the founding generation dies out and ownership atomises across its scions, their relationship to the business might well transform from a profound emotional commitment to a simple financial nexus, with an attendant transfer of power to the firm's stewards (the C-suite) and a change in risk appetite. A fissiparous brood of ever more distantly related owners can also result in significant strategic uncertainty – and pose significant credit risks.

Finally, we should certainly encourage doubt that there is anything genetic about good managerial skills. The success of a father or mother in developing a business is no guarantee of a son or daughter continuing that success. Anybody who still has faith in the hereditary principle should study the history of Europe's royal families.

Ownership is too atomised to exert control

One of the key features of the liberal market economies (LMEs) of the USA, UK, Ireland, Canada, Australia and New Zealand, where the bulk of tradable corporate credit originates, is that corporate ownership is for the most part both international and increasingly institutional.

If we look at the £1.8trn UK stock market by way of example, we find that while individuals own about 10.7%,[18] UK institutions (including unit trusts and investment trusts) own about 30.7%[19] and non-UK owners own around 53.2%[20] – the lion's share. It was not always thus. The same figures for 1963 would have shown over one half of the value of the UK stock market in the hands of individuals and less than 10% in the hands of non-UK holders.[21] In this sense, while the market of 1963 was more atomised than today's, more of its shares were in the hands of individuals who could exert their personal influence on the board and management, whereas today this duty lies largely with institutional investors, many of them from outside the UK. It is telling that nearly 60% of the UK stock market is now in the hands of multiple-owned pooled accounts where the identity of the beneficial owner is unknown.[22]

A fundamental change in the power dynamic

Broadly, though, two trends are apparent: the institutionalisation and internationalisation of shareholdings. These twin developments have changed the attitude toward share ownership and the power dynamic between the owners and their agents.

---

18 ONS (2013). *Ownership of UK Quoted Shares, 2012.* [Online]. Available at **www.ons.gov.uk/ons/rel/ pnfc1/share-ownership---share-register-survey-report/2012/stb-share-ownership-2012.html** [Accessed 25 September 2013].
19 ONS (2013).
20 ONS (2013).
21 ONS (2013).
22 ONS (2013).

FIGURE 3: GEOGRAPHIC OWNERSHIP OF BRITISH STOCK MARKET

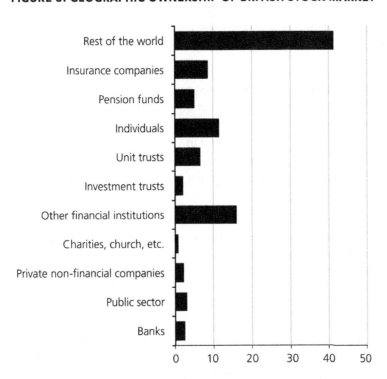

Source: Office for National Statistics; Statistical Bulletin; Ownership of UK Quoted Shares, 2012. 25 September 2013

The institutionalisation of the equity markets has further eroded the notion of ownership by creating a powerful fiduciary agent who deals with the corporate stewards on the equity owner's behalf. When I buy a fund for my ISA, or stocks are purchased for my pension plan, I have no ownership relationship with the equities that will be bought. My concern is purely financial – I want the stocks selected to increase in value such that the value of my fund increases and I want them dumped and replaced with other stocks if they don't. I have even surrendered the most basic rights that an individual shareholder would enjoy, such as attendance and voting rights at an AGM. These I have conferred upon the fund manager.

It is fair to assume that the international investor – more often than not also an institution – enjoys an equally financial interest in the stock. If the investors' only interest is to buy low and sell high, what implications does this have for the occupants of the C-suite and, more importantly, for those debt-investors who extend credit to the organisations they steer? There is, of course, a material difference between the ultimate power of shareholders and debtholders. The former have the 'nuclear option' of exercising their ability to hire and fire senior managers and even deciding to sell control of the company to third parties, while the latter's rights are restricted only to the contractual terms of the specific debt instrument they own.

And yet more power devolves to the C-suite

Let us hear what US Supreme Court Associate Justice Louis Brandeis had to say on this matter:

> "Such a wide distribution of the stock dissipates altogether the responsibility of stockholders, particularly of those with five shares, ten shares or 50 shares. They recognise that they have no influence in a corporation of hundreds of millions of dollars' capital. Consequently they consider it immaterial whatever they do, or omit to do. The net result is that the men who are in control of it become almost impossible to dislodge, unless there should be such a scandal in the corporation as to make it clearly necessary for the people on the outside to combine for self-protection."[23]

Brandeis was speaking in the years before the Great War but his analysis is still trenchant. Think of some recent corporate failures that have harmed shareholders and bondholders alike. Dick Fuld went down on the good ship Lehman (as did its creditors). Fred 'The Shred' Goodwin had to be blasted out of RBS and its creditors are only hanging on thanks to the generosity of the UK taxpayer. Aubrey McClendon clung on for some time at Chesapeake Energy despite actions that saw the company's benchmark 2019 bonds lose 8pts in value over the course of a week, its five-year credit default swap (CDS) contract widen 300 basis points (bps) over the same period and its stock lose approximately 22% of its value. The e-behemoth, Facebook, has in place a shareholders' agreement that effectively allows the CEO voting control and therefore the ultimate say on the corporation's strategy, while its stock approximately halved in value in the six months following its initial public offering (IPO) amid disclosures of pre-IPO communications between the SEC (Securities and Exchange Commission) and the company which cast doubt on the growth forecasts on which the stock's initial pricing was based.

Generally speaking, we feel the owners of corporations have a poor track record at reining in their wayward stewards.

3. Regulatory response

So far, so ineffectual?

Politicians and their advisors have attempted to step into the fray, rightly sensing the strength of public displeasure at the excesses of some corporate titans. Every corporate scandal has precipitated a torrent of (after-the-fact) moral outrage from our elected

---

23 Guide to a Microfilm Edition of the Public Papers of Justice Louis Dembitz Brandeis, in the Jacob and Bertha Goldfarb Library of Brandeis University, Document 128. Testimony before the Senate Committee on Interstate Commerce, 62nd Congress, 2nd Session, Hearings on Control of Corporations, Persons, and Firms Engaged in Interstate Commerce, 1 (pt. XVI) pp.1146–91. (Dec. 14–16, 1911). Cited in, Monks, Robert A.G. and Minow, N. (2004). *Corporate Governance*, third edition, p. 127. Malden: Blackwell Publishing.

representatives, reams of reports and recommendations and some legislative and or regulatory responses.

Most famously, in the wake of Enron's fall from grace (and solvency) in 2001, the US House of Representatives appeared ready to introduce a governance standards bill proposed by Congressman Michael Oxley (R-Ohio), which, while proposing the creation of a new regulator for auditors, was otherwise something of a milquetoast of an act. However, as Tyco and WorldCom followed – with disclosures of shocking shortfalls in governance standards, accounting oversight and outright peculation by members of the C-suite (in conference, Rep. Oxley remarked: "Make no mistake, this is a difficult period for those who love and cherish the free enterprise system"[24]) – the US Senate sponsored a less-timid version from Senator Paul Sarbanes (D-Maryland), which underpinned the final Sarbanes-Oxley legislation (SarbOx).

The US - a curate's egg

In contrast to the original rather toothless Oxley bill, SarbOx did have a bite. That said, a good number of its provisions were surprising only inasmuch as they had not existed before. Real-time disclosure of events material to investors' buying and selling decisions and disclosure of off-balance-sheet transactions and material transactions with unconsolidated subsidiaries seem an article of common sense. Reconciliation of pro forma numbers to GAAP and the disclosure of corrections to prior financial statements required by an auditor seem fairly rudimentary levels of disclosure. Did independent auditors really not have to report to audit committees on critical accounting policies and disagreements with management over accounting principles before SarbOx? Did it really take corporate governance this long to make it a criminal offence to mislead, coerce or manipulate an auditor, or insist upon the barring of violators of securities laws from serving as officers or directors of public companies (the corporate equivalent of allowing a compulsive gambler to run a casino)?[25]

That said, we should not underestimate this major federal initiative, which not merely sought to introduce some sunlight into the smoke-filled conference rooms of a cosy corporate club but also to shake up its board and meaningfully sanction those that transgressed its rules. Auditors could number no more than two of the five board members, curbing the ability of accounting industry lobbyists to court-pack the board with industry insiders. The board could set auditing, quality control and independence standards and investigate the standards of ethics and conduct of the accounting profession; it mandated lead (and coordinating/reviewing) partner rotation, if the partner had audited a company for five

---

24 Capitolwords (2002). *Conference Report on H.R. 3763, Sarbanes-Oxley Act Of 2002.* [Online]. Available at: **capitolwords.org/date/2002/07/25/H5462-2_conference-report-on-hr-3763-sarbanes-oxley-act-of** [Accessed 24 November 2014].

25 For a discussion and comparison of the main points of H.R 3763 (House) and H.R. 3763 (Senate) and the Conference Version, please see Jickling, M. (2002). The Sarbanes-Oxley Act of 2002: A Side-by-Side Comparison of House, Senate, And Conference Versions. Updated 26 July 2002. *Congressional Research Service. The Library of Congress.* [Online]. Available at: **www.law.umaryland.edu/marshall/crsreports/crsdocuments/rl31483.pdf** [Accessed 24 November 2014].

consecutive years and forbade accountants serving as external auditors to a company whose top officer had worked for the accountant within the prior twelve months. Ultimately, it could deem an auditor unfit to audit public companies and subject it to fines and other censures. Moreover, it fell to the board to set standards for auditing, quality control and independence and gave it the ability to impose fines and censures and even suspend firms from auditing public companies.

The act further instructed the SEC to adopt rules for stock analysts, which over time, have influenced the regulation of credit analysts and sharply curtailed their coercion into writing puff pieces for new issues. But some of the act's truly reforming initiatives were reserved for the C-suite. Again, however, if a sharp intake of breath is to be drawn, it is over the non-existence of these provisions heretofore. The act required certification of the adequacy of a company's internal accounting controls and established criminal penalties for *wilful* violations (something we believe quite difficult to prove). Contrary to popular perception, while it prohibited firms from making loans to executives and directors, such a prohibition only applied to loans on preferential terms and not extended in the ordinary course of business. That this provision was informed by the specific outrages of Messrs Kozlowski (Tyco) and Ebbers (WorldCom), who trousered $88m and $408m respectively in company loans,[26] could make one question why so much latitude still remained. However, it did expose the CEO and CFO of a public corporation to forfeiture of trading profits and bonuses received in the 12 months prior to the restatement of financial reports as a result of misconduct. It also increased the severity of penalties for those caught tampering with documents; it prevented bankruptcy courts from discharging debts incurred through securities fraud; and it raised fines and custodial sentences for a range of corporate fraud-related infractions, most notably lifting the maximum sentence from five to ten years.

The UK – the Cadbury Code: hard chocolate with a soft centre

In response to Britain's main domestic corporate scandal of the 1980s (Robert Maxwell), the Financial Reporting Council, London Stock Exchange and accountancy profession set up a committee to report on the financial aspects of corporate governance.

Its terms of reference were narrow – to consider in relation to financial reporting and accountability and to make recommendations on good practice in:

- responsibilities of executive and non-executive directors for reviewing and reporting on performance to shareholders and other financially interested parties – specifically the frequency, clarity and form of reporting

- the case for audit committees, their composition and role

- the principal responsibility of auditors and the extent and value of the audit

- the links between shareholders, boards and auditors.[27]

---

26 Monks, R.A.G. and Minow, N. (2004). *Corporate Governance*, third edition. p.272. Malden: Blackwell.
27 Report of the Committee on the Financial Aspects of Corporate Governance (1992). [Online]. Available at: **www.icaew.com/~/media/Files/Library/subjects/corporate%20governance/financial%20**

Moreover, while the committee's members were individuals of unquestionable talent, experience and probity, they were, in contrast to the Messrs Sarbanes and Oxley, consummate insiders. The composition of the committee included:

- the chairman of the Institute of Directors

- the chairman of the London Stock Exchange

- the vice president of the Institute of Chartered Accountants of Scotland

- the chairman of the Financial Reporting Council

- the chairman of the 100 Group of Finance Directors

- a council member of the Confederation of British Industry.[28]

The committee was chaired by Sir Adrian Cadbury and took contributions from no fewer than 51 senior executives or board members of corporations. Again, this is not to call into question the ability or intentions of the committee but with such a narrow remit and exclusive composition, its findings and recommendations were never likely to be revolutionary.

Nor were they. The committee recommended a code of best practice, compliance with which should be explained in a statement reviewed by the company's auditor before publication. The basis for reporting is 'comply or explain', forcing the companies to elucidate any reason for non-compliance. The code was to be enforced indirectly through becoming a requirement of the London Stock Exchange for ongoing listing and through a request from the committee that the Institutional Shareholders' Committee use its influence as an owner's representative to encourage companies in which its members were invested to comply.

Focus of regulatory responses

The code itself addressed and made recommendations concerning four broad areas.

1. The board of directors

Again, most of the recommendations regarding the board of directors are remarkable only as statements of the obvious: boards should meet regularly, maintain control over the company and monitor management. Boards should include non-executives of adequate calibre and number; the board should have a formal schedule of matters; directors should have an agreed procedure to take independent advice in the furtherance of their duties (paid by the company if necessary); they should have access to the advice and services of

---

aspects%20of%20corporate%20governance.pdf [Accessed 24 November 2014].

28   *Report of the Committee on the Financial Aspects of Corporate Governance (1992), The Committee's Membership and Terms of Reference.* (December 1992). p.60ff and p.85ff. [Online]. Available at: **www.icaew.com/~/media/Files/Library/subjects/corporate%20governance/financial%20aspects%20of%20corporate%20governance.pdf** [Accessed 24 November 2014].

the company secretary, the removal of whom should be a matter for consideration of the entire board.

While we would agree that it would be an egregious dereliction of duty for a company *not* to comply with these practices, they are largely exercises in box-ticking, which can be honoured in the observance without providing any greater substantive security for a would-be investor. While failure to comply with the basic requirements would constitute a huge red flag, compliance in and of itself does not guarantee good practice in anything other than form: absence of evidence is not evidence of absence.

2. One key recommendation

In our view, the Cadbury Code did make one key recommendation about the board in terms of the division of responsibilities at the head of the company, one that we also view as a very obvious red flag with regard to the standards of governance within corporations. This recommendation was that the same person should not occupy the roles of both CEO and chairman of the board – with the latter properly overseeing the CEO's activities and those of other senior executives.

Despite the code, this is a practice that is still witnessed (viz., albeit an American rather than British example, Aubrey McClendon at Chesapeake Energy – see page 29) and it is one which we regard as worthy of investigation.

However, as we shall see from the case study, in the concentrated social networks that often characterise C-suites and boards, formal separation of these roles does not guarantee the independence of the chairman from the CEO's influence.

3. Non-executive directors

No surprises from Cadbury regarding non-executive directors: non-executives should bring independent judgment to bear; they should be free from any business or other relationship which could materially interfere with their exercising independent judgment; they should be selected through a formal process and their selection should be a matter for the entire board. They should be appointed for specified terms with no expectation of automatic reappointment.

4. Executive directors

When it comes to executive directors, the code gets more interesting. Not merely does Cadbury advocate maximum three-year terms for executive directors without shareholder approval of an extension but it calls for "full and clear disclosure of directors' total emoluments ... including pension contributions and stock options."[29] It also counsels that

---

29 Report of the Committee on the Financial Aspects of Corporate Governance (1992), The Committee's Membership and Terms of Reference. (December 1992). p.58 [Online]. Available at: **www.icaew.com/~/ media/Files/Library/subjects/corporate%20governance/financial%20aspects%20of%20corporate%20 governance.pdf** [Accessed 24 November 2014].

executive directors' pay be "subject to the recommendations of a remuneration committee made up wholly or mainly of non-execs."

One would have thought that the combination of the sunlight of disclosure and the disinterested perspective of unswayed non-executives would have kept the remuneration of corporate executives in line with the returns that they managed to deliver to shareholders. Sadly, this has not always proved to be the case and the relationship between the two has proved enduringly cosy.

5. Reporting and controls

In the field of reporting and controls, too, the commission's recommendations are relatively tame. Boards are duty-bound to present a "balanced and understandable assessment of the company's position."[30] As opposed to one that is biased and incomprehensible? It should ensure an objective and professional relationship with auditors. The directors should explain their responsibility in preparing the accounts next to the explanation given by the auditors about their reporting responsibility. (Copy … paste.) They should report that the business is a going concern with supporting assumptions or qualifications.

Prudent circumspection begs the question whether they would report anything different from the auditors; if they did, how would they square that with the maintenance of a professional relationship with the auditors? It would imply a breakdown of communication between the two parties and would call into question the activities of the audit committee, which Cadbury also promotes, being composed of at least three non-execs with clear written terms of reference. The directors should further report on the effectiveness of the company's system of internal control, although again it strikes us that they are unlikely to do so in a critical fashion *proactively*. Any such reports that go beyond ticking the 'internal controls disclosure' box are likely to be post-mortems, instigated after a major failing.

Overall, regulation is likely to remain behind the curve

Whether it is senators and congressmen from the most powerful democratic legislature in the world or the great and the good of the British corporate establishment, how could they do so little in response to such dreadful acts of corporate mismanagement and, in some cases, outright fraud and peculation?

The powers that be in the LMEs are inclined to view failures of corporate governance as irregularities in an otherwise functioning market rather than manifestations of a deeper structural or conceptual problem. Given the infrequency with which major instances of corporate malfeasance have been brought to light, this is probably, broadly speaking, a fair starting point. Their response is therefore to tweak those aspects of market practice that the corporate failures have brought to light – a bit of extra disclosure here, some additional checks there, a few new oversight bodies somewhere else – rather than reform the way the market functions. In practice, this means leaving the main constituents of

---

30   See footnote 28.

the market – corporations, their investors and the market sentinels (accountants, rating agencies, etc.) to sort it out between themselves and to continue as far as possible to self-police and self-regulate.

We suspect that this fails to account for the fact that far from being independent competing interests, the corporate world often operates as a dense social network – collusive or at least cooperative rather than adversarial. In such an environment, entrusting good governance to self-regulation runs the risk of entrusting the chicken coop to the fox. As free-market paladin Adam Smith noted:

> "People of the same trade seldom meet together, even for merriment and diversion, but the conversation ends in a conspiracy against the public … "[31]

4. Tying these themes together from a credit perspective

However, our purpose here is not to change the world but to guide the credit investor through it. By all means review the boxes to ensure that they have been appropriately ticked; that is laudable due diligence. But the sorry threnody of failings of corporate administration continues despite the best efforts to regulate it away – witness Lehman, Countrywide, AIG, RBS, Barclays and, before the Justice Department is done with LIBOR and foreign exchange fixing, doubtless many more – and demonstrates that the credit investor dare not rely on the regulator's good offices alone.

This takes us back to the central theme of this chapter: the corporation is an extension of the individuals who run it and not an entity in its own right. It is the C-suite that determines the culture of a corporation, particularly its risk appetite and ethical approach, partly through senior management's hiring and promoting people in its own image, partly through crafting remuneration structures and HR policies that motivate and reward the behaviour they deem appropriate. Such activities, especially the inculcation of a corporate culture and ethics, defy regulation. If this all sounds a bit 'frustrated liberal arts graduate', consider the following submission regarding Barclays by Andrew Bailey, Head of Banking Supervision at the FSA, to the parliamentary select committee investigating LIBOR fixing:

> "The sort of words that we would frequently use were [sic] that there was a sort of culture of gaming … Although I could not find evidence that he [Bob Diamond] personally had his hands on these things, you really could not escape the fact that the culture of this institution was coming from the top … Whatever the form [of the governance] was, it was not working."[32]

---

31 Smith, Adam (1776), *An Enquiry into the Nature and Causes of the Wealth of Nations*. London: W. Strahan and T. Cadell.
32 House of Commons Treasury Committee (2012). *Fixing LIBOR: some preliminary findings. Second Report of Session 2012–13, Volume II Oral and written evidence*. p. ev 89 ff. [Online]. Available at **www.publications.parliament.uk/pa/cm201213/cmselect/cmtreasy/481/481.pdf** [Accessed 24 November 2014].

And the goal of the credit investor must be to pierce the veil of the form and get to the substance. No model will do this – it is an essentially qualitative and judgment-based exercise.

In the next section of the book, we give two case studies offering recent and concrete examples of the kinds of failures of governance that can dangerously undermine a company's credit standing, one from early in 2012 and one from the dark days of 2008: Chesapeake Energy and the Royal Bank of Scotland. We also offer two case studies that examine different aspects of the interaction between formulaic management compensation schemes and the exercise of executive powers that can impact a company's credit standing: Smithfield Foods and Sallie Mae.

2

Management and Governance: Case Studies

Case study I: Chesapeake Energy

Background

AUBREY McCLENDON CO-FOUNDED CHESAPEAKE ENERGY (CHK) IN JULY 1989 AND assumed the roles of chairman, president and CEO (something that, in itself, should have been a concern). Unlike many occupiers of these roles at major US corporations, therefore, he is a genuine entrepreneur, who put up his own capital to found the company and drove its growth from a humble start-up to the US's second-largest natural gas producer.

The course of 2012 was not smooth for natural gas prices, McClendon or the owners of CHK stock and bonds. In late April, it was revealed that he benefited from an executive perk called the Founder's Well Participation Programme (FWPP), allowing him a percentage share (up to 2.5%) in every active hydrocarbon-producing well run by the company as long as he paid a proportionate share of its development costs. This arrangement ran in addition to the remuneration he was receiving for his work as CEO and chairman.

At this time, with the company's operating results under pressure from continued weakness in US natural gas prices, it emerged that McClendon had borrowed significant amounts of money using his share in CHK's wells as collateral. As the company's drilling activity had expanded significantly over recent years, this required material investment in the wells from McClendon, which led him to borrow up to $846m through affiliate companies ArcadiaResources, Larchmont Resources and Jamestown Resources, which held all of the CEO's interests under the company's FWPP. After the initial revelations, there were further blows to McClendon's credibility as it became apparent that he had benefited from perks at the company that appeared egregious in the context of CHK's operational and financial straits.[33]

He ran a personal hedge fund on company property with staff whose remuneration was paid by CHK. In 2010, he and his family used company jets for a mixture of business and personal travel to the tune of $2.25m. Seventy-five purely personal flights were also taken alongside the 155 flights making up this figure, at an additional estimated cost of $830,000 to $875,000. From 2009 to 2011, Chesapeake Energy paid $13.3m in total compensation

---

33 Shiffman, J., Driver, A. and Grow, B. (2012). 'Special report: the lavish and leveraged life of Aubrey McClendon'. [Online] Available at: **www.reuters.com/article/2012/06/07/us-chesapeake-mcclendon-profile-idUSBRE8560IB20120607** [Accessed 7 June 2012].

to ten non-executive board members. By comparison, Exxon Mobil, the world's third-most-profitable company in 2011, paid 13 non-executive board members a collective $9.9m during the same period. The list goes on, painting a picture of a company whose CEO was allowed by a supine board to flaunt the usual norms of corporate governance.

Changes to the board

The powerful negative market reactions to what appeared to be a potential conflict of interest (although it was argued that McClendon's and CHK's interests were aligned to an extent) brought about a reaction from the company. It was announced that McClendon would relinquish his joint CEO/chairman role and that a new non-executive chairman would be appointed. The FWPP would also be terminated.

Subsequent to these announcements, further actions on the part of the company shored up its liquidity, fulfilled its intention to appoint a non-executive chairman and, under pressure from shareholders, replaced five members of its nine-member board. (Further negative press attention focused on the generosity of the pay schemes that had previously been in place for the former board members.)

Board members who were replaced

The following five board members were replaced: Richard K. Davidson, Kathleen M. Eisbrenner, Frank Keating, Don Nickles and Charles T. Maxwell.

New board members

And the following five new members were appointed: Archie W. Dunham, former chairman of ConocoPhillips and former chief executive officer of Conoco, Bob G. Alexander, Vincent J. Intrieri, R. Brad Martin and Frederic M. Poses.

Boardroom relationships hinted at risk appetite

It is possible to establish the pathways of professional connections between the members of corporate boards. What we have done is to compare the 'new' and 'old' CHK boards and look for connections between their members that lay outside the direct CHK link.

Overall, we found a total of 18 connections linking different members of the CHK board to activities outside their formal CHK roles. Besides these interpersonal connections between board members, a number of other important conclusions can be drawn from an examination of its constituents. Firstly, a simple statistical analysis of the board members' other affiliations should give us some insight into which industrial sectors their expertise lies and how diverse, complementary and balanced the board's professional experience is.

TABLE 3: CHK ORIGINAL BOARD MEMBERS – OTHER AFFILIATIONS BY SECTOR

Individuals	19	
Average # board memberships	9	
SECTORS		
Energy	74	44%
Financial	38	22%
Communications	13	8%
Engineering/tech	9	5%
Transportation	8	5%
Building	7	4%
Consumer/retail	6	4%
Nonprofit	6	4%
Healthcare	5	3%
Hospitality/gaming	3	2%
Total	169	

Source: Capital IQ, authors' research

Unsurprisingly, perhaps, the greatest concentration of expertise on the CHK board lies in the energy sector, where 44% of all board memberships are held. On closer examination, however, this statistic is misleading, since 21 of the 74 board positions in the sector pertain to one individual. If we exclude him from our calculations, the revised percentage of total board memberships for energy falls to 36% – still a preponderance, but now significantly closer to the 26% share of the financial sector in the board's composition.

TABLE 4: CHK ORIGINAL BOARD MEMBERS - OTHER AFFILIATIONS BY SECTOR (REVISED)

Individuals	18	
Average # board memberships	8	
SECTORS		
Energy	53	36%
Financial	38	26%
Communications	13	9%
Engineering/tech	9	6%
Transportation	8	5%
Building	7	5%
Consumer/retail	6	4%
Nonprofit	6	4%
Healthcare	5	3%
Hospitality/gaming	3	2%
Total	148	

Source: Capital IQ, authors' research

We acknowledge that finance is an important part of running a large company, and particularly one like CHK which is capital-intensive and often free cash-flow negative for long periods of time. Many of the board members hail from deeply financially conservative and highly rated companies such as Royal Dutch Shell and ConocoPhilips. But many others do not.

Indeed, if we scrutinise the corporations from which the CHK board is drawn, either in its later or its former incarnations, it can be seen that many of the board members are also on the boards of a number of corporations that are scarcely known for their financial conservatism. Among the list of companies that feature among the board members' activities are names such as the now-bankrupt Caesars Entertainment, Dynegy and a number of companies associated with activist investor Carl Icahn.

None of these associations is a decisive determinant of the board's likely course of action going forwards, but what it does usefully provide is an important qualitative marker that should clearly be factored into the potential credit risks facing this corporation and an indication of the potential future actions of the individuals who have stewardship of the company.

What lessons can we draw?

In this case there are lessons to be drawn that chime with our general, governance-driven approach to the activities of corporate boards and that are valuable as red flags for the credit investor:

- the prevalence of a dense social network at board level, with overlapping backgrounds
- excessive executive freedom for the CEO, who was not effectively supervised by the board
- the composition of the board hinted at its potential appetite for financial risk
- a formulaic link between production volumes and the CEO's personal wealth heightened his appetite for risk
- the combination of a supine board and the CEO's remuneration structure resulted in the company's finances becoming stretched, leading to a liquidity crisis in May 2012.

As a footnote to the foregoing, McClendon announced his intention to leave the company by the end of April 2013.

Case study II: Royal Bank of Scotland

To those who traded credit through the summer of 2008, so vivid are the memories of that period that it is sometimes hard to believe the time that has elapsed since what Ken Rogoff and Carmen Reinhart have named the Second Great Contraction nearly claimed the scalp of one of the largest and oldest British financial institutions, the Royal Bank of Scotland.[34]

Readers will be familiar with much of the detail of what ensued day-by-day as the bank's share price collapsed and the British government took pragmatic steps to recapitalise the institution – enabling the Bank of England to extend emergency liquidity to RBS as its market access rapidly dried up. For all that has been written on the subject, we still believe it is appropriate to focus on one crucial aspect of the end of the ill-fated career of Fred (formerly Sir Fred) Goodwin. In hindsight, this too can be seen to be, in part, as a failure of corporate governance.

In the BBC's series on the crisis, *The Love of Money*, former Chancellor of the Exchequer, Alistair Darling, expresses his incredulity at realising, in the heat of the crisis, that among the ranks of RBS's senior figures there were few who seemed to have a practical grip on the mechanics of how a bank actually worked. According to Darling, many apparently were unaware that they were facing a solvency rather than a liquidity crisis.

Corporate grandees and their shortcomings

If we stop to examine the professional experience of the board members, perhaps it is not so surprising. Many of these people belonged to an upper echelon of the corporate world that has had limited experience of getting involved in the minutiae and performs largely symbolic

---

34 Reinhart, C. M. and Rogoff, K. (2010). *This Time It's Different: Eight Centuries of Financial Folly.* Princeton: Princeton University Press.

roles on a variety of corporate boards. Such figures are able to move comfortably within the corporate stratosphere of senior politicians and company bigwigs, but are a long way from the crude mechanics of the banking trade. RBS's solvency crisis in 2008 can be seen as the sudden crystallisation of the dangers that a company embraces when selecting its board from a coterie of corporate figures who are detached from the fundamentals of the businesses they are overseeing and operate at a permanently high level across a range of corporate boards.

Scotland's financial services industry, founded on a hard-won reputation for financial prudence that has become a positive national stereotype, was done few favours by the problems of RBS. How did this happen? Again, once the composition of the board has been examined in some detail, a familiar pattern of overlapping board memberships and relationships outside the context of RBS, together with a low weighting of board members with industry-relevant skills, can be seen to emerge.

Another old boys' club

Take a look at the names of 15 of the 37 former board members of RBS who show up in a screen of the Goodwin years and ask yourself, 'Other than being on the RBS board, what, at first glance do these people have in common?'

TABLE 5: 41% OF RBS BOARD MEMBERS 2006-8

Buchan, Colin Alexander Mason (prior board)
Cameron, Johnny (prior board)
Currie, James (prior board)
Goodwin, Fred (prior board)
Grossart, Angus Mcfarlane Mcleod (prior board)
Hunter, Archie S. (prior board)
MacKay, Eileen (prior board)
Mathewson, George Ross (prior board)
McFarlane, John (prior board)
McKillop, Tom (prior board)
McLatchie, Cameron (prior board)
McLuskie, Norman C. (prior board)
Robertson, Iain Samuel (prior board)
Sutherland, Peter Dennis (prior board)
Younger of Leckie, Viscount (prior board)

Source: Capital IQ

Think global, hire local

Without putting too fine a point on it, the RBS board of 2008 had a distinctly Scottish flavour, and was replete with Scottish grandees and captains of industry, many of whom had little technical background in banking, but who collectively sat on a total of 231 different corporate boards, 82% of which were in the financial sector.

We find it hard to believe that these individuals would not have been seeing each other with great frequency in the fulfilment of their various board duties. It is, of course, to be expected that a corporation with ancient Scottish roots such as RBS should carry a reasonable number of board members of Scottish origin.

The area of concern here is that, at this point in its life story, RBS's balance sheet was approximately four times the size of total British (i.e. not just Scottish) GDP, and, as a major global financial institution, it could reasonably be expected to have a more diverse board which manifested an appropriately global perspective. All the more so as its CEO was allowed to launch a near-fatal takeover of ABN AMRO, a major Dutch financial institution with global reach.

At the times when these individuals met outside the context of RBS, we are asked to believe that, whilst spending long periods in each other's company in the execution of their board duties, they were able to compartmentalise their behaviour and overlapping knowledge to the exclusion of any potential conflicts of interest or breaches of fiduciary duty. Many of them sat not only on four to six of the RBS group's own internal boards, but also overlapped at a total of 26 other corporate boards.

TABLE 6: RBS BOARD MEMBERS – OTHER AFFILIATIONS BY SECTOR (2006-8)

Individuals	37	
Average # board memberships	6.25	
SECTORS		
Finance	190	82.3%
Energy	13	5.6%
Travel/tourism	10	4.3%
Manufacturing	5	2.2%
Retail	5	2.2%
Technology	4	1.7%
Media	4	1.7%

Source: Capital IQ, author's research

Testing the limits of compartmentalisation

It is surely stretching credulity to assume that people who were discussing RBS's ABN AMRO bid at the RBS corporate board meetings would put this out of their minds altogether by the time they got to another of the board meetings.

It is perhaps possible, we grant you, but it would take an almost hermetic power of abnegation not to carry the pre-existing relationships from outside activities from board to board. To clarify, we are not suggesting that any impropriety occurred; merely that it is not compatible with human nature to so completely compartmentalise oneself.

Now take a look at the names on the list below, detailing the members of RBS's board as of late 2012. Notice anything different? The new board appears to have a less pronounced Scottish accent. Could the new board be less of a dense network of mutually reinforcing relationships than it was in the days of the erstwhile Sir Fred? Reassuringly, from the point of view of the British taxpayers who own RBS stock that initially cost them £25bn, it would appear so.

TABLE 7: RBS BOARD MEMBERS 2012

Crombie, Alexander Maxwell (board)
Davis, Alison (board)
Di Iorio, Tony (board)
Hampton, Philip R. (board)
Hester, Stephen A. M. (board)
Hughes, Penelope L. (board)
Liu, Sherry (board)
MacHale, Joseph Patrick (board)
McCormick, John (board)
Nelson, Brendan R. (board)
Noakes, Baroness Sheila (board)
Ryan, Arthur F. (board)
Scott, Philip Gordon (board)
Van Saun, Bruce (board)

Source: Capital IQ

TABLE 8: RBS BOARD MEMBERS - OTHER AFFILIATIONS BY SECTOR (2012)

Individuals	14	
Average # board memberships	8.5	
SECTORS		
Finance	67	56%
Technology	9	8%
Consumer/retail	9	8%
Telcos/communications	8	7%
Non-profit	4	3%
Other	22	18%

Source: Capital IQ, author's research

In the rear-view mirror of history, the CEO's stacking the board with members of an elite and interconnected social group can be seen as one of the factors that lay behind the poor oversight and massive overreach that ultimately undid RBS.

This was exacerbated by a chauvinist pride taken by the Scottish political class in RBS's disproportionate growth relative to the rest of the Scottish economy. For example, First Minister Alex Salmond's enthusiastic backing of Royal Bank of Scotland's disastrous takeover of ABN AMRO is shown in a letter released on 11 January 2011.[35] Salmond wrote that he "would like to offer any assistance my office can provide". Scotland's secretary for finance, John Swinney, said in a separate letter at the time that the deal was "an enormous achievement for RBS" that helped make Scotland seem "an attractive place to do business".

What lessons can we draw?

Again, there are lessons to be drawn from this disaster that chime with our general, governance-driven approach to the activities of corporate boards and that are valuable as red flags for the credit investor:

---

35   Channel 4 (2012). *Salmond: You keep Scots bank debt, we'll keep the oil money.* [Online]. Available at: **www.channel4.com/news/salmond-you-keep-scots-bank-debt-well-keep-the-oil-money** [Accessed 24 November 2014].

- the prevalence of a dense network of individuals at board level

- the hard-driving CEO who is free to pursue strategic objectives largely set by himself

- the lack of checks and balances on his activity from a supine board

- the overweening ambition that led to the series of takeovers culminating in the ABN AMRO deal.

All of these factors should have sounded a note of caution to RBS's investors but, at the time, were largely overlooked. In the course of 2007–8, the percentage of equity analysts who had a sell rating on RBS ahead of the crisis rose from 0% in September 2007 to a high point of 34% in March 2008, by which time the stock price had roughly halved. The percentage of analysts with a sell rating thereafter diminished to 17.2% by November, by which point the stock had lost a further 85% of its remaining value.[36]

Management compensation and its influence on credit

Gauging management's alignment with stakeholders

At the heart of management's fiduciary responsibilities towards both equity and credit investors lies a deep-seated conflict of interest. This varies depending on jurisdictions. We believe, under English law, their duty is, rather unhelpfully, towards the company; the law has generally interpreted this as meaning the shareholders. Under US law, their duty is more literally to shareholders. In most corporations, the C-suite is rewarded financially for its performance in the form of a base salary, stock and options, potentially creating an embedded bias towards the interests of the shareholder over those of the company's credit investors. Compensation is often driven by formulae linked, at least in part, to the market performance of the company's stock, among other measures.

There are exceptions to this rule. In financial institutions, for example, there are precedents for compensation being paid in the form of subordinated debt rather than equity or options, and some industries reward the C-suite based on the notion of Economic Value Added (EVA®)[37] and other measures of capital efficiency, which take into account the mix of different types of capital on the company's balance sheet. All the same, it is a rare company in which management's own financial interests are not more aligned with those of the shareholder than those of the credit investor. While management is in part motivated in alignment with shareholders, they are also motivated to hang on to their jobs. There is usually a tension between these two motivations.

Ultimately, if managements forget their duty to shareholders they will be subject to the judgment of the market for corporate control – and will be replaced. However, given the

---

36 Source: Bloomberg.
37 EVA is a trademark of Stern Stewart Management Services.

atomised nature of corporate ownership, it can be quite hard for that market to operate effectively, particularly if managements have dense social relationships with, say, asset managers, who are also agents of a kind. Then there are other devices such as management's use of poison pills to frustrate that market. For example, in late 2014, Hertz adopted a one-year rights plan to frustrate the initiative of activists to wrest the decision about the sale of Hertz Equipment Rental away from them.

Disclosure is patchy

Disclosure of management compensation and, hence, their financial motivation to act either in or against the interests of credit holders is inconsistent from company to company and jurisdiction to jurisdiction, which does restrict the range of potential examples that we can bring to bear to illustrate this point. However, there are companies out there that offer a valuable amount of data on this potentially vexed subject. One company with a very high level of disclosure is the US pork producer, Smithfield Foods (SFD), which in 2013 agreed to be acquired by China's WH Group (at the time called Shanghai International Holdings) for an estimated $7.1bn including outstanding debt.

Management compensation case study I: Smithfield Foods

It is fair to say that, with 36 pages of material on the topic of executive compensation in SFD's 2013 10-K/A filing to be analysed, the company's level of disclosure is admirably high. At the time of the deal, SFD management was accused by shareholder activists – including Starboard Capital – of selling the company at a time when its fundamentals were weak and its potential future value was not fully reflected in WH's offer price of $34 a share. Ultimately, however, no alternative deal was tabled and the activists lined up with other SFD shareholders to accept the initial proposal. When we examine the compensation arrangements disclosed in the 10-K, what light does it shed on this accusation?

Principles seem sound

SFD's 10-K sets out the general precepts on which the CEO's compensation is based. The basic principles behind the statement seem reasonable enough. To summarise, there are three elements of total direct compensation: salary, annual cash incentives and long-term equity-based incentives.

- Smithfield seeks to align management pay levels with measures of operating and market performance.

- These measures are subject to peer-group comparison.

- The compensation programme is subject to regular assessment by the compensation committee to more closely align executive rewards with shareholder interests.

- The majority of management compensation is performance-based (82% in 2013, not counting the value of existing shareholdings).

- The company uses guidelines for management stock-ownership.

- An independent consulting firm advises the compensation committee, and does no other work for Smithfield.

- There is a three-year minimum holding period for stock acquired through the deferred cash-incentive programme.

- The company pays no severance benefits except in the event of a change of control (i.e. they are insured against the market for corporate control), and can claw back compensation awarded in the event of misconduct.

- Executives have no employment contracts and the company does not re-price stock options without shareholder approval.

- All executive compensation packages are put to shareholder vote, achieving 82% and 83% support in both 2012 and 2013.

By the standards of some corporations, such strictures are fairly tight, and disclosure is good enough to enable us to work through the detail on compensation in the Smithfield 10-K and work out what financial benefits actually accrued to the management team as a result of the WH Group acquisition.

FIGURE 4: COMPANY PERFORMANCE AND CEO COMPENSATION

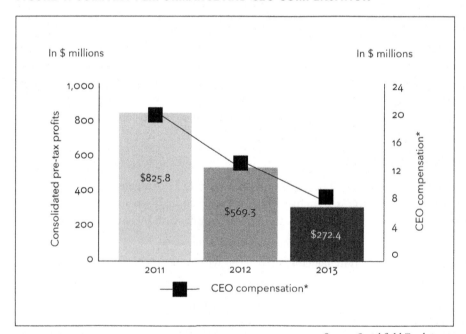

Source: Smithfield Foods inc 2013 10-K/A

* Mr Pope's total compensation as reported in table 9, excluding change in pension value.

Smithfield then highlights changes to the CEO's compensation package over the past two years, generally increasing the correlation between the CEO's performance, as measured by a series of operational and market benchmarks, and his earnings. This section of the 10-K also outlines the company's general compensation practices that apply to all of the executive team, including pay-for-performance and guidelines on management stock-ownership levels, the use of an independent consulting firm to determine compensation levels and limits on other perquisites. All of this is subject to shareholder approval.

But what did it mean in practice?

The question for credit investors when the deal was proposed – and one that should be asked in any M&A situation – was what did this mean in financial terms for the C-suite, and would it be enough to tip the balance on the deal one way or the other? Thanks to SFD's high level of disclosure, we are able to draw out some interesting colour on this topic.

Firstly, it is important to understand that SFD's incumbent management stood to keep their jobs under the terms of the proposed deal. The deal came at a time (May 2013) when SFD's stock market performance had been in-line with the S&P 500 in the course of the year. In the previous 17 months, Smithfield's stock had actually under-performed the index by 10.5%, though it had again performed in-line on a 29-month view.

We have chosen these periods of time because they start on 1 January of each year and therefore fit with many investors' performance-measurement periods. Overall, while not stellar, SFD's market performance appears to have been reasonable. Over this period, management were earning a very comfortable living – perhaps not egregious by the standards of large US corporations in our view, but nonetheless ample – with rewards ranging between a maximum of $20m per year for the CEO and $2.7m for the lowest-paid executive whose compensation is disclosed over the previous three years.

We mention this not so much to weigh in on the moral or social issue of executive compensation as to illustrate the relative attractiveness of their doing a deal in which they would be obliged to leave the company or one in which they would keep their jobs. Our concern is merely the alignment of their interests with those of the company's equity and credit investors.

TABLE 9: SMITHFIELD FOODS EXECUTIVE COMPENSATION 2011-2013

Name and Title All numbers (US $)	Year	Salary	Bonus	Stock Awards	Option Awards	Non-Equity Incentive Plan	Change in Value	All Other Compensation	Total (US$)
C. Larry Pope	2013	1,100,000	–	4,420,000	–	2,724,076	2,201,377	332,937	10,778,390
President and CEO	2012	1,100,000	–	6,128,000	936,000	4,707,032	3,314,395	332,368	16,517,795
	2011	1,100,000	250,000	3,514,000	655,000	13,015,880	1,492,642	200,727	20,228,249
Robert W. Manly, IV Executive Vice	2013	750,000	–	2,210,000	–	1,362,038	4,323,221	50,997	8,696,256
President and CFO	2012	700,000	–	3,556,750	468,000	2,353,516	4,242,027	38,318	11,358,611
	2011	600,000	250,000	2,196,250	327,500	4,693,455	440,405	37,482	8,545,092
George H. Richter President and COO,	2013	800,000	–	576,900	–	3,225,455	1,387,062	68,367	6,057,784
Pork Group	2012	800,000	–	2,083,112	374,400	3,342,159	1,519,305	63,866	8,182,842
	2011	800,000	250,000	–	262,000	3,582,315	902,675	44,711	5,841,701
Joseph B. Sebring	2013	735,000	250,000	1,075,864	–	1,219,021	648,418	80,598	4,008,901
President of John	2012	719,519	–	1,041,556	234,000	1,121,080	1,993,937	176,361	5,286,453
	2011	700,000	250,000	–	163,750	1,791,157	807,822	78,767	3,791,496
Joseph W. Luter, IV	2013	700,000	–	1,084,262	–	1,232,022	1,062,222	166,729	4,245,235
EVP, Sales and	2012	700,000	–	2,045,242	234,000	1,342,290	1,010,801	155,946	5,488,279
Marketing, Pork	2011	700,000	350,000	–	163,750	972,129	335,877	171,283	2,693,039

Source: Smithfield Foods inc 2013 10-K/A

It seems fair to say that the C-suite's annual compensation was indeed variable and performance-driven, though it is also the case that, by most standards, the executives were certainly making plenty of money. Were they, however, being offered a deal that would deliver vast, life-changing wealth to them overnight? Well, not really, in the context of their substantial ongoing annual income. Using the details from the 10-K, we have calculated the sums accruing to the executive team in the form of vesting options and stock holdings at the $34/share offer price:

TABLE 10: SMITHFIELD FOODS VALUE OF VESTING OPTIONS AND STOCK

	Bid Price Per Share	Profit Per Option	Options	Profit on Options	Shares
C. Larry	$34.00	$12.06	33,334	$402,008	$5,186,000.0
		$18.57	66,667	$1,238,006	$3,241,250.0
		$20.70	100,000	$2,070,000	$0.0
		$10.25	0	$0	$0.0
		$1.09	250,000	$272,500	$0.0
		$4.00	50,000	$200,000	$0.0
Robert W. Manly, IV		$12.06	16,667	$201,004	$2,593,000.0
		$18.57	33,333	$618,994	$652,866.0
		$20.70	33,000	$683,100	$1,620,625.0
		$10.25	0	$0	$0.0
		$1.60	50,000	$80,000	$0.0
George H. Richter		$12.06	13,334	$160,808	$1,037,200.0
		$18.57	0	$0	$971,208.0
		$10.25	15,000	$153,750	$0.0
		$2.14	25,000	$53,500	$0.0
		$4.00	25,000	$100,000	$0.0
Joseph B. Sebring		$12.06	8,334	$100,508	$518,600.0
		$18.57	0	$0	$311,705.0
		$10.25	0	$0	$485,591.0
			0	$0	$0.0
Joseph W. Luter, IV		$12.06	8,334	$100,508	$518,600.0
		$18.57	16,667	$309,506	$314,453.0
		$20.70	33,000	$683,100	$581,428.0
		$10.25	0	$0	$324,125.0
		$4.00	25,000	$100,000	$0.0
				$7,527,292	$18,356,651
Total Value					**$25,883,943**

Source: SFD 2013 10-K/A, authors' calculations

It appears that the one-off stock benefits of the deal for management do not amount to significantly more than the annual returns of their keeping their jobs. This changes the basis for assessing management's motivation for backing the deal. In Smithfield's case, rather than riding off into the sunset with a vast haul, management is motivated to stay on board and keep on bringing home the bacon.

In terms of investors' ability to handicap potential outcomes in such a situation, the question really becomes, 'Would Smithfield's C-suite not wish to continue to keep working at this high level of remuneration under the aegis of a new foreign owner, rather than face mounting shareholder pressures as the equity continues only to deliver returns similar to those available in the broader market?' In this instance, management was perhaps not so much tempted to cash out as to cash in on the potential future financial rewards of the deal.

Credit investors were themselves not faced with the same kind of choice. The Smithfield buyout took the company's leverage from 2.1x before the deal to a pro-forma figure of 3.8x after it, moving the company's five-year CDS spread from 190bps to 350bps in the process.

Management compensation case study II: Sallie Mae

As we have illustrated, M&A activity and financial engineering can be materially deleterious to a creditor's interests even if they are enormously beneficial to stockholders. Since a company's leading chief executives are the architects of its strategy with regards both to corporate combinations and the choice of capital structure, it is worthwhile – although not always easy – to investigate the extent to which their remuneration structures encourage them to engage in such activities. We would re-emphasise that we do not approach this issue from a position of advocacy. It is not our intention to engage with the old saw of whether executives manage companies for the benefit of stakeholders or shareholders. Rather, we seek to identify where executive remuneration structures might encourage corporate actions that undermine the position of creditors, especially if such structures are coupled with a 'dealmaker'-style chief executive or executive team and/or a weak board. When such a situation prevails, even companies that one might otherwise think safe from such activity can prove vulnerable.

Let us consider the case of SLM Corp. The Student Loan Marketing Association (SLMA) or Sallie Mae was a US government-sponsored enterprise (GSE) akin to others with down-home monikers, such as Fannie Mae and Freddie Mac – created in 1972 to provide a secondary market and warehousing facility for student loans (originally it was prohibited by Congress from providing loans directly to students). Sallie Mae was, in the opinion of the US Treasury "generally successful in managing political risk"[38] and succeeded in persuading Congress to extend its ownership from the banks and educational institutions that originally participated in the federally guaranteed student loan programme. Hence, in 1983 non-voting stock was listed on the NYSE, and Congress permitted the conversion of all stock to voting stock in 1992. External factors pushed them – or allowed them to create the impression of being pushed – in the direction of privatisation. The offset fee of

---

38 Quinn, P., Stauffer, L. and McQueen, S. (2006). *Lessons Learned From The Privatization of Sallie Mae, draft, US Department of the Treasury, Office of Sallie Mae Oversight,* p.7. [Online]. Available at: **www. treasury.gov/about/organizational-structure/offices/Documents/SallieMaePrivatizationReport.pdf** [Accessed 24 November 2014].

30bps on federally guaranteed student loans acquired for the GSE's portfolio was surely a crimp on profitability that applied to no other student-loan holder; however, it did not apply to private loans or to loans consolidated under the federal student-loan programme. The Office of Sallie Mae Oversight therefore adjudged its financial impact on Sallie Mae as "never greater than 15bps overall for on-balance-sheet student loans."[39] That said, the introduction of the Federal Direct Loan Program in 1993 threatened to eliminate the need for a secondary market altogether. Such political risk precipitated a 56% decline in Sallie's stock price between year-end 1991 and year-end 1994, during which time it under-performed the S&P financials by 64%.[40]

This under-performance did not sit well with Sallie's management, which was characterised by the Oversight Office as possessing an "opportunistic or entrepreneurial spirit, which included an alertness to opportunities, and a will to act on insight".[41] As such they were "culturally oriented toward privatization"[42] for which they had been angling as far back as the Reagan administration. Unsurprisingly, they began a process of privatisation in 1996 and finally terminated Sallie's federal charter in 2004, ahead of the deadline originally set, reflecting SLM's success in replacing federal agency debt with corporate debt and ABS and also in growing earnings. In the four years from 2000–2004, the federally insured student loan market grew to $328bn from $200bn, while private student loan origination underwent fourfold growth between 1996 and 2003.[43] Consequently, SLM's stock price increased almost eightfold from the beginning of 1996 to the end of 2004, outperforming the S&P financials by 78%.[44] Leading the company from July 1997 to May 2005 as CEO was Albert 'Al' L. Lord, a longtime Sallie Mae staffer, who had been with the company since 1981 and was a major proponent of the company's privatisation.[45]

Having reorganised in 1997, the now SLM Holding Corp. sought to vertically integrate and move into origination, in order to capture the federal interest payment subsidy that banks had traditionally recouped by charging a premium when they sold loans to Sallie Mae. The company also acquired companies that made private loans (non-federally supported student loans) and engaged in mortgage banking operations. However, the GSE still had to be wound down and a trust established to ensure that any GSE-related obligations could be settled after SLMA's dissolution (originally planned for 2007). The GSE was overseen during this period by the Office of Sallie Mae Oversight, which undertook annual examinations of the GSE. This body advocated stricter internal controls to separate the GSE and holdco (SLM Corp) to ensure that the holdco did not avail itself of GSE benefits for its own gain. There was concern that the GSE was inadequately capitalised because, as

39 Quinn, P., Stauffer, L. and McQueen, S. (2006).
40 Bloomberg.
41 Quinn, P., Stauffer, L. and McQueen, S. (2006). *Lessons Learned From The Privatization of Sallie Mae, draft, US Department of the Treasury, Office of Sallie Mae Oversight*, p.7. [Online]. Available at: **www.treasury.gov/about/organizational-structure/offices/Documents/SallieMaePrivatizationReport.pdf** [Accessed 24 November 2014].
42 Quinn, P., Stauffer, L. and McQueen, S. (2006).
43 Quinn, P., Stauffer, L. and McQueen, S. (2006).
44 Bloomberg.
45 Bloomberg.

investors might recall, securitisation accounting allowed the company to finance student loans off balance sheet, while holding the higher risk residuals on balance sheet. Moreover, the entity became increasingly involved in higher risk activities. However, the Oversight Office's enforcement powers did not stretch too far beyond reporting to Congress, and SLM management was recalcitrant in its attitude towards oversight and the delivery of information.[46] Either way, on 29 December 2004 the GSE was dissolved and in 2005 SLM became a fully privatised company.

Did remuneration influence strategy?

It is at this point that a glance at management remuneration might elucidate what happens next. Disclosure on SLM executive remuneration is fairly generous but is only referenced in the company's 10-k filings and the investor has to refer to the proxy statement to get an insight into the gen. In addition to providing specific detail, the proxy outlines SLM's philosophy with regards to executive compensation. Thus, as far back as 2001, we learn SLM's executive compensation policy is based "on a belief that compensation tied to corporate performance and share price will enhance shareholder value".[47] This is standard, mom's-apple-pie stuff for shareholder-owned companies but, given that SLM at the time was *not* fully privatised and owned a GSE that benefited from federal subventions, the lack of a nod to other objectives might seem a little surprising. The policy goes on to state that the total compensation package is designed "to attract and to retain executive officers who are *entrepreneurial* [our italics] and desire 'a risk and reward' compensation structure that is based on ownership principles, not the traditional employee-employer relationship."[48]

Sensibly, the proxy goes on to state, SLM benchmarks compensation to that of peer companies, which include: AFLAC, Ambac Financial Group, American Express, American General Finance, CIT Group, Citigroup, Fannie Mae, Freddie Mac, Franklin Resources, MBIA, MBNA, MetLife, Moody's, Morgan Stanley, Stilwell Value, T. Rowe Price and USA Education. Interestingly, the executive compensation philosophy for some of these companies, while making the usual obeisances to shareholder value, is a lot more nuanced. Thus, while SLM awarded performance bonuses linked to " 'core cash basis' earnings per share growth, 'core cash basis' net income growth, loan acquisition volume and control channel origination volume",[49] Fannie Mae's executive compensation was linked to fuzzier general objectives such as "risk management, housing impact, delivery of value through technology and customer relationships, preserving Fannie Mae's franchise and work force development".[50] While the CEO's annual bonus award is admittedly tied exclusively to

46   Quinn, P., Stauffer, L. and McQueen, S. (2006). *Lessons Learned From The Privatization of Sallie Mae, draft, US Department of the Treasury, Office of Sallie Mae Oversight*, p.7. [Online]. Available at: **www.treasury.gov/about/organizational-structure/offices/Documents/SallieMaePrivatizationReport.pdf** [Accessed 24 November 2014].

47   Sallie Mae (2001). *Notice of 2001 Annual Meeting and Proxy Statement*, p.13. [Online]. Available at: **www.salliemae.com/assets/about/investors/shareholder/annual-reports/2001proxy1.pdf** [Accessed 24 November 2014].

48   Sallie Mae (2001).

49   Sallie Mae (2001).

50   Fannie Mae (2002). *Notice of Annual Meeting of Stockholders, May 21, 2002*, p.11. [Online]. Available at:

year-on-year earnings-per-share (EPS) growth, his long-term incentive compensation reflected pre-established goals including financial results but also:

- "implementation of industry-leading financial safety and soundness initiatives;

- "achievement of the highest level of affordable housing finance activity in its history;

- "improvements in its technology management and customer service;

- "successful management of credit and interest rate risk; and

- "attention paid to the development and diversity of its work force".[51]

Thus, the philosophical underpinnings of executive compensation at SLM guide management with a laser focus on enhancing shareholder value whereas those of former peer GSEs encourage other objectives, including the maintenance of asset quality and the promotion of the GSE's public policy role. Even American Express, a peer of SLM with no public policy aims, weighted its annual incentive awards 50% towards enhancing shareholder value and 25% apiece towards customer and employee satisfaction, respectively.[52] SLM executives had few such distractions.

Consistent with Sallie Mae's transition to a fully privatised company, in 2000 the Compensation Committee granted options to Al Lord and other senior executives for the first time since 1997.[53] These were designed to vest on the stock price reaching 120% of the grant price but no earlier than a year from the grant of the options. They would, in any case, vest after five years or on a change of control.[54] In the latter event, SLM would also make up certain tax gross-ups for the executives involved. The change of control provision effectively insulated the beneficiaries from any financial losses resulting from a change in ownership. It could be argued that this is an example of the corporation's stewards protecting their own interests ahead of those of shareholders, who, after all, only have an incentive to sell for a better price than they can currently command, i.e., if a new team believes it is better placed to maximise shareholder value than the current one and backs it with an offer higher than the current share price. Moreover, if we assume the current management team was economically rational (a gross oversimplification – human motivation is far more complex and often unconscious), then the change of control clause almost creates a perverse incentive for them to find an external buyer since it would both increase the value of their stock and accelerate the vesting.

During the course of 2000, Sallie Mae granted Al Lord options on 463,691 shares of the company (225,000 on 13 January and 238,691 that vested one year from their grant date

---

www.fanniemae.com/resources/file/ir/pdf/proxy-statements/proxy.pdf [Accessed 24 November 2014].

51 Fannie Mae (2002).

52 American Express Company (2001). *2001 Notice of Annual Meeting and Proxy Statement*, p.19. [Online]. Available at: www.onlineproxy.com/amex/2001/amex-proxy.pdf [Accessed 24 November 2014].

53 Sallie Mae (2001). *Notice of 2001 Annual Meeting and Proxy Statement*, p.13. [Online]. Available at: www.salliemae.com/assets/about/investors/shareholder/annual-reports/2001proxy1.pdf [Accessed 24 November 2014].

54 Sallie Mae (2001).

on 15 November).[55] The strike prices on the options were set at $43 and $55 per share, respectively, which were the market prices of the stock at the time of issuance. Note that the market price of the shares at the time of the second issuance was already 127.9% of that which prevailed at the time of the first issuance, such that Mr Lord was already in the money to the tune of $2.7m on his first option allocation,[56] provided the stock price held up through the first vesting date approximately two months later. As it happened, it reached $60.75 on the close of 16 January,[57] equal to 141.3% of the market price on 13 January 2000 and constituting a gain of $3.99m or over six times his base salary of $650,000.[58]

Although not vested, Mr Lord also had a book gain of $1.37m on his second option allocation at the same date. This second allocation was a grant of replacement options to replace those that Mr Lord had exercised during the year having retained the shares obtained in this way except for an amount necessary to cover the cost of exercising the options and the associated tax. In other words, if executives hung onto shares after acquiring them through exercising options, they would be given further options to compensate. In 2000, Mr Lord, we learn, acquired 347,459 shares through the exercise of options for a realised value of $6.23m[59] (we do not know what the original strike prices were) and had unexercised in-the-money options totalling almost $29m of which $10.2m were exercisable. Finally, he was granted a stock award in 2000 of $1.57m, which, as long as he stuck around for just over two years, he got to keep.

Mr Lord's compensation structure (and that of his fellow senior executives) accentuates management's focus on share price above all else in two ways. First, by weighting their compensation towards elements that are stock price-sensitive and away from cash base-and-bonus. Second, by encouraging them to build ownership stakes in the company by granting replacement options for those exercised options where the underlying shares were retained. And nobody could accuse SLM of having a hidden agenda. This was completely consistent with the compensation culture adumbrated in the Proxy Statement, which stated that it held Mr Lord's 2000 base salary at sub-25th percentile for the CEOs of peer-group companies, emphasising instead 'at-risk' compensation and that it sought to promote the principle of executives as owners by adopting targets in 1999 that would aim to have the CEO, president and executive vice president own stock equal to a ten-times multiple of their base salary.[60]

Between 2001 and 2005, Mr Lord was granted the following options:

---

55 Sallie Mae (2001).
56 Authors' estimates.
57 Yahoo Finance (2014) [Online]. Available at: **finance.yahoo.com/q/hp?s=SLM&a=00&b=16&c=2001 &d=00&e=16&f=2001&g=d** [Accessed November 24, 2014].
58 Authors' estimates.
59 Sallie Mae (2001).
60 Sallie Mae (2001).

TABLE 11: OPTIONS GRANTED TO AL LORD BY SLM FOR PERIOD 2001-2005

	Initial	Replacement	Grant date	Expiry date	Exercise price/ market price	Price-vesting targets*
	750,000		15-Jan-01	15-Jan-11	$20.17 $24.20	120% of the grant price for five trading days, no earlier than 12 months from their grant date.
		590,019	14-Feb-01	13-Aug-07	$22.97 $27.56	
		413,310	14-Feb-01	13-Jan-10	$22.97 $27.56	
2001		496,356	01-Aug-01	13-Aug-07	$26.62 $31.94	
						One-third One-third One-third
			24-Jan-02	24-Jan-12	$28.67	$35.83 $38.12 $43
2002	3,000,000	459,951	21-May-02	15-Jan-11	$32.60	$35.83 $38.12 $43
2003	1,500,000		28-Jan-03	28-Jan-13	$35.20	$44 $46.82 $52.80
2004	0	0				
2005	300,000	0	19-May-05	19-May-15	$48.84 $58.60	120% of the grant price for five trading days, no earlier than 12 months from their grant date.

*All numbers adjusted for a three-for-one stock split on 20 June 2003.

Source: SLM Proxy statements 2001–2006

In addition, Mr Lord received a further 100,000 'restricted stock units' (RSUs) over this period (300,000 adjusted for the stock split), valued at a total of $9.58m at the time of granting. These vested on 31 December 2004, but converted into stock one year after Mr Lord's departure from the CEO position. In fact, they converted on 3 January 2006 because Mr Lord retired from the CEO position in the previous calendar year and left on 31 May 2005. Did he leave the company? No. He became chairman of the board (having been vice chairman from 1997), for which he received an option over 300,000 shares for a three-year term of service. At 3 January 2006, with SLM stock trading at $55.81 per share, those 100,000/300,000 RSUs were worth $16.74m, a profit of approximately $7.2m (excluding dividends). By the end of this period, through stock and vested options, Mr Lord owned 2.07% of SLM in his own right.[61] The stock price appears to be set as his central motivation.

One final point of qualitative note: in the company's discussion of Mr Lord's compensation in the 2002 proxy statement, it observes that the Compensation Committee "considered the following accomplishments in awarding Mr. Lord's individual performance-based bonus: the successful completion of the integration of the USA Group and Sallie Mae operations ... [and] extension of the Corporation's student loan business through completion of negotiations for the acquisition of two higher education debt-collection businesses ..."[62] A company can grow its earnings organically or it can grow them through acquisition – a time-honoured path, especially if organic growth looks like it might start to falter at some point. What is worthy of attention here is that SLM identifies acquisitions and their successful consummation as factors that enjoy a positive weighting in Mr Lord's remuneration. Not only is he incentivised to maintain a laser focus on raising the stock price; he is also motivated to take event risk to do so.

---

61 SallieMae (2006). *Notice of Annual Meeting to Shareholders*, p.2. [Online]. Available at **www.salliemae. com/assets/about/investors/shareholder/annual-reports/2005ProxyStatement1.pdf** {Accessed 24 November 2014].
62 Sallie Mae (2002). *Notice of Annual Meeting to Shareholders*, p.11 [Online]. Available at: **www.salliemae. com/assets/about/investors/shareholder/annual-reports/2002proxy.pdf** [Accessed 24 November 2014].

Selling Sallie Mae

There is another way to achieve a rapid hike in the stock price which was very much in fashion in 2006–2007. As indicated previously, easy liquidity had fuelled a growth both in the collateralised loan obligation (CLO) and high-yield markets. Underwriting standards had consequently relaxed, which manifested itself in an increase in issuance of so-called 'cov(enant)-lite' loans (loans with meagre covenant protection for investors) and triple-C bonds (the weakest of the high-yield spectrum, just under 50% of which, on average, default over five years).[63] It also led to a growth in payment-in-kind (PIK) bonds, where interest can be paid not in cash but through the creation of additional debt. Such an environment made LBO-financing very inexpensive and lowered the hurdle rates by which LBO initiatives were evaluated.

One might have thought that SLM's LBO candidacy would have been stymied by the fact that it already was leveraged, with equity to managed assets of barely 4%.[64] Moreover, one's concerns might have been assuaged by earlier perceptions that the company would actually seek to improve its credit profile and ratings. And then SLM needed Prime-1 commercial paper ratings in order to fund at least part of its Federal Family Education Loan Program (FFELP) loans. And, although SLM could securitise, did competitive pricing of securitisations not depend to some extent upon the credit quality of the originator? One might have thought so; tell the truth and shame the devil – this author did. He was wrong.

In April 2007 Sallie Mae accepted a $60-per-share offer for the company that valued it at about $25bn. Behind the LBO were two private equity (PE) firms, J.C. Flowers & Co and Friedman Fleischer & Lowe, and two of Wall Street's behemoths, J.P. Morgan and Bank of America. What made the deal viable was the willingness of the two banks to provide $228bn liquidity support for Sallie Mae. It was fair to say that the market had been blindsided. "Now that we've had Sallie Mae, there's a sense that the whole sector is not immune … " said Moody's analyst, Alexander Dill.[65] Between the announcement and the end of June 2007, five-year CDS spreads widened over 600% and many large investors took losses on Sallie Mae's $108bn of debt, including PIMCO, Capital Research, Jackson National Life and Prudential Insurance.[66] The knock-on effect to other financial issuers, many of whom were now also seen as vulnerable to re-leveraging, affected up to 40% of the $2trn corporate bond market.[67]

63   Moody's Investors Service (2014). *Annual Default Study: Corporate Default and Recovery Rates 1920–2013*. [Online]. Available at: **www.moodys.com/research/Annual-Default-Study-Corporate-Default-and-Recovery-Rates-1920-2013--PBC_166292** [Accessed 24 November 2014].
64   S&P (2007). SLM Corporation. [Online]. Available at: **www.globalcreditportal.com/ratingsdirect/showArticlePage.do?rand=WOfWmZ3cvU&sid=555385&sind=A&object_id=938804&rev_id=38&from=SR** [Accessed 24 November 2014].
65   Pittman, M. (2007). 'LBOs Attack Finance Company Bondholders; SLM Unravels'. [Online]. Available at: **www.bloomberg.com/apps/news?pid=newsarchive&sid=aIXYuiPfwKp8&refer=bondheads** [Accessed 24 November 2014]. Bloomberg. 22 May 2007.
66   Pittman, M. (2007).
67   Pittman, M. (2007).

But timing is everything. The LBO was launched at about the time the US mortgage market started turning sour. In February 2007, HSBC, in a move that shocked markets, increased provisions by 20% against losses at its US subsidiary, Household International, which was heavily involved in the US mortgage market. Stories of losses and growth in non-performing assets began to circulate and, by the end of July 2007, spreads on the US generic high-yield index (remember that LBO loans and bonds are by definition high-yield) had more than doubled to over 500bps.[68] Suddenly, the financing that would support the LBO of SLM appeared to be drying up and buyers were looking remorseful.

Flowers' boss, J. Christopher Flowers, stumbled upon what looked like a get-out-of-jail card. He cited Congress's plans to cut subsidies for student loans (in a measure approved by Congress on 7 September 2007) and called it a 'material adverse event' (see entries *passim* in this book), which he believed allowed him to walk away from the deal without paying a $900m reverse break-up fee, even though, by SLM's estimates, the trim to subsidies would result in a decline in core earnings of only 1.8% to 2.1% annually over five years.[69] Flowers and his partners offered a counter deal of $50 per share in cash and $10 in warrants (dependent upon earnings). Unsurprisingly, the matter ended up in court, where phalanxes of lawyers cavilled on behalf of their clients. (Delaware Chancery Court Vice-Chancellor, Leo Strine, quipped: "It's good to know how many people in America it takes to screw in a light bulb or handle a scheduling conference."[70])

The credit crunch paralysed the global financial markets such that SLM, in common with many other specialty finance companies, faced severe difficulties in funding itself through securitisation channels and drew down on the J.P. Morgan/Bank of America financing facility. The matter was resolved when J.P. Morgan and Bank of America agreed to refinance a $31bn credit line to SLM in February 2008, enabling the company to access the funding necessary to maintain itself in business.

In the end, the SLM LBO was an exercise in value destruction. On 12 April 2007, just before the LBO announcement, the stock price closed at $40.75. One year later, with the LBO consigned to history but funding secured, the stock price closed at $17.85[71] – a 56% decline over a period when the S&P 500 declined by about 8%.[72] True, anybody that, as the saying goes, 'bought on the rumour and sold on the fact' could have traded out in the $50 range after the announcement and made a tidy profit. But neither the equity price nor the morality of LBOs are of concern to us here. The issue is the impact on credit investors (negative) and the extent to which it could have been predicted from an examination of the way in which SLM senior executives were remunerated.

---

68 Bloomberg.
69 Kelly, J. and Evans, E. (2007). 'Flowers Sallie Mae Failure Proves He's No Schwarzman'. [Online]. Available at: **www.bloomberg.com/apps/news?pid=newsarchive&sid=azX_uqK203YE** [Accessed 24 November 2014].
70 Corcoran, G. (2007). 'Strine Unplugged: Live at the Sallie Mae Hearing'. [Online]. Available at: **blogs. wsj.com/deals/2007/10/23/strine-unplugged-live-at-the-sallie-mae-hearing** [Accessed 24 November 2014].
71 Data from **finance.yahoo.com**.
72 Bloomberg.

Management compensation lessons

- Read the proxy statements and executive compensation policies of the company being analysed and those of its peers; this is a useful compare-and-contrast exercise.

- An overarching focus of executive remuneration on the stock price to the exclusion of other variables, as appears to have been the case with SLM, will encourage behaviour designed to increase the stock price, *regardless of the impact on other stakeholders (e.g. creditors) in the corporation and the method used to achieve it.* While executive remuneration in a shareholder-owned corporation should be linked to longer-term, non-market related stock performance, a consideration of other variables is likely to be indicative of a culture concerned with the interests of stakeholders other than shareholders, even if only on a secondary basis.

- It is understandable that companies should wish their senior executives to develop ownership positions to align their interests with those of shareholders. However, we should also remember that they are almost by definition a special class of shareholder with executive authority that other shareholders do not enjoy (beyond the rarely-used nuclear option of firing management, or 'accessing the market for corporate control' as it is sometimes more euphemistically expressed) and that they are in an insider position. Rather than aligning executive interests with those of external shareholders, such strategies may actually exacerbate the agency problem and encourage managements to focus on financial engineering over operational excellence. For instance, option grants that vest on change of control might not be uncommon but, when they are coupled with a philosophy that grants them in generous quantities in order to encourage executive stake-building, they can have the perverse effect of providing a financial incentive for management to seek a change of control. Such incentives can encourage managements to be extremely creative in their approach to financial engineering: SLM's management almost consummated an LBO of an already leveraged company.

- The language in which a company chooses to express its philosophy of executive remuneration is telling. Recall the plaudits and praise ladled on Mr Lord for his deal-making prowess? This was a corporate culture that was happy to encourage event risk.

- Be cautious of companies that formerly had a public policy role. Rarely do managers take such companies private in order to remain civil servants (and be paid like them). The consistent goal of SLM management to shake loose the GSE mantle was a yellow flag for creditors. In addition, once privatised, former public-policy companies rarely continue to enjoy the credit protection afforded to them when they fulfilled a government mandate.

Key governance conclusions for the credit investor

What themes can we tease from these now-familiar patterns?

Separation of responsibilities

Despite our criticisms of Cadbury, we give the commission full credit for identifying the need to separate the roles of chairman and CEO. The board is there to defend the interests of shareholders against potential rentier behaviour on the part of the executive. In order to do so, it makes sense that the chairman of the board is not the chief executive of the company.

Our point is not one of distrust; we do not doubt the probity of most CEOs. However, to merge these roles into one is to create a conflict of interest from the outset. The fact that the CEO might also be a major shareholder does not necessarily give us any more comfort. The elevation of such an individual to chairman effectively creates a new class of super-shareholder, armed with the insider perspective and magisterial authority of the CEO and unfettered by the check and balance of a powerful chairman figure. We should further be cautious of role separation that is formulaic rather than substantive. To separate the role of CEO and chair but vest them in relatives or close friends, especially when one individual enjoys a dominant relationship over the other, might satisfy the Cadbury rules but is in reality mere box-ticking.

In the case of Chesapeake Energy, the FWPP might have been an appropriate incentive when the company was a start-up that depended on its founder but it seems less likely that a strong and independent board would have given unquestioning sanction to its ongoing use.

The lack of a challenging voice, we would contend, is not a good basis for strategic decision-taking and should be a red flag to any credit investor. If such a fusion of roles prevails, the investor would have to be very comfortable with the executive's track record and those of his lieutenants, or should look for additional attendant risk to be baked into pricing (in the company's debt trading at a discount to that of better-governed peers).

Remuneration structures – we're not singing the Red Flag ...

We have no axe to grind on the issue of executive pay, per se. However, it stands to reason that the structure of executive compensation will determine, in part, the way the executive manages the business, since, as rational economic beings, they will run the business in a way that maximises their own take and minimises their risk.

It is therefore very important that credit investors study the manner in which senior executives are remunerated, looking beyond headline numbers of salary and bonus to issues such as performance benchmarks and options vesting. These structures by their nature have embedded biases. Are executive bonuses linked to operating profit targets? Or growth thresholds? If so, then it is reasonable to think that management will manage towards those goals and present financial figures in such a way as to flatter those goals.

With the increased use of stock-option grants, this can be deleterious to the credit investor in encouraging executives to pursue debt-financed stock buybacks to inflate their personal remuneration as options vest. We are not reproaching the moral probity of the C-suite with these observations; we are merely recognising that they are economically rational people.

Chesapeake Energy's FWPP most obviously created an embedded bias towards new well development that became less useful (at least to the company if not to its CEO) as Chesapeake matured. Less obviously, it furnished Aubrey McClendon with a portfolio of equity participations, which he could and did leverage and which led him, we believe, to bypass his duty to shareholders. The greater the embedded emphasis on development, the more McClendon borrowed. With 20/20 hindsight, maybe analysts should have asked what he was doing with these participations. However, we would be the first to acknowledge that data on executive remuneration is often hard to find, especially outside the more open-disclosure environment of the US. Nonetheless, it behooves the investor at least to ask the question 'why'; even if the response is silence, that silence may speak volumes. What the investor cannot do, as we shall see in the next section, is place his or her entire faith in the board's remuneration committee.

... but we are raising one

As we said earlier, ours is not a position of advocacy for reining in executive pay. Rather, we seek to understand how pay packages influence management behaviour. However, were we shareholders, we would probably want to see a relationship between executive pay and stock performance, with the effect of underlying market conditions stripped out.

A 2009 study showed that CEO pay was actually negatively correlated to stock performance, with firms paying in the top decile earning negative abnormal returns over the following five years of -13%.[73] Work by Lucian Bebchuk at Harvard on over 2,000 companies demonstrated that in those in which over 35% of the remuneration paid to the top-five executives went to the CEO, the higher the proportion paid to the CEO, the lower the future profitability and market value of the company.[74]

Clearly, remuneration committees are not adequately aligning corporate executive remuneration to the returns earned by shareholders because, we suspect, they too are embedded in the dense social networks we described earlier. Again, investors need to do their own digging. If they come across C-suite officers earning the riches of Croesus, caution is counselled.

73 Cooper, M., Gulen, H. and Raghavendra Rau, P. (2009). 'Performance for Pay? The relationship between CEO incentive compensation and future stock price performance'. Via *Social Science Research Network*. [Online]. Available at: **online.wsj.com/public/resources/documents/CEOperformance122509. pdf** [Accessed 24 November 2014].

74 Bebchuk, L.A., Cremers, M. and Peyer, U. (2009). 'The CEO Pay Slice'. Harvard Law School. [Online]. Cited in: Zweig, J. (2009), 'Does Golden Pay for the CEO Sink Stocks?' [Online]. Available at: **online.wsj.com/articles/SB10001424052748704718204574615950355411042** [Accessed 24 November 2014].

Board backgrounds matter

Boards need expertise both to be able knowledgeably to challenge management and to offer wise counsel. We would hope that an oil-and-gas exploration and production company such as Chesapeake Energy would have a strong representation of board members from the energy sector and, at 36%, we are not disappointed. We would also expect a large corporation dealing with the capital markets and the complex financial instruments it offers to have board members familiar with such matters. Again, at 26% for Chesapeake's old board, we are not disappointed.

However, closer investigation reveals a possible cause for concern. As illustrated, there seems to be a reasonable concentration of individuals who are also either board members or executives of companies which have shown a significant appetite for financial risk. This may imply something, as a result, about Chesapeake's own tolerance for financial risk. Investors should analyse board compositions to check for an adequate balance of internal industry expertise and outside guidance and focus on the backgrounds of the individuals in question for indicators of the strategic guidance they will be giving in their board role.

Board memberships: independence and expertise

For a board to work properly, its members, especially its non-executives, have to possess the independence and expertise to challenge the executive management. Often boards can lack not merely one or the other but both. What is evident from our analyses both of Chesapeake and RBS is that a good number of board members shared similar roles at other organisations, making the governance structure look less like an independent advocate of shareholder interests and more like an old boys'/girls' club. And, to put it bluntly, it is mostly boys.

The UK's track record in this regard is undistinguished compared, for example, to that of corporate Scandinavia – a BBC report of 13 March 2012 cited findings from the Cranfield School of Management that the percentage of women on the boards of the UK's 100 largest listed companies hit a 'record' 17.3% in 2013.[75] The government's target is to have 25% representation by 2015.[76] These figures compare to figures over 25% for the boards of the largest Norwegian, Swedish and Finnish companies.

We strongly advocate that credit investors go through the process of identifying board and management relationships. When such investigations uncover the kind of mutual and overlapping relationships that characterised RBS's pre-nationalisation board, it should constitute a yellow flag because it calls into question that board's capacity for independent judgment.

---

75 Sealy, R., Turner, C., Vinnicombe, S. (2012) 'Women on Boards: Benchmarking adoption of the 2012 Corporate Governance Code in FTSE 350'. [Online]. Available at: **www.som.cranfield.ac.uk/som/ dinamic-content/research/documents/WomenonBoards2012Code.pdf** [Accessed 26 November 2014].
76 Lord Davies of Abersoch (2014). *Women on Boards Davies Review Annual Report 2014*, p.3.

We are not necessarily suggesting conscious collusion. Rather, humans have a bias towards confirmation. We gather with like-minded folk who share at least some of our values, interests and ideas and, when we are faced with the group moving in a direction that we – as individuals – might perceive to be wrong, the collective self-delusion can mean that we nonetheless confirm the pack's behaviour. Combine this with a powerful CEO figure (and, chances are, if they weren't powerful figures they wouldn't be CEOs) who now has no counter-narrative to their own, and the result, as we witnessed in the case of RBS, can be devastating for investors.

Qualitative investigation is essential

When investors encounter such concentrations, we believe it is worth doing some more digging. How have the individuals in question behaved in their other executive/board capacities? Sources such as Bloomberg and S&P Capital IQ can supply the raw historical material of individuals' board memberships for further analysis. What has been their attitude to financial risk? Have the companies to which they provided their services been tainted with any scandal? How do suppliers and customers view the companies?

We would, as a matter of course, advocate the same approach for a company's executive team: where have they worked before and in what capacity? What kind of strategic direction did companies take under their management? What is their appetite for leverage? What kind of people have they hired? How did the companies they managed perform? What corporate culture did they foster?

A crucial supplement to the financial model

To the charge that such an approach does not lend itself easily to modelling and comparison, we would, frankly, agree. However, we believe that selecting credit is first and foremost a question of one's ability to judge a company's management; it is, at its heart, a qualitative call. When the investing community has lost sight of this and fallen into a blind reliance on its ability to 'model' credit – think of the recent debacle in the structured credit market – it has come unstuck.[77]

---

77 For further discussion of the pitfalls of corporate governance, and suggestions as to areas that should be examined at individual companies, please see the case study on Olympus in chapter 4 of this book.

3

Traditional Credit Analysis: A Necessary Skill Set

Overview of the discipline

TRADITIONAL CREDIT ANALYSIS REMAINS THE MOST WIDELY APPLIED METHOD OF evaluation of corporate credit standing. Despite our cautious perspective on the exclusive application of such methods in the absence of further qualitative filters, it would be rash not to recognise their importance as a means of engaging with standard market practice. Treated as one layer of a deeper and more nuanced analysis, it is a useful constituent part of the process that allows a more complete and accurate picture of the underlying credit to be formed.

1. Economic context

The first steps in analysing any corporation from a credit perspective take the form of an assessment of the economic context in which the company is operating and relating its business mix and current strategy to the macroeconomic context of its end markets and theatres of operation. These allow a *tour d'horizon* of the entity's principal supporting markets and their relative health. The first step is to establish the proportion of the company's operations that each market accounts for. Each market should then be assessed in turn for its economic growth, political and legal stability and the strength of property rights within each context (which we address in the sovereign risk section of this chapter).

The principal economic data points to assess relate to economic growth, the levels of inflation, unemployment and the evolution of the fiscal and monetary policies that are in place within the major areas of the company's operations, as well as the likelihood of significant policy revisions by the central bank of each country concerned.

They also should extend to the availability of credit, and address 'softer' but nonetheless quantifiable factors such as the level of consumer and business confidence in each geographic region. Not all of these data are readily available on a timely basis for all possible geographic combinations – and a company with truly global reach may still be disproportionately reliant for its business on large, developed economies, where data is generally more readily available – but it is nonetheless a valuable if an imperfect exercise.

In this area, as in most of the statistical aspects of credit analysis, it is important to focus not so much on individual data points as on their evolution and their standing relative to peer entities. A credit assessment should not be a point-in-time analysis, whether we are looking at the financial ratios of an individual credit or assessing the economic context in which it is operating.

Table 12 illustrates some of the macroeconomic and market-based data that enable us to form a view of the economic context for each credit analysis.

Having established the general economic backdrop in the key regions in which the company operates, the next step is to apply, where possible (again, granularity is often lacking, this time at the corporate level) a similar framework to the individual corporation's exposure to each geography.

TABLE 12: ECONOMIC AND FINANCIAL INDICATORS

Date Time		Event	Survey	Actual	Prior	Revised	Relevance
01/15/2015 13:30	US	Empire Manufacturing	Jan	5	9.95	-3.58	-1.23	82.7869
01/15/2015 13:30	US	Revisions of the Empire State Manufacturing Activity Index					0
01/15/2015 13:30	US	PPI Final Demand MoM	Dec	-0.40%	-0.30%	-0.20%	--	86.8852
01/15/2015 13:30	US	PPI Ex Food and Energy MoM	Dec	0.10%	0.30%	0.00%	--	68.8525
01/15/2015 13:30	US	PPI Ex Food, Energy, Trade MoM	Dec	0.00%	0.10%	0.00%	--	4.09836
01/15/2015 13:30	US	PPI Final Demand YoY	Dec	1.00%	1.10%	1.40%	--	69.6721
01/15/2015 13:30	US	PPI Ex Food and Energy YoY	Dec	1.90%	2.10%	1.80%	--	68.0328
01/15/2015 13:30	US	PPI Ex Food, Energy, Trade YoY	Dec	--	1.30%	1.50%	--	3.27869
01/15/2015 13:30	US	Initial Jobless Claims	10-Jan	290K	316K	294K	297K	98.3607
01/15/2015 13:30	US	Continuing Claims	03-Jan	2400K	2424K	2452K	2475K	68.8525
01/15/2015 13:45	US	Bloomberg Jan. United States Economic Survey (Table)					0
01/15/2015 14:45	US	Bloomberg Consumer Comfort	11-Jan	--	45.4	43.6	--	64.7541
01/15/2015 15:00	US	Philadelphia Fed Business Outlook	Jan	18.7	6.3	24.5	24.3	77.8689
	US	CPI MoM	Dec	-0.40%	-0.40%	-0.30%	--	94.2623
01/16/2015 13:30	US	CPI Ex Food and Energy MoM	Dec	0.10%	0.00%	0.10%	--	75.4098
01/16/2015 13:30	US	CPI YoY	Dec	0.70%	0.80%	1.30%	--	62.2951
01/16/2015 13:30	US	CPI Ex Food and Energy YoY	Dec	1.70%	1.60%	1.70%	--	49.1803
01/16/2015 13:30	US	CPI Core Index SA	Dec	239.635	239.339	239.332	--	39.3443
01/16/2015 13:30	US	CPI Index NSA	Dec	234.611	234.812	236.151	--	35.2459
01/16/2015 14:15	US	Industrial Production MoM	Dec	-0.10%	-0.10%	1.30%	--	88.5246
01/16/2015 14:15	US	Capacity Utilization	Dec	79.90%	79.70%	80.10%	80.00%	61.9672
01/16/2015 14:15	US	Manufacturing (SIC) Production	Dec	0.20%	0.30%	1.10%	1.30%	11.4754
01/16/2015 15:00	US	U. of Mich. Sentiment	Jan P	94.1	98.2	93.6	--	93.4426

Source: Bloomberg

Geographic spread

For the nameless company whose data is set out below, North America accounts for 60% of its sales and 75% of its EBITDA, while the European Union represents 15% of its sales and 10% of its EBITDA, and China and Brazil collectively amount to 25% of sales and 15% of its EBITDA. We evaluate their relative importance to the health of the company and assign relative risk measures to the company's cash flows from each of these markets, weighing their contribution to the corporation as a whole. (See also 2. Sovereign risk on page 63.)

Our task now is to calculate the impact on the company's leverage and coverage (i.e. the ratio derived, in its simplest form, by dividing the company's total outstanding debt by its total cash earnings and by dividing its cash earnings by its total fixed charges) that would result from the loss of the cash flows from that market. It is also important to bear in mind the status and development of these relationships. For example, if you were looking at potentially taking five-year exposure to this credit, you would want to gauge how important each market would be over that time horizon, given each market's individual particularities. Also, a weak performance by one market (e.g. Europe) may understate the general importance of the region if taken in isolation, rather than over a business or economic cycle.

Assuming that this company is solidly positioned on the credit scale, then a temporary interruption to the cash flow that it derives from each market would only be truly damaging if the markets concerned were those of North America (since they collectively amount to 75% of EBITDA and their removal would leave outstanding debts supported by only 25% of the company's previous cash earnings). However, should the company for whatever reason, lose access to the proceeds of its operations in the European Union, the resulting 10% theoretical fall in its EBITDA would leave its debts supported by 90% of its previous cash flows. In our experience, such a pattern is often to be seen in US multinationals, where the scale efficiencies of the domestic market lead to higher levels of profitability than the company can achieve in more fragmented and more highly regulated, albeit sometimes less mature and faster-growing, foreign markets in which it is able to price more aggressively.

It can be seen, then, that the relative contribution of these markets on a steady-state basis means that this corporation's ability to service and repay its debt is most dependent on its ongoing business in the North American sphere. Assuming that it continues to do business there, the downside scenarios presented by loss of access to its foreign markets present relatively manageable risks to its overall creditworthiness – a comparatively narrow range of leverage scenarios between 2.11x and 3.33x on all but the most punitive assumptions. One of the conventions of credit analysis is that a given level of leverage does not necessarily result in a given credit 'result' – many other factors are also taken into consideration, some of which are a direct function of economic factors in the company's markets. A regulated electric utility with a leverage range of 2.11 to 3.33x would be perceived as having stronger credit standing than a steel manufacturer with the same leverage because of its low level of cyclicality and thus the superior predictability of its cash flows and hence its ability to service debt (we address cyclicality later in this chapter).

TABLE 13: ECONOMIC CONTRIBUTION BY GEOGRAPHIC REGION

	N. America	European Union	China + Brazil	Total	
EBITDA contribution	$600m	$100m	$250m	$950m	
Total debt					$2000m
Total leverage					2.11x
Leverage ex – N. America	N/A	$100m	$250m	$350m	5.71x
Leverage ex- EU	$600m	N/A	$200m	$800m	2.50x
Leverage ex- China + Brazil	$600m	$100m	N/A	$700m	2.86x
Leverage Ex-EU, China + Brazil	$600m	N/A	N/A	$600m	3.33x

Source: Authors' calculations

2. Sovereign risk

Until recently there was relatively little hand-wringing over the impact of a sovereign default or exit from a currency union on corporate credits because such calamities befell small countries that had relatively few debt-issuing, non-parastatal corporates to worry about. Avoiding defaults was easy. Then, in 1998, some European politicians thought it would be a good idea to establish a currency union without imposing the corresponding political structure to ensure fiscal transfers within the distinctly developed markets of the European Union.

The rest is history and we don't propose to bewail or detail it here. However, we were recently faced with the reality that up to five (possibly more) European sovereigns – many formerly investment-grade rated – could perhaps default on their obligations and/or exit the currency union. These countries, for all their troubles, boasted investment-grade corporate issuers – in some cases big ones.

Consider the following non-financial corporations and the amount of public debt they have outstanding:

ITALY

Non-financial corporation	Public debt
Enel SpA	€54.7bn
Edison SpA	€3.2bn
A2A SpA	€4.5bn
Telecom Italia SpA	€32.6bn
Atlantia SpA	€13.8bn
Fiat SpA	€15.7bn
Fiat Industrial SpA	€7.6bn

SPAIN

Non-financial corporation	Public debt
Telefonica SA	€59bn
Gas Natural SA	€17.4bn
Iberdrola SA	€27.1bn
Endesa SA	€5.8bn
Melia Hotels Intl SA	€604m
Repsol SA	€7.4bn

PORTUGAL

Non-financial corporation	Public debt
Portugal Telecom SGPS SA	€6.5bn
Energias de Portugal SA	€16.8bn

GREECE

Non-financial corporation	Public debt
OTE	€3.4bn

IRELAND

Non-financial corporation	Public debt
Smurfit Kappa Group PLC	€4bn

Source: Bloomberg; authors' estimates

We therefore have to consider what consequences would ensue for these companies if the sovereigns in which they are domiciled were to a) default and/or b) leave the euro. This is both virgin territory and, we hope, given that financing conditions for these sovereigns have eased to pre-crisis conditions, purely hypothetical. But here are our thoughts.

Sovereign and corporate outcomes can differ

Sovereign defaults do not spell the end of the road for a corporate domiciled in that country, especially when debts and the wherewithal to service them are denominated in a supranational currency over which the local government has no control. Just because a sovereign cannot service its debt, it does not follow that a corporate would be in the same plight. Indeed, partly as a result of changes in corporate taxation over the last few years, while sovereigns have depleted their finances in spending and bank bailouts, corporates have actually amassed large cash balances from which debt can be serviced. European investment-grade corporates had approximately €750bn of cash on their balance sheets in 2013.[78] In many cases then, corporate credit in the eurozone is stronger than its sovereign counterpart.

There are, however, second-order effects of a sovereign default, both fundamental and technical, that credit investors must take into account. First, it is hard to imagine a situation where a sovereign default is not accompanied by a domestic recession, since part of any recovery package will usually entail a significant cut in government expenditure with a negative outcome for GDP. The IMF anticipated that Greek GDP would decline by 4.5% in 2012 (the new Greek cabinet was toying with a drop of 6–7%), in part due to the austerity measures foisted upon the country. To the extent that a corporation domiciled in the afflicted country also derives its revenues from domestic sources, its earnings, cash flow and ability to service debt will be compromised accordingly.

---

78   Moody's Investors Service (2013). 'EMEA Investment-Grade Non-Financial Corporates: Refinancing Needs Over the Next Four Years Appear Manageable'. [Online]. Available at: **www.moodys.com/ researchdocumentcontentpage.aspx?docid=PBC_156326** [Accessed 24 November 2014].

The preference would therefore be to invest in those companies that enjoy geographically diversified earnings streams.

Second, as the troubled sovereign attempts to increase its revenue base, it will likely look to increase taxation on corporations, even potentially imposing capital controls. However, since corporations that do not need to be domiciled in any given country could leave, government taxation efforts usually focus on the companies whose businesses are tied to the country – utilities being an oft-cited example. Indeed, Portugal raised a (theoretically) one-off levy of 0.85% on various utility assets.[79] These corporations might find themselves subject to 'Robin Hood' tax levies as has been the case in Italy. Again, money paid to the government is money no longer available for debt service. That said, no government would knowingly kill a goose that lays golden eggs so such taxes are unlikely to sound a death knell. In the case of Energias de Portugal SA (EdP), we estimate the net impact of the levy at about €30m on an annual EBITDA of over €3bn. From a positive perspective, the need to realise funds often coerces troubled governments to de-nationalise companies or sell off minority holdings. This can shake up sleepy managements, foster a more commercial perspective and bring in new liquidity from strategic investors to shore up the company against the problems faced by its sovereign host (see China Three Gorges case study).

Corporate and sovereign ratings often aligned

Technical effects usually relate to ratings agency initiatives. It is normal for the rating agencies to peg the foreign currency ratings of corporations to the sovereign ratings of the country in which they are domiciled with a one to two notch allowance for the corporation's stronger credit profile. We will not argue here the rights and wrongs of such an approach (the agencies' methodologies are explained in detail in the agencies' own publications for those who would seek to understand them). However, the implication is that once a sovereign begins the slippery slide towards default and falls (usually quite precipitously) into high yield, those corporations domiciled in the sovereign may well follow it, regardless of their fundamental credit quality.

These developments have technical implications, which will exert decidedly un-technical pressure on the price of the corporations' bonds and the spreads of their CDS. In the first instance, the failure of the host sovereign to maintain investment-grade ratings with one or more agencies could result in the exclusion of the bonds of corporates domiciled in the affected country from certain indices, making them ineligible for holding in portfolios benchmarked to that index. Given the still relatively small scale of the European high-yield market, this could result in severe price pressure as a result of forced selling and a significantly smaller pool of potential buyers. Also, once the corporations' bonds themselves are downgraded to junk, they could become ineligible for those funds designated investment-grade only, prompting another round of forced selling. Moreover, with a smaller pool of investors capable of holding the corporations' debt, raising new

---

79 EdP (2013). 'Portuguese Government proposes energy sector extraordinary contribution for 2014'. (EdP Press Release). [Online]. Available at: **www.edp.pt/en/Investidores/informacaoprivilegiada/2013/Pages/GovernoPortuguespropoecontribuicooextsectorenergetico2014.aspx** [Accessed 24 November 2014].

money for refinancing becomes not merely more expensive but more difficult, all other things being equal, increasing the credit risk associated with these entities.

The International Swaps and Derivatives Association (ISDA) undertakes regular reviews of the definitions by which it establishes the legal basis of whether a credit has defaulted under the terms of its CDS contract. At present, one proposal is to introduce another trigger for default for financial CDS, to be known as Government Intervention or GI which encompasses any action undertaken by a government authority (government, agency, regulator etc.) with respect to a financial institution restructuring and resolution to impair debt, whether this be through write-down, expropriation, conversion, exchange or transfer. It includes any changes to principal, interest, maturity or ranking of preference. The move comes in response to a number of 'bail-ins' in the course of the eurozone crisis – for example, in Cyprus.

Material impact of re-denomination

If the consequences of a sovereign default prove manageable, those of an exit of the sovereign host from the currency union (in this case the euro) may prove less so. At present, such a development would seem to have two immediate consequences, one technical, the other fundamental, but both related and concerned with redenomination. However, regulations based on the 2003 ISDA definitions are evolving and are likely to continue to do so, thus requiring investors to remain apprised of the most recent developments in this process.

According to our understanding of current rules, most bonds negotiated under English law (as tends to be the case with eurobonds), only permit the redenomination of bond liabilities into a G7 currency. Thus, in the event that eurozone countries were to exit the euro and revert to legacy currencies, corporations with English-law bonds would not be able to redenominate their bond liabilities without precipitating an event of default. The possible exception to this rule would be Italian corporates, since Italy is a G7 country and its legacy currency – even if much devalued – would still be G7.

On the same basis, redenomination of debt could also be a credit event under CDS contracts, even if the company was able to remain current on its debt service. However – and this is the fundamental challenge – corporations in other non-G7 countries that exited the eurozone would find themselves in the position of having to service euro-denominated debt from an earnings stream now denominated in a much-depreciated legacy currency. At the very least, this could dramatically increase leverage for many of the companies affected. If, for argument's sake, we assume that Portuguese utility firm EdP has debt/EBITDA of approximately 4×, a 25% devaluation in the redenominated currency, would, *ceteris paribus*, increase leverage to 5.3× (simply because the denominator in the equation would now be worth 25% less). In reality, the deterioration is likely to be more precipitous, since redenomination, at least in the short term, would most likely be accompanied by a sharp contraction in the domestic economy, which may in many cases precipitate capital controls, such as were imposed in the case of Cyprus. Although in this instance the country did not redenominate its currency, the mechanism of the EU bail-in that took place in March 2013 imposed haircuts on the bank deposits of wealthy non-domiciled bank account holders and restricted the movement of capital. The draft definitions that are under consideration would obviate this difficult technicality by shifting the focus to the severity of any haircut of debt, rather than just a redenomination, and is more aligned with the economic impact of the event.

Regional diversification provides credit support

However, fortunately most rated international corporations in the peripheral sovereigns are not wholly reliant on domestic earnings streams and, in extremis, have foreign assets that could be sold to raise hard-currency cash.

EdP, again, derives 45% of EBITDA from Portugal and 25% from Spain; 17% comes from its Brazilian assets and the remaining 13% from activities in the US and elsewhere in the EU.[80] It is, therefore, probably overly punitive to restate the company's leverage as we did in the previous section, since only 70% of EBITDA can be said to be at risk from redenomination. Re-running the numbers accordingly, we arrive at an adjusted leverage ratio of 4.8× – somewhat more manageable.

Spanish hotelier, Meliá Hotels International, derives only 15% of its operating profit from Spain,[81] with the bulk coming from the Americas, the Caribbean and non-peripheral Europe. One suspects that in the event of a redenomination it could bill foreign customers in hard currencies (as do many emerging market hotels) to match its liabilities. Moreover, we believe it has a significant number of foreign properties currently on its balance sheet at below their market value.

EdP has also noted on earnings calls that the value of its foreign assets exceeds that of its euro liabilities, implying that, in extremis, it could extinguish one from the other – an unlikely scorched-earth resolution but a scenario that should give investors some comfort.

China Three Gorges (CTG) bought the Portuguese government's 21.35% stake in EdP at the end of 2011. As part of the deal, CTG agreed to arrange a credit facility of up to €2bn for up to 20 years and invest a further €2bn through stakes in renewables projects.[82] This effectively gave EdP a €4bn liquidity infusion, which, even if a Portuguese default or exit from the euro had happened, and EdP suffered disruption in its ability to access hard-currency financing, would have ensured that the company could service its debt in a timely manner out to end-2014 (conservatively).

---

80 EdP (2014). *Investor Day Presentation*, p.10. [Online]. Available at: **www.edp.pt/en/Investidores/ DiaInvestidor/Pages/InvestorDay2014.aspx** [Accessed 24 November 2014].
81 Meliá Hotels International. (2014). *Investor Presentation*. [Online]. Available at: **www. meliahotelsinternational.com/sites/default/files/informes-financieros/mhi_inversores_aug_14_en.pdf** [Accessed 24 November 2014].
82 EdP (2011). 'EDP and China Three Gorges establish strategic partnership'. [Online]. Available at: **www.edp.pt/en/Investidores/informacaoprivilegiada/2011/Pages/ EDPeChinaThreeGorgesestabelecemparceriaestrategica.aspx** [Accessed 24 November 2014].

TABLE 14: EDP'S LIQUIDITY RUNWAY[83]

Cash	1.90	€353m in Brazil; €267m in Renovaveis
Committed Revolver Capacity	1.50	Expires 11/2015
Committed Term Liquidity	3.40	
CP Availability	0.65	Annually renewable
Domestic Line Availability	0.19	Annually renewable
Total Existing Liquidity	4.24	
New Liquidity		
Chinese Line	2.00	20-year facility to be in place by end-summer
CTG Minority Stakes	2.00	€800m in next 12 months
Total Liquidity	8.24	
Funded Debt Maturities		
2012	2.10	
2013	2.30	
2014	3.00	
2015	2.00	

So, it can be seen from the foregoing that, while a sovereign exit from the eurozone would cause severe dislocation – certainly in a form that we are not in a position to predict – there would be winners and losers among the corporates. Those whose management had proactively diversified revenue streams, found strategic partners with deep pockets (lined with hard currency) and firmed up hard-currency liquidity options will live to fight another day. And, had such a crisis prompted a sell-off in risky assets, there would be bargains to be had in credit products.

Legal and disclosure frameworks

Another layer of uncertainty within the sovereign risk area for corporate credit lies in the widely differing legal and disclosure frameworks that are in effect across different national boundaries. In the event of a corporate default, the status of the creditor is in practice very different under US law than it is under German, French, Italian, Spanish and Portuguese, to name but a few jurisdictions. Thus a further qualitative overlay should be added to the analysis of sovereign risk, taking these factors into consideration when considering potential recovery rates on defaulted debt, although we freely admit that is beyond the purview of this book.

---

83 EdP (2012). We are EdP. Investor Day Presentation. [Online]. Available at: **www.edp.pt/en/ Investidores/publicacoes/apresentacoes/Presentations%202012/Investor%20Day%20-%20May%20 2012.pdf** [Accessed 24 November 2014]

3. Company scale, cyclicality, elasticity of demand

The next two factors that we examine in the context of assessing a company's credit standing are the influence of scale and cyclicality. Although it is widely accepted that larger companies in the same industry are generally more creditworthy than their smaller peers, it is worth highlighting the scale of some of the corporations that have come to grief in the recent past to expose the shortcomings of this comforting assumption.

Enron, WorldCom and Parmalat all had multi-billion dollar business profiles and thousands of employees. Thus, scale is not in and of itself a guarantee of a solid credit profile. However, under normal circumstances and in the absence of fraudulent behaviour by senior management, it is fair to say that, given two otherwise similar companies, the larger will generally be perceived as the more creditworthy. The key here is to take the trouble to actually compare the underlying factors between corporations, rather than simply saying that company A is larger than company B and therefore a better credit.

Scale confers support

What scale can confer, in a well-managed business, is institutional support. Thus, in the absence of fraud, a corporation with thousands of employees in a particular country is more likely to receive the support of its bankers and national politicians, as well as better market access, more readily than a smaller competitor. For example, when Thomas Cook, the UK-based travel operator with 33,593 employees, suffered a liquidity crisis in November 2011, it received the support of its bankers to provide liquidity during a major restructuring programme which remains ongoing. On the other hand, HMV, a smaller British concern with 6,997 employees, also faced a liquidity crisis – and was put into administration in January 2013.

Of course, these were not the only factors in play. Thomas Cook, for example, had a far greater number of realisable non-core asset sales with which it could provide cash flow to fund an ongoing turnaround process. Nonetheless, the local scale argument does seem to be a factor in many instances, especially when looking at Europe-based credits. For example, historically, the so-called 'French Put' has been relied upon for support for ailing French corporations from the French state, though this is becoming less of a factor as EU rules concerning sovereign aid to domestic companies are more stringently applied. However, we note that this has yet to prevent the French state from participating in the bailout of beleaguered auto manufacturer, Peugeot S.A. Nonetheless, this phenomenon is becoming more and more idiosyncratic, depending on the underlying economic health of the country concerned, even within the EU, whose members are showing divergent responses to supporting domestic corporations.

Cyclicality

The other principal factor to analyse, cyclicality, is more quantitative in nature and an important means of nuancing the crude financial metrics that arise from the calculation of a company's leverage. Take, for example, the nameless corporation below, which presents a mixed picture, with the following observations holding true:

- In its home market, the USA, the company has established market share and scale and markets are efficient, with good price transparency. Its operating profitability therefore fluctuates in a direct relationship with the economy as a whole, with greater sensitivity on the downside suggesting that its products can be considered to be cyclical.

- The company is more recently established in Europe than in the US, and, while the relationship of sales to GDP growth is fairly clear, profitability is more uneven, due to the mix of countries, tax regimes and labour regulations in play, as well as the acuteness of recessionary forces in a number of countries.

- In China, the robust pace of sales growth, coming from a low base, has a strong positive correlation to the country's GDP trajectory, while a clear relationship exists between increasing scale in the market and increasing profitability.

- Brazil, the company's other major growth market, is also exhibiting a strong positive correlation with GDP growth at the level both of sales and of profitability, but the business here is more fragmented regionally and this has led to upward pressure on operating costs, particularly transportation, due to infrastructure issues.

Thus a picture emerges of the drivers of cash flows with reference to the company's major market concentrations, allowing us to weight the quantitative historical positions in an overall appraisal of its creditworthiness and frame this against the economic outlook in each region.

This is, in our view, by no means a scientific process. In all credit decisions, there is a degree of subjectivity. One of the authors of this book remembers a meeting with a Brazilian investor who refused to lend money to a major local corporation based on nothing more than the fact that the company was based in the state of Bahia, against whose inhabitants he bore a strong personal prejudice. Clearly, this was not a suitable basis on which to found a credit decision, but it does, however imperfectly, illustrate the 'soft' factors that can weigh heavily on lending outcomes.

Elasticity of demand

Armed with macroeconomic data and a sense of the company's cyclicality, this segment of the credit assessment should conclude with an examination of the elasticity of demand for the company's products or services, which feeds into the micro analysis of a company.

A pharmaceutical company offering consumers vital healthcare or a utility providing water are clearly higher priorities to the consumer than more discretionary or aspirational purchases and thus have lower demand elasticity in times of economic hardship. This, in turn, feeds into the robustness or otherwise of company's cash flows and should influence management in its choice of capital policy. In an emerging market, high priority products will typically consume a greater share of disposable income than in a developed market, leading to greater elasticity of demand for a provider of discretionary goods/services.

TABLE 15: GDP % GROWTH VS. COMPANY PERFORMANCE BY MARKET

Market	2011	2010	2009	2008	2007
USA	2.7	3	-3.5	-0.3	1.9
Sales growth	3.5	4.5	-9	-3	2.1
EBIT growth	11	10.5	-22.2	-3.5	8
Sales delta	1.30	1.50	2.57	10.00	1.11
EBIT delta	4.07	3.50	6.34	11.67	4.21
EU	1.5	1.8	-4.2	0.3	3
Sales growth	1.2	2	-12	0.1	2.5
EBIT growth	3.7	7.2	-31	-4.5	3
Sales delta	0.80	1.11	2.86	0.33	0.83
EBIT delta	2.47	4.00	7.38	-15.00	1.00
China	10.99	10	9	10	14
Sales growth	14.3	11.5	13.2	12.5	21.1
EBIT growth	23.0	17.8	14	12.4	17.8
Sales delta	1.30	1.15	1.47	1.25	1.51
EBIT delta	2.09	1.78	1.56	1.24	1.27
Brazil	2.7	7.5	-0.3	5.2	6.1
Sales growth	9.7	15.5	11.1	14.8	8.9
EBIT growth	12	17	10	3	6
Sales delta	3.59	2.07	-37.00	2.85	1.46
EBIT delta	4.44	2.27	-33.33	0.58	0.98

Source: IMF, authors' estimates

4. Maturity and growth prospects of business

A company's stage of development – or rather, both its own and that of the industry in which it competes – is another important area of investigation in establishing creditworthiness. Both factors play together. It is of little help to a company's credit to become the dominant player in an industry that is facing looming obsolescence but an early-stage company in a more enduring industry will still present different credit challenges than one that is in the middle of its evolution or one that has gone 'ex-growth' (i.e. a firm that has exhausted its growth opportunities at a given return on capital employed).

Essentially, each of these three phases requires a shift in financial policy that stresses different areas of the capital structure.

The early years of a company's life, when it is focused on the quest for scale, typically require intensive capital expenditure (capex) and marketing spend, usually causing negative free cash flow and, at very best, stable leverage. This may be accompanied by a period of rapid diversification of the company's funding sources – from early-stage angel investment to stock market listing and bank financing to bond issuance – during which time gauging the market's appetite for a company's stock or bonds is an opaque process that will determine its success to an almost parallel degree to its actual operating performance and growth.

As the company attains scale and becomes an established player in its market, so it would be expected to attain a somewhat greater stability in its capital structure, with established institutional shareholders/lenders, a clear financial policy with regard to dividend payments, diversification through M&A and the emergence of a dividend and shareholder returns policy.

Assuming that the company reaches terminal scale and goes ex-growth, its capital policy should also accommodate the new reality. No longer obliged to devote large amounts of its cash flow to additional plant, it can move towards a maintenance level of capital expenditures while potentially increasing the amount of capital it returns to shareholders or pursue larger-scale M&A activity. Such activity can be highly accretive to both credit standing and earnings, depending on financing, but it can be hugely detrimental when it goes wrong. An ex-growth company faces diminishing support for the trading multiples in the stock, which can leave it facing the prospect of potentially diluting its earnings while it is striving to improve them.[84]

This situation, which is increasingly common among mature companies in Europe, Japan and the USA, can lead to aggressive financing of M&A targets. This, in turn, increases the likelihood of significant 'financial engineering' – increasing financial complexity, often to the detriment of credit standing – in an attempt to improve performance statistics such as return on equity (ROE), return on assets (ROA) or return on capital employed (ROCE). Such measurements and their variants are often embedded in the remuneration formulae of senior management, but can ultimately lead to the undermining of the long-term credit status of the acquirer, and indeed can be an indicator of potential LBOs and management buyouts (MBOs).

5. Obsolescence and substitution risk

A company's earnings sustainability and its ability to continue servicing its debt depends on its ability to keep producing goods and services that customers want to buy at a price that provides a sufficient return on investment for a company to continue offering that particular good or service.

---

84 For example, if company A trades at an EV/EBITDA of 5× and acquires company B, which trades at 6×, then every dollar of company B's EBITDA 'costs' more than every dollar of company A's – resulting in the arithmetical destruction of value for the merged entity.

In a competitive marketplace, a good that commands a high price due to unique characteristics or absence of other providers is likely to encourage consumers to look for (cheaper) substitutes. The fewer potential substitutes that exist for a good, the higher the price (and probably the higher the margin) the producer will be able to command. Indeed, in such a situation, the producer is likely to be a price-setter rather than a price-taker and should be able to pass through to customers increases in costs relating to raw materials or labour. An example of such a good would be a newly patented drug or medical treatment, where other therapies are likely to be non-existent or inferior.

Conversely, the producer of a good or service for which many substitutes exist will not enjoy the same ability to pass through costs and will take its price from that set by the cheapest of its substitutes. Continuing with the pharmaceutical theme, a generic drug for which there is a plethora of substitutes (e.g. a minor analgesic) cannot command a significant price premium to alternatives, nor pass through increased costs that are specific to it. When analysing a company, the investor should contemplate the goods and services under offer and consider what substitutes not merely currently exist but might be under development.

As technological developments accelerate, spotting obsolescence risk will constitute an ever-more challenging task for investors and analysts, and products and services may be freighted with obsolescence risk to which not merely investors but management themselves may be oblivious. By way of example, digital cameras appeared on the scene in the early 1990s. A number of direct and indirect factors – price, connectivity (enabling the sharing of digital photos), the growth of social media, integration of digital cameras in phones and PDAs – have led digital cameras to dominate photography, outselling all film cameras by the middle of the first decade of the subsequent millennium. This change took the world's leading manufacturer of photographic film, Eastman Kodak,[85] into bankruptcy in 2012. As late as 1993, it was AAA-rated.

Today, the main obstacle to the growth in purely electric vehicles (EVs) is their relatively limited range. A breakthrough in battery technology could materially extend their range, which could, quite possibly, completely change consumer preferences for electric versus internal combustion/hybrid offerings. The consequences this would have not merely for the auto OEMs and parts suppliers but also for industries such as fuel retail and electricity generation and distribution is hard to fathom.

Management again is a guide

It would perhaps be advisable to focus not merely on the possibility of product/service obsolescence but management's attitude and approach to the development of such threats, since they will play a key role in determining whether a company can negotiate the obsolescence of its offerings or go to the wall as a result. Investors should examine senior management for evidence of careers or roles in other companies that successfully negotiated product obsolescence. The track records of senior management as agents of change is therefore a factor that potential investors should monitor closely. The fate of Eastman

---

85 Ironically, the charged-couple device image sensor was first developed by Eastman Kodak in 1975.

Kodak contrasts sharply with that of IBM, which, threatened with the migration of computing from mainframe to desktop, nonetheless negotiated the transition by refocusing its activities on technology and business services and finance – activities that had developed as a corollary to its original development of mainframes. Investors should also take into consideration the degree of diversification in the company's offerings, since the less the reliance on a single product or service, the greater the insulation from the obsolescence of one product.

A company with a product that is at the mature stage of its cycle (possibly on its way to obsolescence) should also be subject to careful scrutiny. With limited growth opportunities, management will be forced to placate equity investors either by branching into new areas with all the attendant management and execution risk or by leveraging the company's cash flows to enhance shareholder returns through higher dividends or share buybacks.

With an open market for corporate control, management's failure to use cash flows to enhance shareholder returns could result in their being replaced in a leveraged or management buyout, in which the new management team would significantly leverage the company's cash flows to buy out existing equity-holders. Thereafter, the company is run to service the buyout debt and maximise returns to the new owners. Existing bondholders can, depending on the covenant language in their bonds, find themselves profoundly disadvantaged and almost certainly structurally subordinated. Without appropriate covenants (unlikely in investment-grade credits), there is little incentive for the new owners to take out the existing debt, since it will typically be cheaper than new buyout debt, reflecting the more creditworthy, less-leveraged balance sheet of the pre-buyout company.

6. Capital, asset and labour intensity

Companies require capital, physical assets and labour to varying degrees, with traditional heavy or 'rust belt' industries having among the most intense requirements of all three, and asset-light industries such as online services or asset management firms potentially at the opposite end of the spectrum. This has implications for the manner in which we need to examine these entities from a credit perspective.

The challenges that capital-intensive industries face in credit are sizeable. Their need to install, maintain and upgrade significant physical assets – blast furnaces, production lines, mines, railway lines, paper mills etc. – while operating within often volatile competitive environments (with little ability to foresee the future profitability of the business), places significant stress on their credit standing. Similarly, they require large workforces which it has traditionally been necessary to train, keep onside, and provide for in retirement and support when unwell. To be fair, these paternalistic characteristics are on the wane in modern corporate life, especially in the Anglo-Saxon economies. (Many US companies provide no pensions to employees, and British companies do not have to provide healthcare because this cost is externalised onto the state through the NHS.) All the same, these two factors generally still go a long way to explain their ongoing need for large amounts of capital to support traditional business models.

On the other hand, these industries tend to be highly cyclical and generate large amounts of free cash flow in the growth phases of the economic cycle while incurring significant cash outflows during periods of recession. These factors call for conservative financial policies and operational scale to mitigate such credit challenges, though in practice many companies have sought to circumvent them with the help of financial engineering, especially through the use of off-balance-sheet vehicles to reduce the appearance of capital intensity. Seeking these out through the notes to the accounts is really the only way to get close to the true credit standing of the corporation (see *Chapter 5. Behind the Numbers*).

For all this, capital-intensive industries have intrinsic financial flexibility in the form of the valuable physical assets that can be used as collateral for financing in extremis and may have significant pools of unrealised non-core assets such as housing for a now-diminished workforce or artefacts pertaining to the company's historic evolution. This is at variance with the challenges of the asset-light model from a credit standpoint. For all their fat margins, earnings visibility and supplier-funded inventory, ultimately asset-light firms have little beyond their brands on which a lender can secure his loan. Mitigating this to a degree, insofar as their brands represent a company's operating franchise (e.g. for hotel chains such as Marriott), they do still offer potentially valuable securities to lenders.

7. Numbers focus – key touchstones for creditworthiness

Although we argue strongly in favour of overlaying simple statistical analysis with more nuanced interpretations based on an examination of corporate governance, all credit analysis must involve an interpretation of a company's reported financials and, more importantly perhaps, the trends that they reveal. Credit analysis in practice is about spotting potential transitions in the credit standing of a company and re-positioning your portfolio before the positive or negative credit events that these trends point to actually materialise in asset pricing. Thus, it is appropriate to outline the fundamental numerical areas that are the focus of corporate credit analysis and demonstrate some of the ways that they are calculated.

At this stage, our purpose is merely to provide the basic definitions and calculation methodologies that are used for each metric. We return to discuss more sophisticated approaches, interpretations and modifications to these ratios in sections 4 and 5 of this book. However, alongside the operating metrics of the company that vary industry by industry, the most important numerical areas of financial focus in our view are:

a) Gross leverage

This is perhaps the most basic building block in the credit toolkit. In its simplest form, this is a static ratio that is generally calculated as follows:

```
Total debt ÷ trailing 12-month EBITDA
```

Total debt includes both long- and short-term obligations. Trailing 12-month EBITDA is defined as the EBITDA generated over the previous 12 month calendar period, whether this coincides with a fiscal year end or not. In practice, especially in the context of European and Asian companies that only report full financials once or twice in a calendar year, this will involve either adding together the last two half fiscal years or simply taking the figure from the annual report and accounts.

Note that we focus on gross rather than net leverage (i.e. we remove any cash on the balance sheet from our calculations), as this figure is subject to huge seasonal fluctuations and the cash may prove hard to access in extremis. The focus for the gross leverage figure is on its evolution over a period of years, and, if possible, quarterly or semi-annually, in order to assess whether there is any discernible pattern of credit improvement or deterioration over this time as well as to understand seasonal or cyclical effects.

b) Cash flow measurements

The starting point for this is to define operating cash flow, which is generally accepted to be as follows:

```
Net income + depreciation & amortisation + other non-cash adjustments
+ changes in working capital
```

This figure is then divided by gross debt to derive an expression of the statistic on a percentage basis. Then it is analysed over a substantial time frame to track its evolution and establish whether the company's debt protection measurements are moving in one direction or the other.

More restrictive definitions of cash flow, that aim to remove the funds required to maintain the company's assets and service its equity dividends, include terms such as discretionary cash flow or retained cash flow, in which the credit's dividend payments and maintenance capital expenditure requirements are respectively added back to and deducted from the operating cash flow measure. This figure, when positive, can be divided into the gross debt figure to show how many years it would take for a company to de-lever to 0x leverage, another simple yardstick of financial flexibility which is fairly intuitive.

c) Coverage ratios

Coverage is a measure of a company's ability to pay the interest due on its bonds and loans. Arguably, it is even more pressingly significant than any leverage ratio since a company that is unable to pay its interest costs is in more imminent danger of bankruptcy than one with extremely high leverage but ample coverage. Broadly speaking, there are two definitions that are in common use: EBIT interest cover and EBITDA interest cover, which are, respectively defined as:

```
Earnings before interest and tax ÷ total interest
```

and:

```
Earnings before interest, tax, depreciation and amortisation ÷ total
interest
```

Both of these ratios commonly feature in bank loan performance covenants (subject to often tortuous definitions and exclusions), where minimum thresholds have to be maintained by the company concerned in order to retain access to bank lines. Often they appear in combination with a maximum leverage covenant in this context.

d) Liquidity

It is often said that companies do not go bankrupt because they have too much debt, but because they have too little liquidity – access to readily available funds to service their obligations of all kinds. In assessing a company's liquidity, it is important to establish how accessible the stated cash balance is and what potential restrictions may exist on bank lines that the company describes as "available" (i.e. performance covenants, MAC clauses, BAW language etc.). We cover this topic in detail in Chapter 5. Behind the Numbers: Adjusted Debt and Liquidity on page 127, but outline the key concepts below.

Ratios commonly employed in the analysis of liquidity are:

```
Unrestricted cash ÷ short-term debt
```

and:

```
(Unrestricted cash + Undrawn bank lines) ÷ Short-term debt
```

Other commonly-used liquidity ratios include:

The cash ratio

```
Cash and cash equivalents + marketable securities ÷ current liabilities
```

The current ratio

```
Current assets ÷ current liabilities
```

The quick ratio

```
Liquid assets ÷ current liabilities
```

A particularly informative liquidity ratio sets the company in the context of a complete loss of market access while it continues to operate, generating cash flow and incurring maintenance capital expenditures while restricting dividend payments. The formula for this ratio is, for year n:

```
(Unrestricted cash + available credit lines + OCF in n - maintenance
capex in n + disposal proceeds in n) ÷ (interest cost in n + debt
maturities in n)
```

As in all ratio interpretation, so with liquidity ratios; the important thing is to observe the evolving trends over time.

e) Debt adjustments

A company's published balance sheet debt figures, visible on every corporate balance sheet, rarely give an accurate picture of its true leverage and liabilities. We go into detail to address getting a more accurate picture in chapter 5, but, in brief, it entails assigning a value to off-balance-sheet liabilities such as pension deficits, operating leases and liabilities relating to defective products, industrial accidents, environmental and health liabilities – so-called 'contingent' liabilities – and aggregating them to the stated balance sheet debt figures and making corresponding adjustments to the cash flow statement. Stated in its simplest form, the adjusted leverage ratio is calculated as follows:

```
(Balance sheet debt + NPV operating leases + pension deficit + contingent
liabilities) ÷ (EBITDA + ⅓ annual operating lease payment)
```

8. Cash cycle and seasonality

The variation in a company's credit metrics is influenced not only by its competitive position within its industry, its sensitivity to the economic cycle and general macro context, but also, and to a large extent, by its own cash cycle and seasonality. These vary greatly across the industrial spectrum.

Thus a speciality retail company with a large toy franchise will feel the greatest pressure on its credit metrics in the build-up to the Christmas selling season, with the peak in its borrowings and the weakest point in its metrics coming, logically enough, at the same time as the high point in its inventories and the low point in its cash flow generation. For a retailer, these metrics then rapidly reverse to their annual high point over the Christmas period.

Other industries have longer, multi-year cash cycles that are strongly influenced by the underlying volatilities of the economies in which they operate, requiring a range of different financial policies. An oil exploration and production company, for example, may need to invest large sums in new projects over a lengthy time frame with only uncertain results. The creditworthiness of such a company is largely based on the extent to which its existing portfolio of production assets is capable of generating sufficient cash flows to fund investment in such new projects and balance demand from equity holders for access to these cash flows.

Construction and capital goods companies are obliged to fund multi-year infrastructure projects on a similar basis to these oil companies, though they are able to mitigate the ongoing cash flow requirements by billing for work as it is completed in stages. For a more detailed examination of these topics, please refer to pages 96–126 in chapter 4 of this book.

One key indicator of a company's efficiency and competitiveness and an indicator of potential problems is the efficacy with which it manages its working capital and the speed with which it converts working capital into cash. The principal constituents of working capital are *inventory*, which is turned into finished goods; *accounts receivable*, which is the trade credit the company gives to customers; and *accounts payable*, which is the credit it is able to wring from its suppliers. To the extent that it can accelerate the pace at which it turns inventory into sales, or minimise the payment terms it gives customers or, indeed, maximise those it gets from suppliers, it will reduce its own financing needs.

Receivable and payable terms tend to be quite common across industries, which allows the investor, with a few caveats, to compare the cash-conversion cycle of industry peers. The calculations for such analysis are the number of times these assets 'turn' within a given period or, conversely, the number of days on hand of each working capital item the company has. Since inventory and accounts receivable are assets that the company will have to finance, it should be its goal to maximise the number of 'turns' or minimise the number of days on hand of these items; conversely, since trade credit from suppliers is a form of (up to a point) free financing, a company should try to maximise it.

Turns are calculated as follows:

Accounts receivable turns

```
(Credit-based) revenues over a period ÷ (Average receivables for the
corresponding period (receivables at the beginning + receivables at
the end) ÷ 2)
```

Accounts receivable days on hand

```
365 ÷ Accounts receivable turns (or 90 ÷ Turns if the period is a
quarter)
```

Inventory turns

```
Cost of goods sold over a period ÷ Average inventory for the
corresponding period
```

Inventory days on hand

```
365 ÷ Inventory turns (or 90 ÷ Inventory turns if the period is a
quarter)
```

Accounts payable turns

```
Cost of goods sold over a period ÷ Average accounts payable over the
corresponding period
```

Accounts payable days on hand

```
365 ÷ Accounts payable turns (or 90 ÷ Accounts payable turns if the
period is a quarter)
```

If these figures show the number of times inventory, receivables and payables 'turn' in a year, then the number of days that these items are on hand is simply the number of days in the year divided by the number of turns.

Caveats

Comparing like-for-like: different industries have different working capital cycle characteristics. For instance, a bookmaker will typically take cash payments for its services whereas an advertising agency would bill possibly on 90-day terms or even longer. Thus, bookmakers typically have *de minimis* receivables days on hand while an advertising agency might have hundreds. Comparison across industries is therefore not meaningful.

By extension, comparisons across conglomerates or companies with multiple business lines are also less than useful, since the numbers show a 'blend' of receivables, inventory and payables across a range of business activities, precluding an industry-specific comparison.

However, assuming we are comparing like-for-like, we can begin to make useful deductions. Materially slower receivables turns at one company compared to another could indicate slack working capital management. Deteriorating inventory turns might well highlight that a company is having problems selling its goods and is building inventory backlogs that will require a significant reduction in prices to clear. Ultimately, if the inventory cannot be sold, some impairment charge will have to be applied. While lengthening payables are generally a sign of efficient working capital management, a sudden deceleration in turns/ increase in days on hand could betoken that a company is having cash flow difficulties and being forced to delay payments to suppliers; conversely, a sudden reduction could indicate that suppliers are losing confidence in the company's credit and have changed terms to cash-on-delivery.

Relative size and market power also influence working capital cycles. A large customer upon which a smaller business is dependent can typically dictate receivables terms and vice-versa. At the top of the food chain, any company treating with a government must expect to be paid on the government's terms, all the more so if it is a domestic corporation. This is the reality for companies dealing currently with peripheral European economies. Another useful tool in the accounting analysis of cash conversion is the comparison of EBITDA to operating cash flow. One would expect EBITDA – a measure that has eliminated the principal accrual (non-cash) items – to correlate closely to operating cash flow, given some reduction for working capital consumption, cash taxes and finance costs. However, if operating cash flow is repeatedly a very small proportion of EBITDA, then the company is not converting sufficient accounting earnings into cash and must be leaking cash elsewhere. This is, more often than not, a warning sign and requires further analysis to see where the company's cash is going or why the earnings are of such poor quality that they cannot be monetised.

Cash cycle analysis should be used in combination with liquidity analysis (see 3. Liquidity analysis on page 148) to ensure that a company has sufficient financial flexibility to cope with the seasonal fluctuations in its financing needs. The cash cycle can be extreme in cases of severe seasonality and requires bank lines which are sufficiently flexible to accommodate these severe swings, and should be scrutinised to ensure that they are truly committed facilities with as few elements of conditionality as possible.

9. Growth, margin and capital formation

A starting point for much corporate credit analysis is the extent to which a company is able to grow its revenues and the profitability of any revenues that it gains or loses. Self evidently, a company that posts ever-declining sales or that cannot derive adequate profits from its sales to cover its debt-service costs (interest payments) will ultimately not survive. However, more typically, analysts can examine trends in sales growth/decline and in profitability to highlight underlying trends in the company's business that have longer-term import for the attractiveness and, hence, the pricing of its credit.

The calculation of period-to-period sales growth/contraction is straightforward:

```
(Current period revenues ÷ comparable prior period revenues) - 1
```

First, one needs to distinguish between the revenues gained from sales and the underlying units of the product which are sold. A company might report a significant decline in revenues on a small decline or even an increase in units sold. This implies falling revenue per unit, which could betoken one or more of a number of negative trends: increasing competition either in the form of substitute products or predatory pricing; discounting in response to a weak economic environment; the onset of product obsolescence. Conversely, while rising revenues on static or falling unit sales might be preferable, it could just reflect the passing through of rising raw materials costs in a concentrated market with few competitors rather than a truly favourable trend. There is no formulaic interpretation; rather, disparities between changes in unit volumes and revenues should prompt the analyst to dig further into the drivers for any trends they might reveal.

Growth patterns in both revenues and unit sales will differ from product to product. Double – even triple – digit year-on-year revenue growth might be readily achievable for a piece of the latest branded personal technology but highly improbable for, say, toothpaste or units of electricity, the former moving over the longer term with population growth (and over the shorter term with discounting, marketing and formula engineering) the latter, broadly, with changes in economic activity (for industrial and commercial load) or new home builds (for residential) as well as changes in tariffs. However, even here, analysis must be contextualised against the underlying market. In a frontier economy experiencing rapid growth in personal incomes, growth in toothpaste shipments might indeed be in double digits, while a rapidly industrialising economy could also see double-digit growth in electricity delivery. Investors must consider revenue/unit-shipment growth in the context of macroeconomic drivers and product- and market-specific factors. Where numbers do not correlate to what the investors would expect, they should exercise prudent circumspection.

While revenues are clearly important, it is the profit earned from the sales of goods and services from which debt is serviced and returns made to shareholders. There are a number of metrics which measure the margin – the proportion of revenues that remain once principle costs have been paid. Costs for a typical non-financial corporation fall into two categories:

Cost of goods sold (COGS)

COGS are the direct costs of the products a company has sold during any given period and include outlays necessary to bring the products into inventory and thence to sale viz., raw materials, labour, energy and any overhead that can be allocated to the product.

Selling, general and administrative expenses (SG&A)

SG&A are the selling and administrative expenses that can be linked to the sale of a particular good or a proportion of overall selling and administrative expenses that can be allocated to a good or product. They would typically include marketing/advertising expenses, warranty provisions, facility charges, charges for indirect personnel, etc.

Analysts typically examine margin contributions using the following metrics:

Gross margin

```
(Revenues - cost of goods sold) ÷ revenues
```

The gross margin typically shows the proportion of profit generated from sales once core costs involved in the production of the good (usually raw materials, fuel and labour) have been met.

Again, comparisons across different products and industries might not be particularly meaningful, since they will inherently have different margin profiles, reflecting different inputs. Rather, it is in the longitudinal study of a single company or the comparison of companies in the same industry that gross margin analysis becomes meaningful. A consistently declining gross margin in the same company is clearly a red flag. Analysis of the gross margin across a couple of economic cycles will demonstrate the kind of swings in profitability that the investor can expect as a result of the company's cyclicality. Vulnerability to fluctuating raw materials prices and/or energy prices will, to the extent that these cannot be passed onto the consumer, be evident in gross margin movements (with a lag depending on inventory accounting – see chapters 4 and 5).

Gross margin analysis across an industry may reveal which companies have been better at managing structural and/or labour costs. Again, there is no mechanical linkage between a given gross margin number and an assessment of a company's performance; rather, changes are prompts for the investor to further investigate management's actions.

EBIT and operating margins

```
Either earnings before interest and taxes or Operating earnings ÷ revenues
```

These metrics are useful because they allow the investor to gain insight into a company's core profitability from its operations, undistorted by the impact of direct taxation and capital structures (since they are calculated on earnings before tax, interest cost and dividends have been deducted). They can therefore be used to make comparisons across players in the same industry regardless of national boundaries or financing structures. EBIT and operating income and their associated margin calculations are often used interchangeably, but can contain meaningful differences, especially when dealing with companies that are undergoing significant restructuring with attendant costs. Also, EBIT is a non-GAAP measurement.

Operating income is the sum of revenues less COGS and SG&A expenses and thus addresses a company's core earnings. (For some enterprises, such as consumer goods or services, SG&A expenses can be a principal cost. For instance, the manufacturer of a mature consumer item in a developed economy with concentrated competition – e.g. feminine hygiene products – may only be able to boost sales and market share with significant marketing initiatives, the cost of which would show up in SG&A).

EBIT may include other non-operating income/expenses such as equity earnings in affiliates, restructuring charges, gains on sales of assets, etc. Frequently, these sources of income/expenditure may be non-cash and/or unrelated to the day-to-day operations of the business, and, in understanding the core profitability of the business, are therefore better excluded. However, in the case of a company that, for instance, regularly books gains/losses on asset sales (for instance, a hotel chain) or has been in lengthy, multi-year restructuring with high associated cash outgoings, it may be more economically verisimilar to use EBIT. It is also valuable to see how a company reconciles non-GAAP metrics such as EBIT and EBITDA to GAAP metrics.

EBITDA margin

```
Earnings before interest, taxes, depreciation and amortisation ÷
revenues
```

As we have emphasised elsewhere in this book, cash is king. Companies must service their debt from cash earnings and, while accrual earnings might better reflect a distribution of revenues and costs over time, if they are not cash, they must be adjusted accordingly.

In the income statement, the two largest accrual (non-cash) cost items are usually depreciation and amortisation, which reflect the allocation to given accounting periods of costs associated with the usage of tangible and intangible assets, respectively. In some cases the choice of an asset's life for depreciation/amortisation purposes may bear more resemblance to the idea of 'forty days and forty nights' in the Bible, than the real economic life of the asset. The depreciation/amortisation number can also be manipulated by the choice of methodology (more of this in chapters 4 and 5).

Either way, their exclusion (together with that of other non-cash/one-off items in the income statement) produces a margin that is a better proxy for a company's cash-based profitability. It is not without flaws: EBITDA makes no allowance for the cost of making long-term investments and the use of a firm's investment capital. An acquisition can boost EBITDA and the EBITDA margin but it has a capital cost associated with it.

Net margin

```
Net income before distributions to shareholders ÷ revenues
```

Net margin is beloved of companies but of limited use to the credit investor, given that it reflects profitability after debt service (interest) has been deducted and after tax, which is also paid after the deduction of interest. It is also very much an accrual number: depreciation, amortisation, non-cash and one-off charges and non-cash tax figures are all contained within the net income number. Also, given differences in national taxation regimes and in the use of more or less aggressive capital structures across industries, it provides a poor basis for comparison.

10. Shareholders and shareholder activism

Founding families/foundations

As we demonstrate elsewhere in this book, the hereditary principle is no guarantee of sustainable stewardship of a company. Nonetheless, many of today's largest and most successful corporate behemoths continue to have controlling, or at least still-influential, family shareholdings. As well as creating multi-generational wealth, the maintenance of family participation in businesses can enhance business continuity and adherence to certain principles which lead to favourable conditions for creditors.

In the classic case, a founding family may retain a long-term stake in a company over generations, often with voting rights that are considerably in excess of their actual economic stake in the company, like the Sulzberger family's historical ownership of the *New York Times* or the Kellogg or Hershey Foundation's stakes in their eponymous companies. In many of these cases, the long-standing shareholding can act as a brake on aggressive changes of operational or financial strategy.

All of the aforementioned companies can be characterised as conservatively financed. However, this is far from universally the case simply because of the presence of a controlling family. To take another example from the print and media sectors, it was the Chandler family's desire to monetise their stake in the diminishingly profitable Tribune Company that led to the very aggressively financed LBO in 2007, which ultimately caused the company to file for bankruptcy in 2008. Thus, an understanding of what is motivating family or foundation shareholders is very important in interpreting whether their stake implies greater or lesser financial conservatism.

Another factor to consider in this context is the use of super-voting share structures, which are a means of maintaining family control of the business. Depending on the objectives of family members, these structures are a double-edged sword from a credit perspective, since they can allow the family either to stymie strategic progress or push the company into quixotic misadventures. Where they do exist, it is important to analyse the family's attitude towards the C-suite and the extent to which they are willing to give professional management teams free rein to run the company in the interests of all stakeholders. Also, under some jurisdictions, such as France, shares accrue additional voting power year by year, if held over time by the same shareholder or foundation, which can, gradually, turn a minority stake on an economic basis into a controlling stake on a voting basis.

A company's selection of its key officers – CEO, CFO and COO – can often be a revealing indicator of its direction, or, indeed, lack thereof. Does the board nominate an insider to the CEO role – a 'safe pair of hands'? This could well be a vote of confidence in the existing strategy and a welcome vote for continuity; however, it is a welcome vote only if the current strategy is delivering. For example, Peugeot embarked on a capital-raising exercise that diluted the Peugeot family's controlling stake and equalised it with that of its co-investors, the French state and Chinese auto manufacturer, Donfeng Motor Group, at 14% apiece.[86] Contemporaneously, the company elected a new chairman to its managing board and shortly afterwards appointed representatives of the French state and Dongfeng to vice-chair positions on the supervisory board, in addition to appointing other new members.[87] We would expect these changes to herald strategic change rather than 'business as usual'.

By contrast, a company that operates in a highly specialised industry, and whose equity performance is basically satisfactory, might be expected to select an industry specialist, steeped in operational expertise and capable of articulating a long-term view. In the case of Shire plc, a UK pharma company specialising in genetic therapies, medications for attention deficit disorder and hyperactivity, and drugs for renal and gastrointestinal ailments, what should we make of its selection of Susan Kilsby as the next chairman? A glance at her CV on Bloomberg indicates that, far from being a lab rat, Ms Kilsby is a 30-year M&A veteran at Credit Suisse who headed and chaired their M&A division. The choice could indicate that Shire is about to embark upon a phase of M&A either as acquirer or acquiree; either way, it would seem to indicate a change in tack for Shire, which could be meaningful for investors.[88]

Shareholder activism

Figures such as Carl Icahn, Kirk Kerkorian, Bill Ackman and their ilk have caused palpitations among credit investors for decades. Large concentrations of shareholders can

---

86   PSA Peugeot Citroën (2014). 'Final Agreements Between PSA Peugeot Citroën, Dongfeng Motor Group, the French State, EPF and FFP'. [Online]. Available at: **www.psa-peugeot-citroen.com/en/media/press-releases/final-agreements-signed-between-psa-peugeot-citroen-dongfeng-motor-group-the-french-state-and-the-family-owned-etablissements-peugeot-freres-and-ffp** [Accessed 24 November 2014].

87   PSA Peugeot Citroën (2014). 'Completion of Share and Rights Issues Reserved for Dongfeng and the French State, New Supervisory Board'. [Online]. Available at: **www.psa-peugeot-citroen.com/en/media/press-releases/completion-of-share-and-rights-issues-reserved-for-dongfeng-and-the-french-state-new-supervisory-board-structure** [Accessed 24 November 2014].

88   Subsequent to our noting this, Shire attempted to sell itself to Abbvie for £32bn.

effectively be co-opted by activists with relatively tiny economic stakes in the company into signing up for the latter's agenda in the hope of a quick turn on their long-term holding.

A typical activist scenario would involve a medium-sized, relatively sleepy investment grade corporation with a stock price that has been somewhat lagging the market over recent quarters. Out of the blue one morning comes the announcement across the news wires that a shareholder activist has taken a relatively modest stake in the company's equity with the intention of buying more and seeking to appoint new board members to represent their intentions. These intentions are rarely (with notable exceptions) credit-friendly, and often take the shape of divesting assets that the activists deemed to be 'non-core' (reducing collateral for creditors), raising additional debt to finance share buybacks or special dividends (increasing financial risk) or, at the extreme, seeking to buy out the whole company (potentially subordinating existing debt beneath a mountain of new, secured facilities and at the back of the queue when it comes to getting obligations serviced).

There is rarely time to trade out of positions before the market has priced in a number of credit-negative outcomes, so what is important is to undertake a thorough analysis of which of the wide range of possible scenarios is most likely to be the eventual outcome. A rapid run-up in the share price on the day of the announcement, for example, is actually a material obstacle to increasing his stake. A robust rebuttal of the activist's proposals by management, with the backing of significant shareholders, would also represent a potentially insuperable problem. Market conditions may not favour the activist's proposals for financing or divestments. We refer you to chapters 6 and 7 for a fuller discussion of the factors that need to be assessed. However, in practice, we actively screen the data available on services such as S&P Capital IQ and Bloomberg to check shareholder registers for the presence of such investors and changes in their shareholdings.

Institutional shareholders

An awareness of the composition of the shareholder register can alert the credit investor to potential threats to a company's creditworthiness long before they actually arise. Significant concentrations of shareholdings confer the ability to exercise corporate control in an open capital structure. Even if this right is not habitually exercised, it poses a threat to credit insofar as large shareholders may be open to persuasion by activists to force the pace of strategic or financial change at the company. Significant changes in a company's shareholder base can presage more radical change at the company, especially when there is potential for collusion between like-minded shareholder groups. We discuss the atomisation of institutional shareholdings and the change in the nature of their historic role in exercising corporate stewardship in depth in chapter 2.

Thankfully, changes in the shareholder register are a matter of public record and can be monitored through the relevant stock exchanges or through wire services such as Bloomberg and Reuters. We give an example of the quarterly changes among one company's (US department store JCPenney) institutional shareholders in figure 5.

FIGURE 5: EVOLUTION OF MAJOR INSTITUTIONAL HOLDINGS OF JCPENNEY STOCK

	Holder Name	Portfolio Name	2011 Q4	2012 Q1	2012 Q2	2012 Q3	Amt Held↑
1.	- PERSHING SQUARE CAP	n/a	38.7MLN	39.1MLN	39.1MLN	39.1MLN	39,075,771
2.	VORNADO REALTY TRU	n/a	No Report	23.4MLN	No Report	No Report	23,400,000
3.	- DODGE & COX	DODGE & COX	No Report	No Report	16.1MLN	20.3MLN	20,316,550
4.	- STATE STREET	n/a	No Report	No Report	No Report	No Report	18,094,911
5.	- FMR LLC	n/a	No Report	No Report	No Report	No Report	17,935,226
6.	J C PENNEY PROFIT SH	n/a	14.6MLN	No Report	No Report	No Report	14,639,712
7.	EVERCORE TRUST COM	EVERCORE TRUST C	15.2MLN	13.8MLN	12.9MLN	12.2MLN	12,188,385
8.	- BLACKROCK	n/a	No Report	No Report	No Report	No Report	10,349,882
9.	- HOTCHKIS & WILEY CAP	HOTCHKIS AND WILE	8.7MLN	4.7MLN	7.3MLN	9MLN	8,978,475
10.	- VANGUARD GROUP INC	VANGUARD GROUP I	8MLN	8.4MLN	8.7MLN	8.9MLN	8,872,428
11.	SASCO CAPITAL INCOR	SASCO CAPITAL INC	5.8MLN	4.8MLN	5.9MLN	6.5MLN	6,498,613
12.	- UBS	n/a	No Report	No Report	No Report	No Report	5,905,801
13.	- DEUTSCHE BANK AG	DEUTSCHE BANK AK	5MLN	6MLN	5MLN	5.1MLN	5,054,273
14.	MAVERICK CAPITAL LT	MAVERICK CAPITAL	2MLN	989,118	2.6MLN	4.7MLN	4,709,263
15.	GLENVIEW CAPITAL MA	GLENVIEW CAPITAL	No Report	No Report	No Report	4.5MLN	4,457,212
16.	ORBIS HOLDINGS LIMI	ORBIS HOLDINGS LI	No Report	No Report	No Report	3.9MLN	3,918,590
17.	HSBC HOLDINGS PLC	HSBC HOLDINGS PL	22,677	3.1MLN	5.4MLN	3.5MLN	3,545,322
18.	WELLINGTON MANAGEM	WELLINGTON MANAG	1.7MLN	1.6MLN	2.3MLN	2.8MLN	2,815,278

JCP US Equity · 29) Settings · 99) Feedback · Holdings: Historical · JC Penney Co Inc · CUSIP 70816010 · 1) Current 2) Historical 3) Matrix 4) Ownership 5) Transactions 6) Options · Search Name -- · 21) Save 22) Delete 23) Saved Search 24) Refine Search · Text Search · Holder Group All Holders · 30) < 2011 Q3 · Zoom · 100%

Australia 61 2 9777 8600 Brazil 5511 3048 4500 Europe 44 20 7330 7500 Germany 49 69 9204 1210 Hong Kong 852 2977 6000
Japan 81 3 3201 8900   Singapore 65 6212 1000   U.S. 1 212 318 2000   Copyright 2013 Bloomberg Finance L.P.
SN 860223 GMT GMT+0:00 H382-570-0 23-Jan-2013 11:45:05

Source: Bloomberg

11. Quantitative and market-based credit systems

Traditional methods of credit analysis can now be further supplemented by a number of market-based predictors of default such as Moody's KMV®, Bondscore® and their competitors.

The KMV model translates publicly-available pricing information into an Expected Default Frequency in three stages:

1. estimation of the asset value and volatility of asset return – driven by market values, or by the option-pricing formula

2. calculation of the distance-to-default, which, according to KMV, occurs when the asset value reaches a level somewhere between the value of total liabilities and the value of short-term debt and

3. the derivation of the probability of default, in which 1 is mapped to 2.

Variations in the stock price, leverage ratio and asset volatility are all important inputs into the formulae, but, whatever the strengths of their methodologies, their dependence on stock market information flows does tend to highlight the heroic assumption that lies at their heart: that the equity markets operate on information flows that are at least as good as the bond and CDS markets. Given the degree to which the latter are directly influenced by bank trading books, this is a questionable assumption in our view.

Furthermore, the market-driven approach is vulnerable to self-reinforcing false positives since the market value of a company's traded debt and equity becomes more volatile the more risky the company is perceived to be, and the reliance on equity volatility that is integral to the operation of some of these models can skew their output significantly.

The Altman Z-Score® has become perhaps the most widely accepted of these systems and is readily available on many financial market data terminals at no additional charge. In its initial test, the Altman Z-Score was found to be 72% accurate in predicting bankruptcy two years before the event, with a Type II error (false negatives) of 6%.[89] In a series of subsequent tests covering three periods over the next 31 years (up until 1999), the model was found to be approximately 80%–90% accurate in predicting bankruptcy one year before the event, with a Type II error (classifying the firm as bankrupt when it does not go bankrupt) of approximately 15%–20%.[90] It can thus be seen that these quantitative, market-based models can be helpful in highlighting potentially vulnerable companies in a portfolio.

The Altman Z-score formula for predicting bankruptcy was published in 1968 by Edward Altman, who, at the time was an assistant professor of finance at New York University. The Z-score is a linear combination of five common business ratios, weighted by coefficients which are estimated by identifying firms that had declared bankruptcy and then collecting a matched sample of firms within the same industries that had survived.[91] The models, which vary according to whether the company in question is publicly listed or private, have varying degrees of accuracy in predicting defaults. From the mid-1980s onwards, the Z-scores have gained wide acceptance.

None of the variations of the Z-score is designed for use with financial companies because of the latter's frequent use of off-balance-sheet structures, which renders much of the publicly available data on the companies inaccurate as a means of predicting default. Herein lies one of the weaknesses of dependence on such quantitative models in isolation.

---

89 Altman Edward. I. (1968) 'Financial Ratios, Discriminant Analysis and the Prediction of Corporate Bankruptcy' [Online] Available at **onlinelibrary.wiley.comdoi/10.1111/j.1540-6261.1968.tb00843.x/full** [Accessed 18 February 2015]

90 Altman Edward. I. (2000) 'Predicting Financial Distress of Companies: Revisiting the Z-Score and Zeta® Models' [Online] Available at **citeseerx.ist.psu.edu/viewdoc/download?doi=10.1.1.25.1884&rep=rep1&type=pdf** [Accessed 18 February 2015]

91 The original Altman Z-score formula was as follows:
$$Z = 0.012T1 + 0.014T2 + 0.033T3 + 0.006T4 + 0.009T5.$$

T1 = Working capital ÷ total assets. Measures liquid assets in relation to the size of the company.

T2 = Retained earnings ÷ total assets. Measures profitability that reflects the company's age and earning power.

T3 = Earnings before interest and taxes ÷ total assets. Measures operating efficiency apart from tax and leveraging factors. It recognises operating earnings as being important to long-term viability.

T4 = Market value of equity ÷ book value of total liabilities. Adds market dimension that can show up security price fluctuation as a possible red flag.

T5 = Sales ÷ total assets. Standard measure for total asset turnover (varies greatly from industry to industry). Altman found that the ratio profile for the bankrupt group fell at -0.25 avg, and for the non-bankrupt group at +4.48 avg.

Elsewhere in this book, we reinforce the point that the inclusion of such vehicles in corporate credit assessments is the most accurate way of divining the true underlying creditworthiness of the company.

12. Disclosure

Information, goes the cliché, is power. Companies are well aware of this and consequently are often unwilling to release any more about themselves than the details about their business that are required by the letter of securities law in their regular filings. Yet the level and quality of corporate disclosure are other factors that are in and of themselves an indication of the company's relative standing as a credit.

Disclosure, of course, cuts both ways, since it punishes most the companies that have most to hide, but every credit investor worth their salt is aware of this and it is incumbent on them to push the limits of what companies are happy to discuss – within the boundaries of full public disclosure, of course. Credit analysis is a discipline in which asking awkward questions of senior management is a fundamental responsibility, and one might expect the senior figures of corporate C-suites to wish to avoid the potential embarrassment of public interrogation on quarterly conference calls and just publish more detail on the composition of their businesses' earnings, cash flows, bank covenants etc. Old habits, however, die hard, and many companies still release too little information for public scrutiny too late for a thorough analysis to be undertaken, leaving the investor with the choice of making an uncomfortable leap of faith or simply avoiding the investment altogether.

This problem varies in intensity with location. The disclosure requirements for US corporations are usually more stringent than those under which their European counterparts are obliged to operate, though even the latter fluctuate greatly between different legal jurisdictions. Volume of disclosure is really no substitute for quality, with many companies being all too willing to publish reams of operational data while remaining more reluctant to give away any details of more sensitive areas of corporate policy. This is an area in which the availability of timely information can be vital in ensuring that investors avoid rapidly deteriorating credit.

Investing in publicly traded companies can mitigate a cultural aversion to disclosure, since some regular financial data is required by most stock markets to retain listings, but many companies are culturally more attuned to using bank financing than the public markets and continue to be reluctant to improve their levels of disclosure. (We wonder if the current trend in Europe towards the de-levering of bank balance sheets will begin to reverse this habit over time.) This is particularly the case among large family-dominated concerns and parastatal companies, used to cosy financing relationships that have lasted many years. All the same, from a credit investor's perspective, good disclosure is a clear positive, allowing decisions to be based on appropriate levels of timely information and tends to help facilitate market access for companies to undertake opportunistic re-financings and establish longer-term sources of funding and efficient capital structures.

13. Relative positioning on a scale of creditworthiness

In the final phase of credit assessment, each of these elements should be considered relative to one another, resulting in a kind of mental matrix in which the judgments are combined. All of the following factors must also be assessed against peer companies within the industries in which the firm under assessment competes, and against other companies with which it has common characteristics:

- a credit's position vis à vis its economic context

- its scale, cyclicality and the elasticity of demand for its products

- the business's maturity and growth prospects

- its obsolescene and substitution risk

- its capital, asset and labour intensity

- its financial ratios

- its cash cycle and seasonality

- its margins and capital formation

- the liquidity at its disposal

- the composition of its shareholder base.

The credit rating agencies have gone some way to systematising their approach to this process, and nowadays publish ratings rationales, which show that company X has, for example, the financial ratios of an investment-grade credit but the scale and cyclicality of a high-yield credit. The other factors we list above are all thrown into the mix to provide notchings and other differentiating shades in order to arrive at a rating. Ultimately, in practice, some of these factors weigh more heavily than others, and so it must be with our own credit assessments. Liquidity, for example, with its decisive role in corporate survival in a crisis, should be given particular importance.

Sometimes this can be, relatively speaking, a straightforward process, with pure-play companies that make for easy comparison within their industries. But in many cases corporations combine elements of different industries even if they do not perceive themselves as traditional conglomerates, and elements such as the financing arm of a large corporate may require an analysis that has more in common with the way one would assess a bank than its corporate parent. In summary, it may be more straightforward to present the kind of decision-making matrix we are describing in literal terms, which we attempt to do in table 16. However, so mechanical an approach is only useful as a guide, since, in practice, the weightings and credibility that are attributed to each factor will remain highly subjective and nuanced by the interpreter.

TABLE 16: CREDIT MATRIX EXAMPLE

Economy	Scale	Cyclicality	Elasticity	Maturity	Obsolescence	Intensity	Metrics	Seasonality
4	3	5	6	4	5	7	6	8

Margins	Capital formation	Shareholder base	Peer comparisons	Liquidity	Disclosure	Number of factors	Overall 'score'	Weighted
8	7	8	5	4	7	15	5.8	6

In table 16 we rate each factor on a qualitative scale, from 1–10, with 1 being the strongest from a credit perspective and 10 being the weakest, though even a score of 10 does not imply imminent insolvency.

Our fictitious company, for all its impressive scale and relatively solid cyclicality, maturity and elasticity, its above-average liquidity and favourable standing in its peer group, is dragged down by its capital and labour intensity below-average credit metrics. In the end, the numerical assessment puts it just below the middle of the scale.

The importance of subjectivity in this and any other analysis cannot, however, be overstated. This is what has led us to weight the positives in this case more heavily than the negatives and caused a rounding up to a score of 6/10 from a simple average of 5.8/10, positioning this credit on the positive side of the investment-grade/high-yield divide.[92]

Conclusion

Having read this chapter, the reader should be in a position to make the basic numerical and some of the qualitative credit evaluations that will be needed in approaching real-world investment decisions.

In the next chapter, we look to delve more deeply into the financial side of the equation, examining some of the areas in which management teams seek to present their companies' financial statements in ways that present an unduly positive impression of their companies' creditworthiness.

---

92 Assuming a ten-point scale.

4

How Managements Present Reality

Introduction

IN THIS SECTION WE ATTEMPT TO MOVE ON FROM THE TRADITIONAL APPLICATION OF financial metrics in credit analysis and, armed with an awareness of the governance factors to complement these skills, examine some of the ways in which management's presentation of financial data can frustrate the analyst's attempt to assess a company's creditworthiness.

Initially, we have to turn back to the numbers. Here we discuss management's options and motivations in presenting the figures that they submit for public scrutiny. We spend some time on sell-side practitioners' efforts further to emphasise the supremacy of numbers. We then link this theme to our scepticism over the real value of long-term corporate financial modelling and seek to emphasise the importance of an interlinked narrative between the numbers and other factors, such as the quality of auditors and auditor rotation, in a credit assessment.

In the second part of the chapter we illustrate the importance of interpreting the numbers in the context of the economic realities that they purport to represent, taking each section of the financial statements in turn: P&L, balance sheet and cash flow statement, and highlight areas that merit particular scrutiny from the investor. As we address each successive major area of the financial statements, we will illustrate conventional methods of financial presentation for income statement, balance sheet and cash flow items and highlight some of the inconsistencies they can contain, as well as providing examples that illustrate a more obfuscatory approach, in the hope of leaving the reader better equipped to arrive at a meaningful view on interpretation of management's presentation of the facts, and their implications for the credit behind them.

1. Reducing credit to a numbers game

We feel that the analytical approach of the investment banking community, especially to large corporations that are potentially important clients of these same banks, can sometimes miss the mark.

Management teams will, understandably, use the latitude given to them by accounting rules to present their companies in the most favourable light possible. It is up to the investor – confronted with a surfeit of companies to examine and a paucity of time in which to examine them – to interpret what the numbers really mean. Market practitioners often sing the praises of 'crunching the numbers' but the figures to be crunched do not emerge from nowhere. They are, in their 'pre-crunched' form, the results of management actions and the ways in which they choose to present them.

In comparing one company's revenues to another's, are we actually comparing things that are alike? In short, in analysis, the rule is: garbage in, garbage out.

As credit investors, we are often invited by bank salespeople to meet their bank's 'athletes' and listen to their latest opinions. The sporting imagery here is revealing: it reduces corporate financial analysis to a kind of arithmetical Olympiad where the laurels go to the producer of the most sophisticated quantitative model. In part, this focus on the numbers almost to the exclusion of other factors is a product of financial institutions' own reliance on mathematical modelling for their internal risk-management purposes (an approach whose shortcomings were vividly illustrated during the financial crisis of 2008).

A chief risk officer, usually a highly numerate individual, will typically find himself more at ease with a seemingly quantifiable credit risk, presenting an arithmetical number of turns of leverage and consequent probability of default, than with the complex realities of an actual credit risk, which requires an understanding of interlinked narrative issues that together influence the likelihood and timing of corporate defaults. Moreover, these factors may have limited bearing on the pricing of credit, which, frustratingly for analyst and investor alike is more often than not a factor of macro developments or market technicals.

'Soft' factors can predominate in credit judgments

To illustrate this, for example, depending on the legal domicile of a company with five turns of leverage in an industry where average enterprise value multiples are 5.2×, a management team may be more or less motivated either to file for bankruptcy or restructure debt, a factor that is entirely bypassed by a purely numerical approach.

This is illustrated by the differing timelines, but ultimately similar outcomes, that featured in the fates of the US telephone directories publisher, R.H. Donnelley, which filed for Chapter 11 bankruptcy in 2009, and its Italian counterpart, Seat Pagine Gialli, which, facing similar competitive and financial challenges, has laboured to stay out of formal bankruptcy while teetering on its very brink for some time – ultimately only defaulting on its unsecured debt in January 2011, having more or less exhausted its refinancing options.

In addition to our misgivings about the value of long-term corporate modelling, the awareness that management's actions and financial presentation of a corporation might be informed by their own incentive structures or a desire for job security as much or more than by the interests of the shareholders for whom they act is an issue which investors need to bear in mind when assessing management's motivation for taking decisions over financial policy and strategy.

This lies at the crux of the stewardship problem that we identified in chapter 2, and is illustrated by the examples of the behaviour of management at Nortel Networks and Waste Management later in this chapter, as well as being subject to deeper examination in chapter 6. To establish whether or not there is an actual threat posed to the company's creditworthiness from such apparent conflicts arising requires a significant investment of time and analytical detective work. The scope for material distortions of presentation to flatter the appearance of accounting reality is extremely broad.

But numbers can still be revealing

Bearing the above in mind, we detail below some of the many areas in which such creativity and flexibility can be used to distort perceptions of corporate health, illustrating fields of particular focus with relevant case studies in the three main sections of companies' financial reports.

2. Manipulation of the income statement

The income statement is perhaps the most apparently straightforward of the major financial reports that companies are obliged to disclose to public scrutiny – a simple matter of additions and deductions relating to a finite period – that solves to a number for the stock market to then divide by the average number of shares outstanding in the year to derive the headline-grabbing EPS figure.

This figure, if it deviates materially from a 'Street' consensus built on an average of an indeterminate number of analysts' estimates, can lead to material impacts on stock prices and credit spreads.

To give a dramatic example of the impact of such an 'earnings miss' on asset prices, US department store JCPenney reported earnings well below the market's expectations on 15 May 2012, on the back of which the company's stock price fell by 20% and its five-year CDS spread rose by 165bps to 620bps, its highest level since December 2008. Same-store sales fell by 18.9% in the course of what was to prove to be an ill-starred attempt by the company to address a younger and more affluent customer base via a strategy of store revamps and in-store 'shops' highlighting individual brands (see figure 6). The results were sufficiently out of line with the market's expectations and management's previous guidance to also trigger downgrades from the ratings agencies.

More famously, the accounting trickery that enabled WorldCom (see later in this chapter) to inflate its income statement by $3.8bn in 2001 and 2002 involved improper transfers of costs from the income statement onto the balance sheet.[93] The impact of this shift in costs was sufficient to artificially inflate its quarterly profitability to the tune of several hundred million dollars.

FIGURE 6: JCPENNEY STOCK AND CDS LEVELS

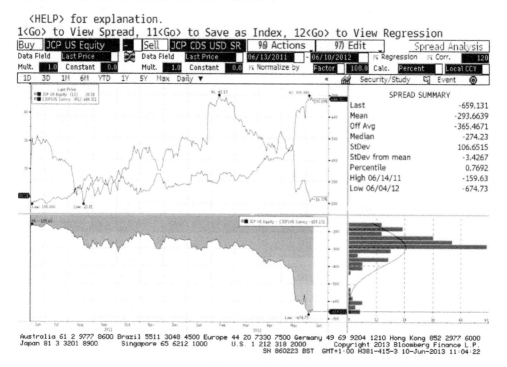

Source: Bloomberg

Application of management discretion

Beneath the income statement's apparent simplicity, then, lie huge variations in corporations' definitions of underlying terms and material differences in accounting policies. Part of one company's SG&A expense is included by another firm in its cost of sales, flattering its operating costs by comparison. One firm's revenues are recognised on receipt of payment, another's well in advance, flattering the latter's top-line compared to that of its peer.

The fact that executive (and employee) remuneration are often formulaically linked to specific measurements can encourage them to 'manage' the presentation of accounts to flatter those numbers. For instance, a change in depreciation policy can be used to impact EBIT or operating margins if these are bogeys for remuneration calculations. This is not in and of itself problematic – digging through the notes buried in the annual report or 10-K will

---

93 For a fuller discussion of this topic, please refer to: Revsine, L., Collins, D.W., Johnson, B. and Mittelstaedt, F. (2011), *Financial Reporting and Analysis*. New York: McGraw-Hill.

usually reveal such a practice. However, such notes usually appear well after the publication of the 'headline' number, which analysts and investors eagerly await and which drive changes in the prices of both equity and credit securities. Thus non-GAAP measurements such as EBIT, EBITDA and their even more malformed variants, EBITDAL,[94] OIBDA,[95] and NOPLATDA,[96] run the danger of becoming shibboleths rather than the useful gauge of corporate performance that was their original purpose. It is therefore necessary to understand the purpose of their use and how they might be manipulated.

Revenue and expense recognition

The International Accounting Standards Board (IASB) and the Financial Accounting Standards Board (FASB) state in their joint 2008 discussion paper on revenue recognition[97] that revenue has been earned, is realised or realisable and therefore eligible to be recognised when all four of the following criteria are met:[98]

1. persuasive evidence of an exchange arrangement exists

2. delivery has occurred or services been rendered

3. the seller's price to the buyer is fixed or determinable and

4. collectibility is reasonably assured.[99]

Even working within these tight definitions, however, issues arise. For example, in cases where a retailer of a product retains the right to return unsold product to the manufacturer, the manufacturer would be unable to recognise the expected revenue attached to the full value of goods shipped until such time as the last item of that shipment had actually been sold to the end consumer.

Similarly, sales of product with delayed delivery dates should not be recognised until the customer takes title for the goods and assumes the risks associated with their on-selling. A further example of this is a retailer that takes a percentage of the cost of a product in the expectation of receiving the rest of its cost at the time the product is handed to the customer.

So far, these examples are fairly intuitive – a strict application of the IASB/FASB criteria is easy enough, but in reality the application of these criteria becomes much more nuanced as the scale and complexity of businesses increases and can lead to significant mismatches between stated and received revenues. As we see later in this chapter, two of the most

---

94 As above but including rental leases.
95 Operating income before depreciation and amortisation.
96 Net operating profit less adjusted taxes, depreciation and amortisation.
97 Financial Accounting Standards Board (2008). 'Preliminary Views on Revenue Recognition in Contracts with Customers', *Financial Accounting Series Discussion Paper*. [Online]. Available at: **www.fasb. org.** [Accessed 24 November 2014].
98 For a fuller discussion of these and other accounting topics, see Revsine et al. (2011), cited in footnote 84.
99 FASB ASC Section 605-10-S25 – Revenue Recognition. [Online] Available at: **www.fasb.org**. [Accessed 26 November 2014].

egregious abuses of revenue recognition in recent history lay behind the collapse of WorldCom and HealthSouth in the early years of the 21st century.

Because there is often a mismatch in timing between the receipt of revenues and the costs associated with them, accounting principles are designed to alleviate the disconnect between these events, with accrual accounting better matching the unevenness of a more cash-based approach in the interests of presenting a more stable picture of a business whose actual income and outgoings may occur several months, or in some cases even years, apart. While this clearly presents a more consistent picture of a company's finances, there is a downside, in that it also gives scope for management to manipulate the timings of actual payments and receipts. Thus a subscription-based business, like a professional journal publisher, will typically recognise its revenues and expenses associated with it over the life of the subscription, rather than at the time it receives the cash in from the subscriber, taking the view that its obligation to the subscriber is discharged over the life of the contract.

Revenue recognition red flags

a) Growth of 'other assets' and investment in intangibles

The technique of growing other assets and investment in intangibles has been used frequently by management teams seeking to flatter the short-term income-generating capacity of a business. If a company recognises a current expense as an intangible asset, it is then able to reduce the reported level of its operational costs while reporting a higher level of intangible assets on the balance sheet. To obfuscate the true nature of these intangible assets, management may choose to categorise them as 'other' assets. Significant growth in this line item should therefore be a cause for concern.

To cite a widely-known example, in the now infamous case of WorldCom, the annual cash outflows relating to the growth of these intangibles flowed through the cash flow statement as part of WorldCom's capital expenditure line. In our view, this kind of recurring investment in intangibles is often a marker of potential accounting manipulation. However, monitoring the ratio of capex as a percentage of sales against the company's industry peers can provide a red flag if a company is engaging in this practice.

In the case of WorldCom, the company flouted accounting convention with regard to the recognition of expenses in this way. The convention is that it is only at the time when expenses actually provide a benefit to the company that they can be recognised as assets on the balance sheet. By classifying its line costs as capital expenditure rather than current expenses (allegedly to the tune of $3.055bn in 2001 and $797m in 2002), WorldCom was able to defer part of its current expenses into the future and enhance the current level of earnings at the expense of those yet to come. According to the *New York Times* on 4 July 2002, a memo prepared by Scott D. Sullivan, the chief financial officer at the time, attempted to justify this capitalisation by spuriously arguing that WorldCom was paying for excess capacity that it would need in the future, i.e., that the line costs in question were a cost of obtaining future customers.[100] In some instances, accounting rules do allow

---

100 *New York Times* (2002). [Online] Available at: **www.nytimes.com/2002/07/04/business/04TELE. html** [Accessed 9 March 2015]

for some of costs of obtaining customers to be capitalised, though never to the degree that WorldCom did. Again, it is a question of degree relative to accepted practices among industry peers that can shine a light on the acceptability of such practices.

b) Changing revenue recognition timings

Another North American Telco, Nortel Networks, offers a further example of manipulative revenue and cost recognition, in this case to enhance measures of profitability and efficiency such as ROE and ROCE with the aim of hitting earnings guidance and thereby increasing senior management's remuneration.

Specifically, the individuals concerned changed the company's revenue recognition policy in order to bring forward revenues that would enable Nortel Networks's results to hit previously announced targets, then selectively reversed some of the results of the changes so that Nortel Networks would not exceed these widely expected targets. Nortel Networks's management also concealed the existence of excess reserves of over $300m which should have been included in the 2002 accounts but were hidden away for later use. They then directed the release of these reserves to bolster profits in the second quarter of 2003, with the effect of turning a US GAAP loss into a profit and enabling the payment of significant management bonuses.

The final denouement in the fraud came when Nortel Networks's management failed to enlighten shareholders as to why Nortel Networks was conducting a purportedly comprehensive review of its assets and liabilities, which resulted in the restatement of approximately $948m in liabilities in November 2003. Management falsely represented that the restatement was caused solely by mistakes relating to internal controls, whereas in reality Nortel Networks's first restatement was the result of "the intentional improper handling of reserves which occurred throughout management's tenure."[101]

c) Other forms of revenue manipulation

HealthSouth, a US-based hospital operator, had apparently enjoyed rapid growth and a steadily growing share price throughout the 1990s. In 2003, the SEC filed civil charges against HealthSouth for misleading public investors by presenting fraudulent financial statements. A forensic investigation of the company's accounts was conducted by PricewaterhouseCoopers to determine the extent and value of such activity that had taken place from 1997 through July 2002. After the investigation was completed, the CEO and key finance officers of HealthSouth were found to have boosted the company's revenues in a variety of ways, including:

- Deferred revenues from prepaid health coverage had been recognised in full rather than applying the key principle of matching cost and revenue within the relevant time frame.

- The amorphously defined 'other' revenues from healthcare coverage had themselves been overstated.

---

101   SEC (2007). 'SEC Charges Four Former Senior Executives of Nortel Networks Corporation in Wide-Ranging Financial Fraud Scheme'. [Online]. Available at: **www.sec.gov/news/press/2007/2007-39.htm** [Accessed 24 November 2014].

- Sundry routine operational expenses had either been capitalised or, alternatively, deferred, thereby understating annual expenses and further inflating the company's apparent profitability.

- 'Cookie jar reserves' – a line item over which management exercised complete discretion – were used to conceal shortfalls in income. By this method, management effectively set aside a reserve of cash in the good times to be deployed to flatter earnings whenever it felt the need.

- An indication of this practice can often be shown by the presence of outsized write-downs, particularly in the final quarter of the fiscal year, which can subsequently be reversed in order to close the gap between actual earnings and earnings targets. Thus, perversely, in practice it can pay to be somewhat suspicious of companies that seem to be almost too reliable at hitting their own earnings forecasts.

At the end of its forensic investigation into HealthSouth's accounts, PricewaterhouseCoopers had uncovered a total of $1.4bn in overstated income, beginning in 1999. A further overstatement of $1.1bn had also previously been identified by the US Justice Department after extensive discussion with executives of HealthSouth's own finance department.

Depreciation policy

Conventional presentation

The choice of a depreciation policy that is appropriate to the life span of a company's assets helps to accurately reflect the absorption of the cost of their initial purchase over a time which reflects their usefulness. The management of two companies with identical profitability in the same industry that use similar physical and intellectual property may, however, choose widely differing estimates of these assets' useful lives, a factor that can materially affect the impact on the companies' financial statements.

In the following table, Company A assigns useful lives of between three and 20 years to its assets, while Company B assigns useful lives of three to ten years. The impact of their policy difference on the balance sheet and income statement are shown in table 17.

This practice is perfectly proper and legal, but again is susceptible to abuse; it is well worth devoting time to digging out the definition of depreciation policy from the notes to the company's accounts in order to identify potential areas of concern. Again, changes in policy are worthy of scrutiny. A sudden extension of the estimated average useful life of assets is a red flag that can indicate that a company is choosing to under-invest in its plant, which may be an indication of more deep-seated troubles. A related area that can also be manipulated to distort economic reality is salvage valuation, any changes in which can be used to increase or decrease the depreciation figure in the income statement (see Waste Management example in the next section).

TABLE 17: DEPRECIATION POLICY IMPACT ON BALANCE SHEET AND INCOME STATEMENT

US$ millions	Company A	Company B
Balance sheet		
Property, plant and equipment at cost	100	100
Less accumulated depreciation	26	37
Net PP&E	74	63

US$ millions	Company A	Company B
Gross profit	40	40
Depreciation	10	20
Other operating costs	15	15
Operating profit	15	5
EBITDA	25	25

Source: Authors' estimates

Depreciation policy abuse

Waste Management - garbage in, garbage out

One example of the distortive effect of depreciation-policy abuse is given by the US corporation, Waste Management.

The company's senior management employed Andersen Consulting to help it present its accounts in a way that flattered its real profitability and led its published figures more closely to resemble the projections that management had shared with the wider market. The company's 1998 accounts assigned significant reappraised salvage values to its truck fleet, the motivation being that the larger salvage value reduced the annual depreciation charge for the asset, thereby overstating both net assets and net profit on lower expenses.[102]

To check for this abuse, simply divide the gross value of a company's tangible assets by the depreciation charge for the corresponding year to derive a figure that shows how long the underlying depreciation assumption is (i.e. how long the asset will be in use) then compare this to the economic useful life (in this case of the trucks) that is disclosed in the company's accounting policies.

---

102 We are indebted to the work of our colleagues at AMBA for their support on the HealthSouth, Waste Management, Nicor, Nortel Networks, China Forestry and Caterpillar examples in this chapter.

A discrepancy between the calculated depreciation period relative to the actual accounting policy number would reveal in this case that the company was indeed being somewhat aggressive in its approach to accounting for waste trucks, thereby flattering its reported earnings and assets.[103]

Alternatively, a simple comparison of the group's assumptions with those of its peers may also be informative. A further red flag to watch out for that may indicate that this practice is being used by a company is the presence of frequent impairments in its quarterly filings. Management teams may feel tempted to optically offset declining profitability by using this accounting device in order to meet targets that have been set for executive compensation, as was the case at Waste Management. Depreciation expenses on garbage trucks were distorted by assigning large amounts of residual or salvage value, while useful lives were extended beyond those prescribed by industry standards.

- 'Other fixed assets', which had previously been attributed zero salvage value, were re-computed on a spurious basis to assign them arbitrary salvage values.

- Landfill sites were given book values that did not correspond with the lower values that would ordinarily be attributed to such sites.

- A policy of expense-capitalisation was implemented in order to distribute the effects of Waste Management's accounting manipulation over a period of ten years. The policy was orchestrated and directed by the company's CEO and chairman of the board of directors, its COO and its CFO.

- During 2002's investigations, Waste Management's senior management cashed in their stock options, exacerbating the 33% fall in the stock price.

103   Cantoria, C.S. (2010). 'Unraveling the Details of 10 High-Profile Accounting Scandals'. [Online]. Available at: **www.brighthub.com/office/finance/articles/101200.aspx** [Accessed 24 November 2014].

TABLE 18: WASTE MANAGEMENT – ADJUSTMENTS TO ACCOUNTS

Waste Management Inc	Pre merger				Post merger		
(USDm)	1994	1995	1996	1997	1997(R)	1998	Notes
Depreciation and amortization	127	144	191	303	1,392	1,499	
Absolute increase	na	17	47	112	na	107	
PPE break-down - Gross							
Land and landfills	487	1,114	1,827	3,307	7,160	8,384	
Vehicles	70	221	405	687	2,676	2,797	
Machinery and equipment	71	154	186	252	3,079	3,072	
Containers	40	134	215	303	1,637	1,845	
Buildings and improvements	29	108	191	250	1,665	1,632	
Furniture and fixtures	13	29	41	46	544	506	
	710	1,760	2,866	4,844	16,761	18,236	
Less: accumulated depreciation and amortization	(187)	(441)	(667)	(889)	(5,572)	(6,598)	
	524	1,319	2,198	3,955	11,189	11,638	
Effective depreciation rate							
Depreciation as % of gross fixed assets	17.9%	8.2%	6.7%	6.3%	8.3%	8.2%	1
Capex-to-depreciation ratio							
Capex restated	187	253	443	436	1,332	1,651	
Capex to depreciation	1.5	1.8	2.3	1.4	1.0	1.1	2

Estimated useful lives		1995	1996	1997	Prior to 1 Oct 97	1 Oct 97 afterwards	
Buildings and improvements		7-30	5-35	20	10-40	10-40	
Vehicles		3-12	3-12	5-10	3-10	3-10	
Machinery and equipment		3-12	3-12	5-10	3-20	3-20	
Containers		3-12	3-12	8-12	8-20	8-12	3
Furniture and fixtures		3-10	3-10	3-7			

Statement made by the company in its 1998 AR   3

"Effective October 1, 1997, WM Holdings discontinued assigning salvage values to collection vehicles and containers, and adopted a process that shortened the estimated useful lives of certain landfills."

"Also effective October 1, 1997, WM Holdings reduced depreciable lives on containers from 15 and 20 years to 12 years, and ceased assigning salvage value in computing depreciation on North American collection vehicles or containers. These changes in estimates resulted in an increase in depreciation expense of $33,700,000 in the fourth quarter of 1997."

	1994	1995	1996	1997	1998	
Asset impairment and unusual items (based on the 2008 AR)	122	394	530	1,771	864	4

Source: Amba Research, Thomson ONE

Notes

1. The decline in the effective depreciation rate could indicate that the company is using an aggressive depreciation policy. Ideally, if such detail is available, the effective depreciation rate for each individual asset class should be calculated and compared to the depreciation rate/period disclosed in its accounting policies. Alternatively, all that can be done is to compare the rate with industry peers, which should highlight the asset categories that are being accounted for aggressively. Since depreciation is not separately disclosed, this figure represents the combined depreciation and amortisation charge for the year. Given that the intangible assets of the company were not material we have ignored the impact of amortisation. In calculating depreciation, land needs to be excluded from the gross value since it is not depreciable. However, again, this is not separately disclosed. But we do not believe that the directional trend in the rate would be materially affected by the exclusion of land.

2. The capex-to-depreciation ratio increased steadily from 1994–1996, indicating that depreciation did not move in line with capex. This is another potential indicator of aggressive depreciation policy.

3. Given the nature of the company's operations, it would have been prudent not to assign a salvage value for collection vehicles and containers, since the salvage values could be highly subjective. It is, perhaps, reasonable to accept the increase in the useful lives of containers, since the company's decision not to assign salvage values may be due to its decision to use the containers for a longer period of time. However, the useful life of containers has actually decreased to 8–12 years from 8–20 years, indicating that the company could have initially assigned unreasonably high salvage values, thereby understating the depreciation for previous years.

4. These are further potential red flags indicating Waste Management's aggressive use of depreciation policy. Waste Management stated that the decision to reduce the useful life of containers from 15 and 20 years to 12 years in 1997 was due to a comprehensive review performed by the management on its operations. No further information was given with regard to the reason for the review. The fall in useful life, however, had a significant impact on Waste Management's operating costs. Waste Management disclosed that the change in depreciation policy has caused costs to increase by $33.7m (14% operating loss). Thus, there may also have been significant understatement of prior years' depreciation charges.

The company recognised asset impairment and unusual items throughout the period 1994–1998. If these impairments related to property, plant and equipment (PP&E), this, too, can be interpreted as an indication of an aggressive depreciation policy that understates the initial depreciation charge and takes subsequent impairments.

Capitalisation of income statement items

Companies may attempt to enhance the appearance of their profitability by capitalising costs that more legitimately should be passed through the profit and loss account.

Capitalisation is yet another acceptable practice that can be misused. Many significant instances of corporate fraud have been based on manipulation of this accounting device, notably the WorldCom fraud, as previously mentioned.

Naturally, the distortions that such improper capitalisations create flow through the company's income statement and cash flow statements, artificially increasing the apparent strength of both. The amounts capitalised are expensed as depreciation, which is in turn added back into cash flow calculations. Red flags signalling potential manipulation of this technique include sudden increases in capital expenditures that take place at the same time as decreases in operating expenses in relation to either sales or PP&E, as illustrated below, where our example company is running a stable gas transportation business whose revenues are fee-based and subject to little seasonal fluctuation.

TABLE 19: CAPITALISATION OF INCOME STATEMENT ITEMS

US$ millions	Period 1	Period 2
Revenues	100	100
SG&A	51	41
EBIT	49	59
PP&E	250	260
Cash from operations		
EBIT	49	59
D&A	25	26
EBITDA	74	85
Maintenance capex	25	35
Dividends	10	10
Discretionary cash flow	39	40

Source: Authors' illustration

In the example of table 19, the upwards distortion of cash flow is minor – only $1m – but the important thing to note here is the ease with which such changes can be used to improve the apparent strength of a company's cash flows. Cumulatively, this can amount to material mismatches between appearance and reality.

Additionally, if we also consider the fact that companies are at liberty to capitalise the costs associated with, for example, the transport and installation of new machinery, or interest associated with new projects before they come on stream (both of which are in keeping with strict accounting principles), then the vital role that auditors play in maintaining appropriate classification of capitalised items becomes clear (see the *Auditors* section later in this chapter).

M&A smokescreen

Royal Ahold[104]

Another potential area of concern, in which managements have significant discretion to distort accounting reality, is created when companies engage in a rolling programme of acquisitions. Of course, far from every company that pursues an active M&A strategy gets into difficulty, but there is an abundance of instances where a hard-driving CEO, with his sights set on transforming the company's geographical reach or its scale within its industry, loses control of the rolling M&A process. After a sequence of acquisitions that have garnered approval from the markets, the quality of a company's due diligence processes can deteriorate, along with the sharpness of the management team's focus, as the backlog of acquisitions builds up, putting stress on internal systems. Suddenly, margins that were forecast to be on an endless upward trajectory thanks to synergies are undermined by the crystallisation of unforeseen costs, or worse, a potentially fatal accounting problem that went unseen during the due diligence process is discovered at a newly-acquired subsidiary.

Rapid M&A activity lays a company open to human error, but can also create the opportunity for unscrupulous management teams to exaggerate and distort the acquiring company's financial performance, motivated by a desire to support the share price and their own remuneration prospects.

Examples of the latter abound, but one of the most conspicuous at the beginning of the 21st century was Ahold, the Netherlands-based international supermarket chain. In this case, the rapid pace of M&A activity, in combination with inadequate due diligence and, ultimately, questionable corporate ethics, led to rapid deterioration in credit quality, though eventually the corporation was able to recover much of the lost ground over a period of lengthy rebuilding and strict adherence to conservative financial policies. Bondholders underwent significant mark-to-market pain in the interim, but a default was avoided.

In common with many of its European retail peers with dominant positions in relatively small domestic markets, Ahold embarked on a strategy of international expansion,

---

104   For further detail, read de Jong, A., Dejong, D.V., Mertens, G.M.H., Rosenboom, P.G.J. (2005) 'Royal Ahold: A Failure of Corporate Governance and an Accounting Scandal'. [Online]. Available at: **econpapers.repec.org/paper/dgrkubcen/200557.htm** [Accessed 26 November 2014].

beginning with the consolidation of a fragmented retail sector in the northeastern USA, then extending its reach globally to Southern Europe, Asia and Latin America. In keeping with other less-than-glamorous companies (viz. Enron, Tyco) that had become investor favourites in the 1990s, the stardust on Ahold had been provided to a large degree by the sheer pace of its M&A activity and the initial impact this had on reported earnings growth. The US was Ahold's most successful venture abroad, and the company sought to maximise this success by diversifying into the parallel sector of food service, making three substantial acquisitions in this sector between March 2000 and November 2002.

Ahold's problems were cumulative, as it pursued a cluster of international M&A opportunities in the course of its rapid growth between 1980 and 2001. Most of this activity was outside the company's core European markets, and was a key driver of Ahold's successful stock market performance over this period. To achieve its targeted earnings growth level of 15%, the company found itself almost unable to resist the temptation of embarking on deal after deal.

Differences in reporting practice between Dutch and US GAAP relating to goodwill accounting began to increase in the late 1990s and made themselves apparent in ever-increasing difficulties in reconciling the Dutch and US accounts, with the former charging goodwill against equity without passing it through the income statement and the latter capitalising the goodwill and amortising it over a period not greater than 40 years. Because of Ahold's dual listing in the US and the Netherlands, it was obliged to amortise the goodwill in its 20-F. The differences between the US and Dutch accounts increased to the extent that in 2001, its reported earnings in its Dutch accounts were €1,113m, while in its US accounts they were only €119m. The introduction of impairment charges, rather than amortisation to goodwill in 2001 under US GAAP only exacerbated these differences, leading Ahold to make a €728m impairment for its Argentine joint venture, rather than amortising the loss over 20 years in Holland.

In the end, it was not the differences in accounting practice themselves that undermined Ahold's credit standing. Far more materially, the company was found to have misreported vendor rebates at one of its recently acquired food service subsidiaries and it subsequently emerged that Ahold did not actually legally control its joint venture partners and therefore should not have fully consolidated them (while simultaneously failing to disclose material off-balance-sheet liabilities to these joint venture partners). The accounting discrepancies were again a smoking gun betraying the existence of other underlying problems. Once the company's accounts had been duly rectified, reported 2000 earnings of €1,115m were reduced to €442m, 2001 earnings fell from profit of €1,113m to a loss of €254m and 2002 earnings from a loss of €1,200m to a loss of €4,300m.

Auditors

Madoff

One of the many scarcely credible features of the $18bn lost in the Bernard L. Madoff Investment Securities fraud in 2008–9 was that the auditing firm that he employed, Friehling and Horowitz in New City, New York, was disproportionately small relative to the Madoff operation. This would ordinarily be a clear red flag to investors as Madoff's firm could (and clearly did) exert undue influence over the independence of so small an auditor.[105] This is perhaps an egregious example, yet there are other instances in which the absence of credible auditing oversight has been a clear marker of potential corporate wrongdoing.

Case study: Olympus

Another recent example of lapses in auditor oversight is to be found in the losses at Japanese consumer electronics giant Olympus, caused by over $1bn of illegal payments that had been overlooked by a compliant board. The arrival of external auditors prompted the then-CEO's dismissal. Some of Olympus's issues have been dismissed as cultural, a lazy accusation in our view that, if taken literally, would have worrying implications for the whole of corporate Japan.

Olympus is renowned for the manufacture of cameras, videos, laser-optical scanners, medical devices, microscopes, printers and, latterly, for the biggest loss-concealing scam in the history of corporate Japan.

We should first provide an important cultural context to the wrongdoings of Olympus senior management. The 1980s were a torrid time for export-led Japanese corporates as the 1985 Plaza Accord put pressure on the government to appreciate the yen, with a deleterious impact on Japanese corporate profitability. In response, Japanese managements – Olympus among them – resorted to *zaitech* – financial engineering through investments in derivatives and other (profoundly non-core) risky activities, helped by the low interest rates that were the corollary of the stronger yen.

Predictably, this ended in tears and Olympus took a ¥2.1bn loss on the value of its investments in 1991. However, it would appear that the scale of losses was greater than this and that Olympus sat on them, waiting for Godot, in the form of a recovery in the fortunes of Japan's economy and capital markets, to come and bail them out. It didn't. What did was a change in accounting standards that would have forced Olympus to mark

---

105 Friehling, it transpired, was not registered with the Public Company Accounting Oversight Board (PCAOB), which was created under the Sarbanes-Oxley Act of 2002 to help detect fraud. Nor was the firm 'peer reviewed', in which auditors check one another for quality control. According to the American Institute of Certified Public Accountants, Friehling was enrolled in their peer-review program, but was not required to participate because he supposedly didn't conduct audits. It later emerged that Madoff's banker, J.P. Morgan Chase, had known that Friehling wasn't registered with the PCAOB or subject to peer review as early as 2006.

to market the value of its investments. Rather than take the pain of doing so, management sought to 'disappear' the losses by selling the investments to fake companies at face value and compensating the principals of those entities through 'advisors' fees' of credulity-challenging dimensions: when the company acquired Gyrus Group (a British manufacturer of medical equipment) in 2008 for $2.2bn, it paid $687m to such advisors,[106] who would customarily command 1% of the transaction value.[107]

Fast-forward to 2011. On April 1 (yes, April 1), Michael Woodford, a British Olympus manager of 30 years, is raised from relative obscurity (he was executive MD of Olympus Medical Systems Europa) to become Olympus's global president and COO. Six months later he was elevated again to the CEO post. Needless to say, the elevation of a non-Japanese and non-Japanese speaking executive to such a key role in corporate Japan was extraordinary and rumours began to circulate. Japanese financial journal *FACTA* volunteered:

> "The fact that the company picked a bottom-ranking foreign executive director with virtually no significant responsibilities from amongst a pool of 25 potential candidates, including the vice-president who was responsible for medical instruments ... set tongues a-wagging".[108]

However, Olympus was able to counter this by asserting its outward-looking selection as a virtue: Woodford was the "new global face of Olympus".[109]

Either way, Woodford proved no patsy. He was irked that the Gyrus acquisition was handled from Tokyo when it should have fallen within his purview and bridled at company leader Tsuyoshi Kikukawa's assertion that the authority to hire, fire and determine board remuneration would remain with him, not Woodford.[110] His awareness of the rumours surrounding losses and suspect payments at Olympus was raised by an article in *FACTA* and he sought to address these issues with Kikukawa and Olympus's compliance officer and group VP, Hisashi Mori, but received no satisfactory answers.

A follow-up article led Woodford to send a letter to Mori (copied to all board members) requesting more information on acquisitions and to pursue this with further questions. Frustrated with the lack of response, Woodford demanded that he be made chief executive officer and that Kikukawa, as chairman, no longer attend management meetings. Although Kikukawa acceded to his request, other board members suddenly began treating Woodford

---

106 Ridley, K. and Smith, A. (2011). 'Special Report: In Japan, a foreigner speaks out'. [Online]. Available at: **graphics.thomsonreuters.com/specials/Olympus.pdf** [Accessed 24 November 2014].

107 Soble, J. (2011): 'Olympus admits to $687m fee for advisor'. [Online]. Available at: **www.ft.com/cms/s/0/317dbd4e-faoe-11e0-b70d-00144feab49a.html?siteedition=uk#axzz3JyK4PFiT** [Accessed 24 November 2014].

108 See note 96.

109 Tabuchi, H. (2011). 'At Olympus, Western Questions for Old School Ways'. [Online]. Available at: **www.nytimes.com/2011/10/27/business/global/olympus-chairman-resigns-amid-widening-scandal.html?pagewanted=all** [Accessed 24 November 2014].

110 Nikkei Business (2011). 'Michael Woodford, ex-CEO of Olympus: "Let me tell the true story behind my dismissal."' [Online]. Available at: **business.nikkeibp.co.jp/article/eng/20111101/223529** [Accessed 24 November 2014].

very icily at the subsequent board meeting and questioned him on his decision to copy some of his later letters of enquiry to the firm's auditors. Woodford's dissatisfaction with the internal response to affairs at Olympus led him to commission PwC to give the manufacturer of endoscopes the equivalent of an accounting colonoscopy, the result of which arrived on October 10 2011. It identified that acquisitions had yielded a combined loss of $1.287bn for shareholders and catalogued a plethora of governance failures.[111]

Woodford copied the report to Kikukawa and Mori and demanded their scalps. At a board meeting on 14 October, Kikukawa appeared (uncharacteristically late), announced a change of agenda, the dismissal of Woodford and a ban on his speaking at the meeting. Every board member supported Kikukawa's decision, whereafter Woodford was stripped of his company mobile, PC and apartment keys and told to take the bus to Narita.

Woodford returned to the UK, passed a file of information to the Serious Fraud Office and requested police protection, allegedly on the grounds that the third-party advisors who had benefited from Olympus's liberality were Yakuza-linked. The FBI, to which Woodford had also passed materials, began an investigation as did other law-enforcement agencies and regulators. Japanese authorities arrested seven individuals in February 2012, including Kikukawa and Mori, plus the formal internal auditor and a number of bankers. Kikukawa and the other executives received three-year sentences suspended for five years (suspended sentences are the norm for false financial reporting in Japan) in July 2013.[112]

Olympus's stock price fell almost 18% on the day of the announcement and over 80% between then and mid-November.[113] A number of key shareholders subsequently dumped stakes. Foreign investors sought to have Woodford reinstated to his position but were blocked by Japanese institutions. However, on 20 April 2012 an extraordinary shareholders' meeting was convened, which proposed a slate of 11 'independent' board members and the approval of restated accounts. Interestingly, the candidate for chair was a former senior executive of Sumitomo Mitsui Bank, one of Olympus's largest domestic creditor banks.[114]

Auditors: Lessons to learn

Corporate culture

What is utterly remarkable about the Olympus case is that none of the senior executives, including Kikukawa and Mori, appeared to undertake their misdeeds for personal financial gain. What drove them was a corporate culture that could simply not abide the loss of face (not just for themselves but for other executives and former managers) that accompanied the conveyance of bad news. Indeed, perversely, they seemed to believe that they were acting honourably in preventing such bad news from surfacing and unleashing a tsunami

111 Nikkei Business (2011).
112 Soble, J. (2013). 'Olympus ex-chairman gets suspended sentence.' [Online]. Available at: **www.ft.com/cms/s/0/a845fc34-e3a5-11e2-b35b-00144feabdc0.html#axzz3JyK4PFiT** [Accessed 2014].
113 Bloomberg.
114 Kelley, T. and Kubota, Y. (2012). 'Olympus eyes fresh start, ex-CEO mulls legal threat'. [Online]. Available at: **uk.reuters.com/article/2012/04/20/uk-olympus-egm-idUKBRE83J04420120420** [Accessed 24 November 2014].

upon the zen-calm pool of consensus corporatism upon which Olympus's internal culture floated. This is not to slight Japan – the same consensualist culture has also spawned unparalleled excellence in manufacturing based on principles of *kaizen* – but it does show the importance of a degree of adversarialism or at the very least an open culture where questioning and debate are welcomed are key at the board level, since as Olympus (and arguably Fukushima) have proven that problems which are allowed to fester can have catastrophic consequences.

There is another lesson that extends well beyond Japan to the boardrooms of the rest of the world. The C-suite may occupy the corner offices at the top of the skyscraper but they are lonely eyries. Especially in liberal market economies, social and peer perception of the success or failure of executives is reduced to the performance of the stock price; a number becomes a reification, encapsulating all the decisions and actions of the executives (while drowning them in the general movements of the market) and reflecting back to the executives the sole measure of their success or failure. In such an environment, executives run the risk of managing the number, not the business.

Finally, while we might ascribe Olympus's opacity to Japanese corporate culture, investors have little excuse for not noticing that Kikukawa had an appetite for risk. In 2001 he told the *Sankei* newspaper:

> "People used to joke that Olympus was so cautious it wouldn't cross a stone bridge even if it pounded on it three times ... But now, what's risky is not taking risk. My philosophy is that if there's at least a 50% chance of success, you should try it."[115]

So Kikukawa effectively told investors that his statistical approach to risk was almost akin to that of coin-tossing. Even if investors were happy with such a risk-disposed individual at the helm, a strong, independent board would be key to harness his energies.

Board independence

This must exist in more than name. Olympus's board was unswervingly loyal to Kikukawa and, when confronted by Woodford's discoveries, sought to round on and exclude the outsider. It is for precisely this reason that we urge investors to look beyond the tick marks in the boxes and examine the substance of board membership: how long have board members served? Are any related? What other boards do they serve on and do companies governed by those boards have a close relationship with this one (for instance, is the board member a representative of the company's leading credit institution?). Does the company disclose related party transactions involving board members? Is one individual a 'kingmaker'? Does the CEO get to anoint his successor?

Whilst Olympus was a study in opacity, some research on some of these issues would have at least raised some questions. Twelve out of the 15 directors of Olympus were either Olympus executives or former executives.[116] Was that a robust, independent board?

115   Dvorak, P. and Osawa, J. (2011). 'Olympus Ex-Chairman Boasted About Appetite for Risk'. [Online]. Available at: **online.wsj.com/articles/SB10001424052970204505304577001600497281284** [Accessed 24 November 2014].
116   Gapper, J. (2011). 'Olympus's deceit was dishonourable'. [Online]. Available at: **www.ft.com/cms/**

Accountants and audit committees

Olympus had been through a few auditors, albeit some of the changes seemed to have more to do with the auditors than with Olympus. The company's first auditor was the Japanese affiliate of Arthur Andersen (of Enron fame) until that company's demise in 2002. Then came KPMG Asza until 2009 when E&Y ShinNihon took the role. Subsequent disclosure revealed that KPMG had questioned Olympus's treatment of the Gyrus acquisition and had been summarily replaced. However, none of this was aired at the time and Olympus did not receive a qualification on any of its audits. Nonetheless, the change of auditor from KPMG to E&Y might have prompted a question, if nothing else. What investors should perhaps have seized upon was the audit committee, which was headed by Hideo Yamada, who subsequently faced charges. The UK's Financial Reporting Council, in its September 2012 guidance, advocates that, "The board should establish an audit committee of at least three, or in the case of smaller companies two, independent non-executive directors."[117] Yamada's role as an executive managing officer and executive officer of Olympus made him less than independent and vitiated any check and balance the committee could have imposed. This should have been at least a yellow flag.

Unusual transactions

Anybody who has worked for a bank or fund manager will have endured interminable training sessions on the subject of money laundering, evidence of which can often be found in clients' unusual and unprofitable transactions. So, too, with corporate actions. Olympus paid a 58% premium for Gyrus in what was designated a friendly takeover[118] in a consideration equal to 4.8 times sales. However, just over a year later, Olympus sold its own blood-testing and chemical analysis unit for only twice revenues.[119] Other acquisitions were singular, to say the least. During Kikukawa's tenure Olympus acquired over 100 businesses, many unlisted and unprofitable, in areas as diverse as pet care and DVD manufacture.[120] Such behaviour would be economically questionable under any circumstances, even in a private, closely held company, which might answer to the caprice of its owner. In a large, publicly traded entity such as Olympus, this should have been a clear red flag.

s/0/60ba6782-0abd-11e1-b9f6-00144feabdc0.html#axzz3JyK4PFiT [Accessed 24 November 2014].

117 Financial Reporting Council (2012). 'Guidance on Audit Committees', Section 2.3. [Online]. Available at: **www.frc.org.uk/Our-Work/Publications/Corporate-Governance/Guidance-on-Audit-Committees-September-2012.aspx** [Accessed 24 November 2014].

118 Robinson, G. (2007). 'Olympus mounts offer for Gyrus'. [Online]. Available at: **ftalphaville. ft.com/2007/11/20/9022/olympus-mounts-offer-for-gyrus** [Accessed 24 November 2014].

119 Cooper, C. (2011). 'Olympus Sale of Growing Unit Helped Hide Balance Sheet Hole'. [Online]. Available at: **www.bloomberg.com/news/2011-11-14/olympus-2009-sale-helped-hide-balance-sheet-hole.html** [Accessed 24 November 2014].

120 Reuters (2011). 'Kikukawa to face questions on Olympus cover-up' [Online]. Available at: **www. reuters.com/article/2011/11/11/olympus-idUSL3E7MB2EJ20111111** [Accessed 24 November 2014].

3. Manipulation of the balance sheet

Perversely, while balance sheet debt must be a key driver of creditworthiness, it is probably fair to say that credit analysts do (and indeed should) spend more of their time trying to establish what a company's exposure is to liabilities that are not on the balance sheet than they do the company's listed debts.

Companies typically have many other liabilities and contingencies which do not appear on the balance sheet but which, if unsatisfied, can cause the company severe financial distress. In that sense, while they might not constitute 'debt' in a narrow legal sense, they have debt-like characteristics. We explore these in detail in chapter 5, but to list some examples, think of factored receivables; operating leases; pension and healthcare obligations; guarantees of unconsolidated JV debt. How about tobacco-related healthcare costs and associated damages? or settlement funds for Hexavalent Chromium poisoning? oil spills in the Gulf of Mexico? asbestosis claims? These are all obligations which a company could be obliged to meet but which would most likely not appear on the balance sheet. All need to be diligently estimated – many are detailed in the notes to the financial statements under 'contingencies' – and at least considered when estimating a company's total debt obligation and ability to service it.

In so doing, credit analysts arrive at adjusted debt (though, typically, most analysts would not adjust debt for all the contingencies outlined above) which, in our view, paints a far more accurate picture of a company's liabilities than a mere assessment of its balance sheet debt. See Chapter 5. Behind the Numbers: Adjusted Debt and Liquidity on page 127 for a full discussion of this important topic.

Inventory valuation: Nicor

One feature of the balance sheet that can be manipulated to flatter a company's earnings potential is the valuation of inventory, which can impact the gross margin that the company reports. One example of this was the SEC's accusation, later settled out of court without the company's accepting or denying the accusation, that gas distributor Nicor had inflated its profitability by accessing lower-cost last-in first-out (LIFO) inventory reserves without disclosing this as a material change in its accounting policy, thereby pushing up its gross margin relative to its peer group.[121] Senior executives at the company were accused of having operated a long-standing fraud whereby the natural gas distributor could profit by accessing LIFO gas inventories, thereby artificially averaging down its input costs and increasing Nicor's apparent profitability, as well as increasing revenue under a performance-based utility rate plan.

The management team was also accused of materially understating Nicor's expenses during the first and second quarters of 2001 by combining the proceeds of a weather-insurance contract with those of an agreement to supply gas to an insurance provider at below-market prices. They were accused of having improperly charged losses realised from the supply

---

121 Taub, S. (2007). 'Nicor Ex-CFO Charged in LIFO Scheme'. [Online]. Available at: **ww2.cfo.com/accounting-tax/2007/08/nicor-ex-cfo-charged-in-lifo-scheme** [Accessed 24 November 2014].

agreement to their utility customers which, in turn, led to the company overstating its income for the years 2000 and 2001. Nicor was also alleged to have failed to disclose in either of the management's 'Discussion & Analysis' sections of its 2000 and 2001 financial statements that it had booked significant increases to income resulting from the LIFO inventory. The company's regulatory filings allegedly did not disclose that the continued liquidation of Nicor's low-cost inventory was not a sustainable part of its business strategy.

Fixed asset revaluation: China Forestry

Our next case study carries many of the tell-tale signals of a corporate accounting fraud – so many, in fact, that it is hard to believe, with the benefit of hindsight, that it went unnoticed for as long as it did. In late 2010 and early 2011, after several weeks of fevered market speculation, it emerged that there were indeed significant accounting irregularities at China Forestry (CF). The company had presented an increasingly complex financial picture which many market participants had interpreted as reflecting potential inconsistencies in its revenue recognition policies. The market caught a whiff of something unsavoury at the company when it was revealed that the CEO, Mr Li Han Chun, had sold his own stake in CF on 12 January 2011 at a 6.9% discount to market value in order, apparently, to devote the proceeds to an investment in copper mining, a field in which he hitherto had no apparent experience. The market was briefly reassured by the subsequent purchase of 12m CF shares by Mr Li Kwok Cheong, the company's chairman. Sadly for the latter Mr Li, and CF shareholders in general, the belief that this investment evinced in CF's future prospects was soon proven to be misplaced.

Ultimately, CF's accounting irregularities turned out to be a simple case of embezzlement and accounting fraud. The company is one of China's largest privately-held forest operators, with 172,000 hectares of reported forest land. On 31 January 2011, CF announced that potential irregularities had indeed been identified by its auditors, KPMG. The auditors resigned from their position on 5 January 2011, suggesting in their resignation letter that the company undertake a broad-based investigation to "identify all irregularities that may have occurred and all management involved in the irregularities, trace where the group spent the proceeds from the initial public offering and reconcile the details of recorded plantation assets".[122] KPMG had discovered that cash proceeds from certain asset sales had never actually been deposited in CF's bank accounts, while reported earnings were being systematically flattered by the reclassification of farmland as forest-land and its ensuing upwards revaluation prior to CF's IPO in 2009.

Farm- and forest-land ownership in China is a politically-sensitive issue, and the reclassification of one to the other required support within the state bureaucracy, which was perhaps available for a share of the embezzlement proceeds. In the context of a weak regulatory framework the company's CEO had been able to keep multiple sets of accounts in order to conceal from CF a fraud amounting to $5m, which he attempted to disguise by registering revaluation profits on the company's plantation holdings (to the tune of $900m),

---

122 Source: Bloomberg.

thereby encouraging investors who were more focused on apparent momentum within the company than on the veracity of its growth story. The fraud became apparent when it was seen to be impossible to reconcile the change in the valuation of PP&E on the balance sheet with the movement of funds on the cash flow statement.[123]

Fixed asset revaluation: FirstEnergy

As part of management's efforts to shift debt from its operating subsidiaries (in this case its generating units) to the parent company, FirstEnergy (FE) sought to transfer the 80% stake of the Harrison plant from the generation company, Allegheny Energy Supply (AES), which it purchased as part of its acquisition of Allegheny Energy (AYE) to Monongahela Power, a regulated utility subsidiary.

When FE bought AYE, it marked up the value of the Harrison plant under 'fair value accounting' from about $565m to $1.16bn. In support of the valuation, the company was able to cite third-party studies valuing the plant in excess of $1.3bn. The transaction that sought to move the plant to Monongahela valued it at about $1.2bn or approximately $760/kw. However, recent transactions involving coal plants suggested transaction prices closer to $300–$450/kw, which would have valued Harrison in the $445–$665m range.[124] We cannot say what the correct valuation of the plant should be but we can cite this as an example of the latitude available to management under acquisition accounting.

4. Manipulation of the cash flow statement

While analysts typically view income statements and balance sheets with prudent circumspection, given the impacts of accrual accounting and the selection of accounting methods on the presentation of economic reality, greater faith is placed in the statement of cash flows, since this is the statement in which all accrual issues 'wash out' of the financial statements.

However, although the cash flow statement probably does provide the most reliable source of information on liquidity available from which to service debt and, indeed, the core information needed to value a company from an equity perspective (the basis for projection of future cash flows), it is not immune to subtleties of presentation and manipulation. What follows is a discussion – by no means exhaustive – of the key areas in which the presentation of cash flows can be manipulated.

123 Kih, S. (2012). 'Pitfalls Investing in Asia – Accounting games listed companies play'. [Online]. Available at: **www.nextinsight.net/index.php/story-archive-mainmenu-60/916-2012/5566-avoid-pitfalls-investing-in-asia-accounting-games-listed-companies-play** [Accessed 24 November 2014].
124 CreditSights (2013). FirstEnergy: Post-Issuance Analyst Day [Online]. Available at: **www.creditsights.com/id/142550?searchSessionID=e95b567f-b8c9-4686-87c9-facc9cc64dd2&rf=28** [Accessed 24 November 2014].

Receivables sales and securitisations

Firms can expedite cash generation through the sale, factoring, securitisation and the pledging of receivables for financing. A receivables transfer that is not treated under GAAP as a true sale remains on the company's balance sheet and the proceeds from any financing transaction are recorded in the cash flow statement as a financing item, below the operating cash flow line. The problem arises with transfers which are treated as sales, which lead to a reduction in the accounts receivables on the balance sheet and, correspondingly, an operating cash inflow, in the 'change in working capital' item on the cash flow statement.

The issue here is one of sustainability and economic verisimilitude. First, the transfer of the receivable merely brings into the current period cash (customarily less a haircut) that would typically have been realised from the collection of the receivable in the subsequent period. The company might be able to repeat the trick on the subsequent period (sell the receivables due for collection in the period after that) but it might not. The future generation of operating cash flow from this source is dependent on the ability to continue selling receivables. Many companies use this as an efficient source of short-dated financing, especially when they benefit from large receivables from well-recognised, high-quality credits. However, such companies typically also have access to other forms of financing.

For more troubled entities, receivables financing may represent the last reliable source of liquidity that they are able to access and the scope for growing future receivables may be limited (with sales likely in decline). Moreover, the pledging of receivables would limit the ability of such a company to access other forms of secured financing (given a smaller pool of reliable assets available for security), the usual lifeline for a distressed entity unable to access unsecured borrowings.

Finally, there is an issue of presentation. A company that relies on receivables securitisation is effectively borrowing from future periods to provide cash for the current period. We would argue that it is more accurate to reflect the proceeds of such securitisations as financing items (below the operating cash flow line), thereby removing their flattering impact on operating cash flow and making clear the extent to which they provide financing for the company's operations.

Meritor has an off-balance-sheet receivables financing arrangement. Movements are shown in the cash flow statement not as short-term financing but as working capital items. Historically, this has flattered the company's operating cash flow. Also, being off balance sheet, this information has to be excavated from the notes and body of the financial reports and, once established, the outstanding balance needs to be added back into the debt figure to show a true picture of Meritor's adjusted leverage, and, in so doing, reducing stated cash flow and increasing leverage.

Here is Meritor's 2013 operating cash flow breakdown provided in Note 25 of its financial statements in the 2013 10-K filing. As can be seen, the borrowings under the off-balance-sheet factoring arrangements are presented not as a financing item but as a positive contribution to working capital (see highlighted line).

TABLE 20: MERITOR OPERATING CASH FLOW

	$m
Net income (loss)	-20
Less: loss from discontinued operations net of tax	-2
Income (loss) from continuing operations	-18
Adjustments to income (loss) from continuing operations to arrive at cash provided by (used for) operating activities:	
Depreciation and amortization	67
Deferred income tax expense (benefit)	-4
Restructuring Costs	26
Loss on debt extinguishment	24
Equity in earnings of affiliates	-42
Stock compensation expense	5
Provision for doubtful accounts	3
Pension and retiree medical expense	151
Gain on sale of equity investment	-125
Gain on sale of property	0
Dividends received from equity method investments	30
Pension and retiree medical contributions	-153
Restructuring payments	-26
Changes in off-balance sheet receivable securitization and factoring programs	43
Changes in assets and liabilities, excluding effects of acquisitions, divestitures, foreign currency adjustments and discontinued operations:	
Receivables	-87
Inventories	19
Accounts Payable	-31
Other current assets and liabilities	37
Other assets and liabilities	0
Operating cash flows provided by (used by) continuing operations	-81
Operating cash flows used for discontinued operations	-15
CASH PROVIDED BY (USED FOR) OPERATING ACTIVITIES	**-96**

Source: Meritor 10-K 2013

Again, there is nothing wrong with receivables factoring as a form of short-term financing. In Meritor's case, we hold the receivables to be of high quality and sustainable in nature. (We believe them to come from Swedish global lorry manufacturer, AB Volvo.) But it certainly has debt characteristics and we would argue that its presentation as a financing item and its inclusion in debt more faithfully represents Meritor's cash flows and leverage. This is best illustrated by showing the company's cash flow, first as presented by Meritor in a company presentation, including changes in off-balance-sheet receivables securitisation as an operating item, as shown in table 21.

And then, adjusting operating cash flow to represent the factoring as a financing item, removing the changes in off-balance-sheet receivables securitisation and factorings as an operating item and recording them as a financial item under "Other Borrowings", we get the result shown in table 22, which presents Meritor's cash-generation in a rather less favourable light.

TABLE 21: MERITOR CASH FLOW AS PRESENTED BY THE COMPANY

Exhibit 1	
	2013
Net income (loss)	-20
Less: loss from discontinued operations net of tax	-2
Income (loss) from continuing operations	-18
Adjustments to income (loss) from continuing operations to arrive at cash provided by (used for) operating activities:	
Depreciation and amortization	67
Deferred income tax expense (benefit)	-4
Restructuring Costs	26
Loss on debt extinguishment	24
Equity in earnings of affiliates	-42
Stock compensation expense	5
Provision for doubtful accounts	3
Pension and retiree medical expense	151
Gain on sale of equity investment	-125
Gain on sale of property	0
Dividends received from equity method investments	30
Pension and retiree medical contributions	-153
Restructuring payments	-26
Changes in off-balance sheet receivable securitization and factoring programs	**43**
Changes in assets and liabilities, excluding effects of acquisitions, divestitures, foreign currency adjustments and discontinued operations:	
Receivables	-87
Inventories	19
Accounts payable	-31
Other current assets and liabilities	37
Other assets and liabilities	0
Operating cash flows provided by (used by) continuing operations	**-81**
Operating cash flows used for discontinued operations	-15
CASH PROVIDED BY (USED FOR) OPERATING ACTIVITIES	**-96**
INVESTING ACTIVITIES	
Capital expenditures	-54
Proceeds from sale of equity investment	182
Proceeds from sale of property	0
Other investing activities	3
Net investing cash flows provided by (used for) continuing operations	131
Net investing cash flows provided by (used for) discontinued operations	6
CASH PROVIDED BY (USED FOR) INVESTING ACTIVITIES	137
FINANCING ACTIVITIES	
Proceeds from debt issuances	500
Repayments of notes and term loan	-475
Other borrowings	**11**
Net change in debt	**36**
Debt issuance costs	-12
Other financing cash flows	0
CASH PROVIDED BY FINANCING ACTIVITIES	**24**
EFFECT OF CURRENCY EXCHANGE RATES ON CASH AND CASH EQUIVALENTS	-4
CHANGE IN CASH AND CASH EQUIVALENTS	61
CASH AND CASH EQUIVALENTS AT BEGINNING OF YEAR	257
CASH AND CASH EQUIVALENTS AT END OF YEAR	318
Free operating cash flow (operating cash flow - capex)	**-150**

Source: Company reports, authors' calculations

TABLE 22: MERITOR CASH FLOW AS ADJUSTED FOR RECEIVABLES SECURITISATION

Exhibit 2	
	2013
Net income (loss)	-20
Less: loss from discontinued operations net of tax	-2
Income (loss) from continuing operations	-18
Adjustments to income (loss) from continuing operations to arrive at cash provided by (used for) operating activities:	
Depreciation and amortization	67
Deferred income tax expense (benefit)	-4
Restructuring costs	26
Loss on debt extinguishment	24
Equity in earnings of affiliates	-42
Stock compensation expense	5
Provision for doubtful accounts	3
Pension and retiree medical expense	151
Gain on sale of equity investment	-125
Gain on sale of property	0
Dividends received from equity method investments	30
Pension and retiree medical contributions	-153
Restructuring payments	-26
Changes in assets and liabilities, excluding effects of acquisitions, divestitures, foreign currency adjustments and discontinued operations:	
Receivables	-87
Inventories	19
Accounts payable	-31
Other current assets and liabilities	37
Other assets and liabilities	0
Operating cash flows provided by (used by) continuing operations	**-124**
Operating cash flows used for discontinued operations	-15
CASH PROVIDED BY (USED FOR) OPERATING ACTIVITIES	**-139**
INVESTING ACTIVITIES	
Capital expenditures	-54
Proceeds from sale of equity investment	182
Proceeds from sale of property	0
Other investing activities	3
Net investing cash flows provided by (used for) continuing operations	131
Net investing cash flows provided by (used for) discontinued operations	6
CASH PROVIDED BY (USED FOR) INVESTING ACTIVITIES	137
FINANCING ACTIVITIES	
Proceeds from debt issuances	500
Repayments of notes and term loan	-475
Other borrowings	**54**
Net change in debt	**79**
Debt Issuance Costs	**-12**
Other financing cash flows	**0**
CASH PROVIDED BY FINANCING ACTIVITIES	**67**
EFFECT OF CURRENCY EXCHANGE RATES ON CASH AND CASH EQUIVALENTS	-4
CHANGE IN CASH AND CASH EQUIVALENTS	61
CASH AND CASH EQUIVALENTS AT BEGINNING OF YEAR	257
CASH AND CASH EQUIVALENTS AT END OF YEAR	318
Free operating cash flow (operating cash flow - capex)	**-193**

Source: Company reports, authors' calculations

In addition, while the off-balance-sheet factoring does not, by definition, appear on the balance sheet, management acknowledges on p.50 of the 2013 10-K under 'Off-Balance-Sheet Arrangements' that it has about $332m utilised under off-balance-sheet receivables securitisations. So, we advocate adjusting net debt for this number to get a more representative idea of leverage.

TABLE 23: MERITOR OFF-BALANCE-SHEET ADJUSTMENTS

Unadjusted debt and leverage calculations	Fiscal year ended 29 September 2013	Source
Short-term debt	$13	10-K balance sheet
Long-term debt	$1,125	10-K balance sheet
Gross debt	$1,138	
Less: cash and equivalents	-$318	10-K balance sheet
Net debt	$820	
EBITDA	$276	10-K note 23
Gross debt/EBITDA	**4.1**	
Net debt/EBITDA	**3.0**	
Adjustment 1. Off-balance sheet debt		
Short-term debt	$13	10-K balance sheet
Long-term debt	$1,125	10-K balance sheet
Off-balance sheet receivables securitization and factoring	**$332**	10-K page 50
Gross debt	$1,470	
Less: cash and equivalents	-$318	10-K balance sheet
Net debt	$1,152	
EBITDA	$276	10-K Note 23
Gross debt/EBITDA	**5.3**	
Net debt/EBITDA	**4.2**	

Source: Company reports, authors' calculations

And this shows us that including off-balance-sheet securitisations as debt lifts net leverage by over a turn – not an insignificant amount. We would note, too, that we have yet to adjust the number for any operating leases or pension underfunding.

Leases: capital vs. operating

Many factors influence the choice of employing capital leases compared to operating leases and the use of one or the other does not, in and of itself, constitute a red flag. However, it is worth remembering that accounting for capital leases flatters operating cash flow relative to that of operating leases. Why?

Payments under a capital lease include both an interest component, which is flowed through the income statement and reduces earnings and operating cash flow, and a capital component, reflecting implied principal repayment, which is recorded as a financing item akin to debt repayment but which does not reduce operating cash flow. By contrast, an operating lease payment consists exclusively of rental expense for accounting purposes, the entirety of which is flowed through the income statement and, by extension, operating cash flow. The use of a capital lease compared to an operating lease will therefore, all other things being equal, flatter the operating cash flow by the amount of principal repayment in any given period's lease payment. Both IASB and FASB have proposed rule changes that would bring operating leases on balance sheet.

Cash flow from asset churning

Typically, unless the prime activity of a business is the buying and selling of assets, we should expect to see operating cash flow provide the bulk of free cash flow and be underpinned by earnings from ongoing operations rather than cash releases from working capital, which might not be sustainable over the long term. This revisits an earlier discussion about convertibility. If a company's core earnings are the driver of its cash generation, cash flow from operations should usually reflect a significant proportional relationship to EBITDA.

However, in the case of hotel company, Meliá Hotels International, in 2013 operating cash flow (including interest payments) amounted to only €32m – about 9% of EBITDAR (i.e. EBITDA plus lease rentals) and failed to cover capital expenditures of €34.8m and investments of €180.3m. Making up the shortfall were disposals of assets and investments of €112.9m (plus issuance of new debt and some cash usage).[125] That is, the company appears to have made more cash from churning assets than it did from hotel operations.

If this were a one-off it might reflect a period of repositioning and restructuring but, in Meliá's case, a similar pattern is seen in previous years. Meliá, in fact, appears to make most of its cash not from operating hotels but from buying and selling hotels and investments in hotel companies. This is not in and of itself a criticism. However, the investor must be

---

125 Meliá Hotels International (2013). 'MELIÁ HOTELS INTERNATIONAL, S.A. AND IT SUBSIDIARIES. Auditor's Report, Consolidated annual accounts at 31 December 2013.' [Online]. Available at: **www.meliahotelsinternational.com/sites/default/files/informes-financieros/mhi_inf_ financiero_13_en.pdf** [Accessed 24 November 2014].

aware that when analysing Meliá they are studying something more akin to a property company than a hotel business in terms of cash flow generation and should, accordingly, look for different peers against which to compare it.

Cash flow from goodwill impairment

Another technique that can be used temporarily to enhance the reported level of cash flow is by using goodwill impairment. On 10 April 2012, Caterpillar acquired Hong Kong-listed ERA Mining Machinery, together with its wholly-owned Chinese mainland subsidiary Siwei.[126] Caterpillar's 10-Q for Q2 2012 shows a fair value of $671m for the tangible assets acquired in the transaction. Fuzzier items such as customer relationships and trade names – intangible assets that are always difficult to value with any degree of accuracy – were valued at $105m. Liabilities taken on were $592m along with goodwill of $461m. To quote the company at the time:

> "Goodwill … represents the estimated future economic benefits arising from other assets acquired that could not be individually identified and separately recognised. … Factors that contributed to a purchase price resulting in the recognition of goodwill include expected cost savings primarily from increased purchasing power for raw materials and a reduction in other manufacturing input costs, expanded underground mining equipment sales opportunities in China and internationally, along with the acquired assembled workforce."[127]

Now, this may sound a little vague. Furthermore, as we have seen in the China Forestry case, there are precedents for having concern about the accuracy of due diligence with a number of China-based companies. The company did sound a note of caution on this topic, as can be seen in the following extract, which comes from the 8-K announcing the impending goodwill impairment charge:

> "Caterpillar first became concerned about an issue when discrepancies were identified in November 2012 between the inventory recorded in Siwei's accounting records and the company's actual physical inventory. This was determined by a physical inventory count conducted at Siwei as part of Caterpillar's integration process. Caterpillar promptly launched a comprehensive review and investigation into the nature and source of this discrepancy. This extensive review has identified inappropriate accounting practices involving improper cost allocation that resulted in overstated profit. The review further identified improper revenue recognition practices involving early and, at times, unsupported, revenue recognition."[128]

---

126 Selling, T. (2013). 'Caterpillar: Another Sad Example of Bad Goodwill Accounting'. [Online]. Available at: **accountingonion.com/2013/02/caterpillar-another-unfortunate-case-of-bad-goodwill-accounting.html** [Accessed 24 November 2014].

127 SEC (2013). 'Caterpillar Inc. Form 10-K for the fiscal year ended 31 December 2012.' [Online]. Available at: **www.sec.gov/Archives/edgar/data/18230/000001823013000075/a10kpdfwithexhibits.pdf** [Accessed 24 November 2014].

128 SEC (2013). 'Caterpillar Inc. Form 8-K. Current report pursuant to section 13 or 15 (d) of the Securities Exchange Act of 1934.' [Online]. Available at: **phx.corporate-ir.net/phoenix.zhtml?c=92466&p=irol-SECText&TEXT=aHRo cDovL2FwaS50ZW5rd2l6YXJkLmNvbS9maWxpbmcueGlsP2lwYWdlPTg2NjQ2NTEmRFNFNFUTowJlNFUTo wJlNRREVTQz1TRUNUSU9OXoVOVElSRSZzdWJzaWQ9NTc%3d** [Accessed 26 November 2014].

Several factors catch the eye here:

- Although it has apparently not yet completed the due diligence process on the acquisition, Caterpillar nonetheless intends to record a $580m charge to goodwill – a figure substantially higher than the original goodwill recognised and almost as much as the actual purchase price paid.

- The write-down will clearly impact other assets (inventory, receivables etc.), but the company does not identify where this will be seen.

- It is apparent that the target's inventories had been mis-stated, and that non-existent or exaggerated receivables and goodwill were recorded. Caterpillar, it appears, was the victim of accounting manipulation, and should not, in our opinion, have recorded the associated losses as a 'non-cash' impairment charge as this clearly would appear to be better defined as cash.

Conclusion

An investigation of a company's accounting practices is the only means of sounding out their impact on its apparent creditworthiness. Often, a thorough reading of the notes to the report and accounts is a first step in seeing what changes of accounting policy a company may have made from one reporting period to the next, serves to highlight potential areas of concern and helps the analyst distinguish between those practices that mask economic reality and those that are merely industry conventions.

5

Behind the Numbers: Adjusted Debt and Liquidity

Introduction

HAVING MADE OUR CRITICISMS OF THE ROLE PLAYED BY AN OVER-RELIANCE ON numerical analysis, in this chapter we promptly reverse tack and acknowledge the importance of interpreting these very numbers – properly. Our stance here is not to advocate the literal application of numerical analysis, but rather to use it in a more interpretative fashion. In order to do this, we give a number of case studies in which we tease out contextual factors that can either support or undermine the credit case for the corporate concerned. We take each part of the financial statements in turn: P&L, balance sheet and cash flow statement, and highlight areas that merit particular scrutiny from the investor.

We then move off balance sheet and introduce and illustrate the important concept of adjusted debt, which will constitute a substantial feature of many of the case studies that follow. We look at pension liabilities, in the context of General Motors (GM) and Ford, operating leases at the Home Retail Group and event risk in the form of the Macondo oil spill and its implications for BP. We also look at liquidity in the context of Clear Channel Communications and examine the nature of committed credit lines. Finally, we look at some of the other factors beyond the scope of pure credit analysis that have a material influence on a company's creditworthiness, and include two case studies of LBOs with very different outcomes.

1. Adjustments for off-balance-sheet liabilities

In order to arrive at figures that more accurately reflect the true level of a corporate's financial status, it is necessary to perform a variety of adjustments to the company's stated levels of debt and cash, usually entailing the re-integration of financial commitments that do not appear in the financial statements. We highlight the principal areas below.

Adjusted debt I: pensions and OPEBs

One of the most important of the adjustments that have to be made is to reflect the value of pension commitments and other post-employment benefits (OPEBs). This is particularly material in labour-intensive industries, especially those in the mature phase of the development cycle, which often have legacy beneficiaries of these programmes that are far in excess of the current workforces and thus constitute a major factor in these companies' financial profiles.

In the US, pensions usually rank alongside other senior unsecured creditors in bankruptcy. That is to say, if the company in whose senior unsecured notes you have invested goes bankrupt, it will not merely be with other unsecured creditors that you will share what remains once senior creditors have been made whole, you will also be divvying up what's left with pensioners and current employees with pension rights.

Pension funds do have their own assets from which to meet their outstanding obligations. However, to the extent that the plan's assets are insufficient to meet its projected benefit obligations (an actuarial assessment of how much the plan will have to pay based on the number of current retirees and eligible employees and their expected mortality present-valued at a discount rate, usually around the current AA corporate bond rate) – what is referred to as the plan's underfunded amount or deficit – this becomes a senior unsecured claim in bankruptcy. Many companies, especially those with higher credit ratings, are fully or nearly fully funded. Many, however, are not. Those that are not have an obligation that looks like senior unsecured debt in bankruptcy, and this should be factored into a measure of adjusted leverage.

Some of the worst cases of pension underfunding can be found among those entities that once boasted large unionised workforces – much larger workforces than those they employ today. In its pre-Chapter 11 incarnation, for example, the old GM was often described as "a pension plan with a company attached". Many rust-belt, labour-intensive industries contain companies with similar characteristics, though most are unlikely to suffer GM's fate.

Although much smaller companies than they once were, they nonetheless are obliged to fund the pensions of all those workers – in some cases multiples of current staffs – that earned rights to pensions while they worked for them. Those workforces that were highly unionised were often able to negotiate the most favourable pension deals, such as defined benefit plans (in which the pension benefit, rather than contribution, is agreed and the company bears the market risk associated with generating enough money to provide it), leaving the companies in question with some of the greatest pension deficits. On the other side, some companies made use of periods of high interest rates (and therefore high discount rates and low PVs of pension obligations) and returns on assets to enjoy pension holidays. Now that returns are more questionable (especially in equities, which, despite some amazing peaks and troughs, have had something of a weak run over the last decade) and discount rates low, their pension deficits have also ballooned. Adjusting debt to reflect these deficits can materially change a company's total debt and leverage numbers.

TABLE 24: PENSION DEFICITS – IMPACT ON ADJUSTED DEBT

$bn	Ford (Auto Only)	GM (Auto Only)	Goodyear
Total Debt**	14.3	10.7	5.1
Cash and Equivalents	24.3	26.1	2.3
Net Debt (Cash)	-10	-15.4	2.8
EBITDA*	10.6	13.1	1.8
Net Debt/EBITDA	N/A -- Net Cash	N/A -- Net Cash	1.6
Pension Underfunding	18.7	26.9	3.5
Pension-Adjusted Net Debt	8.7	11.5	6.3
Pension-Adjusted Net Debt/EBITDA	0.8	0.9	3.5

* Ford & GM - Authors' Calculation; Goodyear -- Bloomberg
** For GM Including Series A Preferred Stock

Source: Company accounts, authors' calculations

Sources: Bloomberg; Deutsche Bank estimates; company filings

Adjusted debt II: leases

One particular area of focus is in the field of operating leases, which is a popular off-balance-sheet funding mechanism in sectors as diverse as retailing, airlines, hospitality and telecoms. This figure does not garner much attention from the equity community and is disclosed only once a year, usually in a note to the annual report and accounts – if it is disclosed at all. Again, US disclosure is usually superior and the rental lease obligations can generally be found in company filings. Historically, the accounting profession has chosen to overlook the cost of leases in financial statements, although there is now increasing pressure from regulators to address this.[129]

Operating leases are a lot like debt but do not appear on the balance sheet. Capital leases, by contrast, do appear under the rationale that in a capital lease transaction a transfer of ownership of the leased asset takes place. However, under an operating lease, a company is still contractually obliged to make a series of payments over a finite time period, an arrangement which resembles debt service and can be broken into interest and principal components. It is true that, in contrast to failure to pay under a loan or bond agreement, welshing on a lease will not automatically trigger default on other obligations if left uncured but it would represent a breach of a legally enforceable contract and such a

---

129 An article in the *Financial Times* of 2 January 2013 sheds some light on this debate: Pollack, L. (2013). 'Operating leases: the old skool of off balance sheet vehicles'. [Online]. Available at: **ftalphaville. ft.com/2013/01/03/1320783/operating-leases-the-old-skool-of-off-balance-sheet-vehicles** [Accessed 24 November 2014]. As does **www.ft.com/cms/s/3/83f1728c-42bf-11e2-a3d2-00144feabdc0. html#axzz2G0407AA8**. 'Leases and balance sheets'. *FT*. 1 January 2013.

breach could pose a serious challenge to a company's ability to keep operating. So, using the rationale that if it waddles and quacks like a duck, a duck it is, we advocate factoring leases into the calculation of total debt. But how?

Methodologies differ, but recognition is vital

There is debate between the ratings agencies as to the correct approach to attributing a net present value to this line item. S&P, Fitch Ratings and Moody's have published lengthy methodologies setting out their own rationales to calculate the annual lease payment across different industrials.

There is also an alternative approach to the capitalisation of operating leases that is more nuanced than the 'factor' approach and is driven by US-style presentation of leases in regulatory filings. This operating lease data can be gathered from the notes to the annual filings found in most US 10-Ks. Here we will use, as an example, the filing of US commercial vehicle parts supplier, Meritor, for fiscal years ending September 2013, 2012 and 2011. By way of comparison, if we were to employ the 'factor' approach for Meritor's 2012 numbers it would give the outcome shown in table 25.

TABLE 25: MERITOR: IMPACT OF FACTOR-BASED LEASE ADJUSTMENTS ON LEVERAGE AND OPERATING STATISTICS

Future Minimum Lease Payment	2013	2012	
2013		17	
2014	32	14	
2015	16	13	
2016	15	12	
2017	15	12	
2018	14		
Thereafter	14	23	
Total Payments	106	91	
Years Remaining	2	3	
Capitalisation Factor		8	
Capitalized Leases		256	Minimum First-Year Payment Multiplied by the Capitalization Factor
Depreciation Component		10.7	Minimum First-Year Payment * 1/3
Interest Component		21.3	Minimum First-Year Payment * 2/3

Impact on Meritor's 2013 Leverage and Operating Ratios

	Unadjusted	Adjustment	Adjusted
EBITDA	276	11	287
Net Debt	820	256	1076
Gross Interest	128	21	149
Net Debt/EBITDA	3.0		3.8
EBITDA Gross Interest Coverage	2.2		1.9

Source: Company reports, authors' calculations

In essence, the alternative methodology calculates a net present value (NPV) of future minimum lease payments discounted at the firm's effective cost of debt (gross interest divided by average total debt). The net present value of the minimum lease payments is added to total debt, since, as we have noted previously, operating leases have significant debt-like characteristics. (For accounting purists in search of a balancing item for this additional debt, it would be appropriate to record an asset of equal size to reflect the benefit that the company derives from the assets it leases, probably as an addition to PP&E.)

The interest component of lease expense is derived from averaging the NPV of future lease payments over the current and previous periods and using the firm's effective cost of debt as a discount rate, as calculated above. This is added to interest expense. Selling, general and administrative expenses (SG&A) are reduced by an amount equal to the average of the first-year minimum lease payments of the current and prior periods and implicit interest is subtracted from this latter amount to arrive at the operating lease depreciation expense. This amount is then added back to EBITDA for leverage calculations.

As nuanced as this approach is, it too is not without pitfalls, especially in the context of complicated accounts or poor disclosure. The calculation of the effective cost of funds is key, since this is the rate at which the future lease payments are discounted. An inaccurate rate can therefore lead to either overstatement or understatement of the implicit debt represented by the operating leases. Capitalisation of interest (if unknown or not added back) and the impact of gains/losses on derivatives can also distort the figure used for interest expense and thus lead to an inaccurate discount rate as can understatement of the denominator (total debt) through the non-inclusion of off-balance-sheet financing. In the case of Meritor, for simplicity of presentation we have used total debt from the company's balance sheet. However, adding back off-balance-sheet debt materially reduces the effective cost of funds, with the effects on the calculations as shown in table 27.

The interest rate is clearly also influenced by the financial position of the company. A company that was flirting with insolvency would have a very high cost of debt, which, perversely, would lead to the debt represented by operating leases being understated. In such a situation it would make more sense to source a cost of funds from a peer company. Ideally, we would use the interest rates imputed in the company's actual leases but such granularity is not usually available.

The underlying logic, with which we agree, is that each lease has a finite life to which, given perfect disclosure, could be attributed a discount rate by which the NPV of the obligation could be determined. Because, in a portfolio of store or aircraft leases, we are unlikely to get anywhere near this level of granularity in company disclosures, rules of thumb have become an imprecise but commonly-used method of approximating this figure. The results can be sensitised by using a higher multiple for more economically sensitive and volatile sectors and lower multiples for more inelastic industries, to reflect an assessment of the typical lease life in each industry. The resulting figure (annual lease obligation × multiple of 4× to 8×) creates another vital constituent of adjusted debt. Operating leases are a call on a company's cash flow and require servicing in manner parallel to its financial debt.

5. BEHIND THE NUMBERS: ADJUSTED DEBT AND LIQUIDITY

TABLE 26: MERITOR: IMPACT OF NPV-BASED ADJUSTMENTS ON LEVERAGE AND OPERATING STATISTICS

Future Minimum Lease Payment	2013	2012	
2013		17	
2014	32	14	
2015	16	13	
2016	15	12	
2017	15	12	
2018	14		
Thereafter	14	23	
Total Payments	106	91	
Years Remaining	2	3	
Annual Gross Interest	128	97	
Total Debt	1138	1060	
Interest Rate	11.2%	9.2%	
PV of Operating Leases	78.0	67.1	
2014	32	14	
2015	15	13	
2016	15	12	
2017	15	12	
2018	14	12	
2019	14	12	
2020	14	12	

	Unadjusted		
2013 Implicit Interest Expense	8.2		Average of current and last year's PV of operating leases * current-year interest rate.
Adjustment to SG&A – Rent	23		Average of first-year minimum lease payments.
Lease Depreciation Expense	14.8		SG&A Adjustment less implicit interest

Impact on Meritor's 2013 Leverage and Operating Ratios	Unadjusted	Adjustment	Adjusted	
EBITDA	276	15	291	This is added to interest expense.
Net Debt	820	78	898	This is subtracted from SG&A
Net Debt/EBITDA	3.0		3.1	This is added to reported depreciation
Gross Interest	128	8	136	
EBITDA Gross Interest Coverage	2.2		2.1	

Source: Company reports, authors' calculations

TABLE 27: MERITOR: DISTORTIVE EFFECTS OF OFF-BALANCE-SHEET ADD-BACKS

Future Minimum Lease Payment	2013	2012	
2013		17	
2014	32	14	
2015	16	13	
2016	15	12	
2017	15	12	
2018	14		
Thereafter	14	23	
Total Payments	106	91	
Years Remaining	2	3	
Annual Gross Interest	128	97	
Total Debt	1470	1345	
Interest Rate	8.7%	7.2%	
PV of Operating Leases	83.1	71.3	
2014	32	14	
2015	15	13	
2016	15	12	
2017	15	12	
2018	14	12	
2019	14	12	
2020	14	12	
2013 Implicit Interest Expense	6.7		Average of current and last year's PV of operating leases * current-year interest rate	This is added to interest expense.
Adjustment to SG&A – Rent	23		Average of first-year minimum lease payments.	This is subtracted from SG&A
Lease Depreciation Expense	16.3		SG&A Adjustment less implicit interest	This is added to reported depreciation

Impact on Meritor's 2013 Leverage and Operating Ratios

	Unadjusted	Adjustment	Adjusted
EBITDA	276	16	292
Net Debt	820	83	903
Net Debt/EBITDA	3.0		3.1
Gross Interest	128	7	135
EBITDA Gross Interest Coverage	2.2		2.2

Source: Company reports, authors' calculations

Operating lease case study – there's no place like HOME

Home Retail Group (HOME), which operates chains of home and general merchandise retail stores in the UK, provides a good example of how taking off-balance-sheet financing in the form of operating leases into account provides a more complete picture of a company's financial health than could be derived from the headline financial statements alone.

FIGURE 7: HOME EQUITY PERFORMANCE 2010-2013

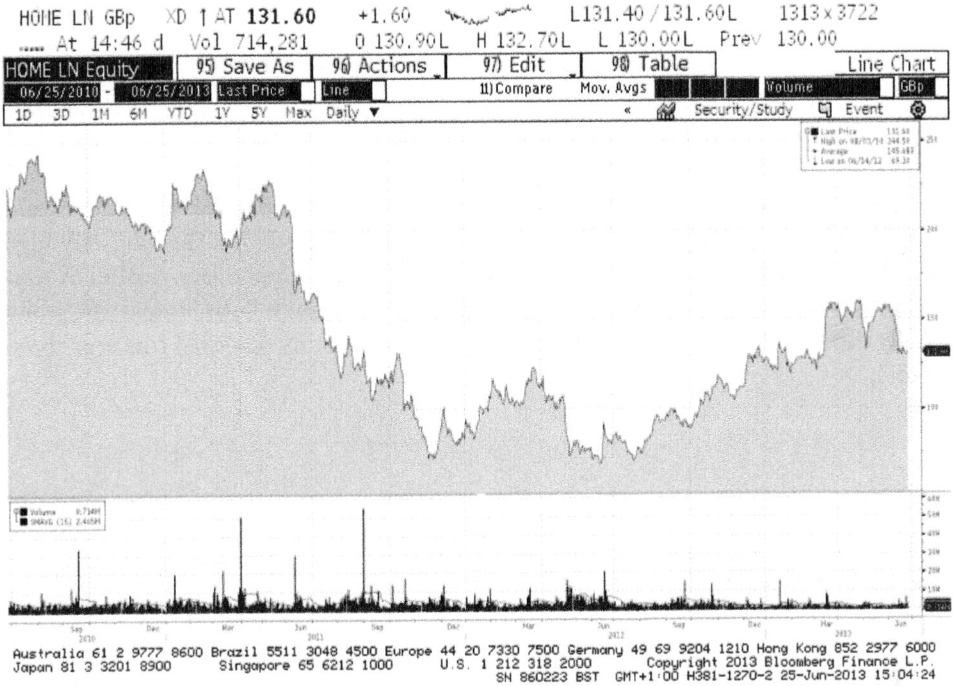

Source: Bloomberg

HOME's operating results have suffered in latter years as parts of its business have been subjected to intensifying competition from the large British food retailers' move into non-food sales and also by the generalised shift in British consumer spending towards the internet, although it has proved to be a doughty survivor in a challenging UK retail environment.

Nonetheless, at first glance, the group's balance sheet looks resilient. HOME has built an unusual retail model in which its own financing is provided by a mixture of positive working capital and a tightly-managed consumer receivables portfolio while its entire store base is rented. Despite operating in a tough environment, HOME has generated positive free cash flow[130] – a key credit concept that we will examine in more depth in the liquidity analysis section.

---

130 Free cash flow = EBITDA - net interest paid - taxes +/- movement in working capital - capital expenditures - other financing activities.

TABLE 28: HOME - INCOME STATEMENT 2006-2010

Income statement (£m)	FY 06	FY 07	FY 08	FY 09	FY 10
Revenue	5,548	5,607	5,985	5,897	6,022
Gross profit	1,862	1,962	2,104	2,024	1,967
Operating expenses	1,516	1,926	1,718	1,732	1,673
EBIT	346	328	386	292	295

Source: HOME

An un-levered balance sheet = a strong credit?

On the liabilities side of the balance sheet, HOME shows zero financial debt. This means that the 'first cut' of HOME's credit statistics is relatively innocuous, showing very high levels of interest coverage (21.3× EBIT ÷ interest in FY 2010, total debt ÷ EBITDA 0.0× since 2008 and total debt ÷ total capitalisation of 0% since 2007). Furthermore, the group typically carries a significant cash balance, further assuaging any potential concerns about liquidity.

TABLE 29: HOME - SUMMARY BALANCE SHEET 2006-2010

In £m	2006	2007	2008	2009	2010
Cash and equivalents	130	284	174	209	364
Inventories	881	906	1,005	930	935
Receivables	1,478	569	598	594	582
Other current assets	8.5	3.0	21.2	143.8	150.0
Non-current assets	2,821	2,763	2,895	5,312	2,246
Total assets	5,318	4,526	4,693	4,190	4,277
Current liabilities (including S-T debt)	373	136	1,811	335	324
Trade payables	863	1,025	1,090	999	1,042
Other non-current liabilities	1,133	286.2	77.0	96.6	44.8
Total debt	1,046	224	0	0	0
Total liabilities	2,368	1,447	1,348	1,431	1,411
Total liabilities + stockholders' equity	5,318	4,526	4,639	4,190	4,277

Source: Company accounts

However, if we take the trouble to dig the company's rental payments out of the notes to the financial statements, pick a multiple from the ratings agencies range (in our example, we have used the Moody's methodology of 8× annual rental leases as the NPV of the lease obligation) and add it back into the adjusted debt figure, quite a different picture of HOME's underlying financial strength and creditworthiness appears.

We could have argued the toss over whether a 6× or an 8× multiple is more appropriate, but what emerges under either methodology is a picture of a company with substantial adjusted debt, carrying an NPV of either £3.03bn under Moody's 8× methodology or £2.2bn under the method favoured by S&P. We should also bear in mind any pension deficit (in HOME's case only a small figure) to arrive at our final adjusted debt calculation.

TABLE 30: HOME - OFF-BALANCE-SHEET ITEMS 2006-2010

£m	2006	2007	2008	2009	2010
Commitments	49	59	60	22	8
Pension adjustments					
Net deficit/ surplus	26	9	84	(46)	(25)
Non-cancellable operating leases					
Annual rental (debited to income statement	299	328	328	373	379
Debt equivalent NPV (8×)	2,394	2,626	2,626	2,982	3,033
P&L adjustments					
Interest (⅓)	100	109	109	124	126
Depreciation (⅔)	199	219	219	249	253

Source: Company accounts, authors' calculations

From adjusted debt to adjusted leverage

Having derived adjusted debt, in order to arrive at a ratio to express the company's adjusted leverage we need to divide its adjusted debt by its EBITDAR, that is to say its EBITDA + ⅓ of its annual rental leases, another market convention which, for all its imperfections, has become a rule of thumb.

We should emphasise that the lease obligation for HOME looks set to diminish over time as it exits less profitable stores and re-shapes its store portfolio. However, as table 31 represents (under the 8× methodology) the company was running a tight (though, so far, sufficient) balance between its operating returns and its financial obligations to its lessors and pensioners.

TABLE 31: HOME – ADJUSTED LEVERAGE

Key ratios	FY 06	FY07	FY 08	FY 09	FY 10
Total debt/total cap.	30.1%	6.8%	0.0%	0.0%	0.0%
Total debt/ EBITDA	2.8×	0.5×	0.0×	0.0×	0.0×
Lease adj. total debt/EBITDAR	3.3×	3.7×	2.9×	3.6×	3.8×
Adj. total debt/ EBITDA	4.5×	5.0×	4.1×	5.3×	5.6×

Source: Authors' calculations

As table 31 demonstrates, while HOME's total and net debt figures have declined dramatically over the period in question, its adjusted debt figures (for leases and for other off-balance-sheet liabilities) have been rising as the denominator in the calculation has remained under pressure. We will now illustrate the adjustments that we have made to this denominator. To complete the picture, table 32 illustrates the workings we used to adjust both debt and EBITDAR in our calculations.

TABLE 32: HOME - RATIO AND DEBT ADJUSTMENT SUMMARY

£m	FY 06	FY 07	FY 08	FY 09	FY 10
Adj. to debt					
Adj. 1 operating leases (8×)	2,394	2,626	2,626	2,989	3,033
Adj. 2 pension surplus/deficit	(26)	(9)	(84)	46	25
Adj. 3 contingent liabilities	48	59	60	22	8
Total adjustments	2,417	2,675	2,602	3,050	3,066
Adj. to EBITDA					
Add ⅓ operating leases	100	109	109	124	126

Source: Authors' calculations

Conclusion

To summarise, we believe that analysing HOME as a credit neatly illustrates two of the major areas of off-balance-sheet adjustment that should be applied to every individual credit that is being considered for inclusion in a portfolio:

• adjustment for operating leases

• adjustment for pension deficits.

It can be seen that without a thorough analysis of off-balance-sheet liabilities, it would be easy to arrive at a very misleading impression of the company's credit standing. Including both the full operating lease liability and the pension scheme is perhaps excessively punitive, as a degree of flexibility exists in relation to payments due on both, but it does help to highlight potential downside scenarios that could be deleterious to the interests of creditors.

2. Event risk

Case study: BP and the Macondo oil spill

In the event of a potentially catastrophic financial liability, it is critical to attempt to establish the impact of a range of scenarios on the credit standing, and indeed the ultimate survival of the companies involved. In 2010, when the Macondo oil well, deep in the Gulf of Mexico, exploded with tragic loss of life at the rig and the threat of environmental and economic catastrophe for the surrounding Gulf Coast region, an attempt to quantify the potential financial liabilities from the disaster was necessary in order for investors to take a realistic view on its impact on the credit standing of the companies that owned and operated the well.

In such situations, where there is a wide range of outcomes in terms of where liability may lie and what the ultimate cost of reparations may be, uncertainties abound. On the other hand, when some of the world's largest oil companies are in the frame, there are deep pockets available to deal with all but the most draconian of punitive damages. As well as BP, Anadarko Petroleum, Mitsui Oil (which all owned the rights to the well on a 65/25/10 basis), Transocean and also potentially Cameron and Halliburton, which were involved in the blow-out preventer design and drilling, respectively, were all potentially implicated.

Clearly, the situation required close scrutiny, though any hypotheses arrived at would remain fraught with uncertainty.

Assessing a moving target

All that could be done was to attempt to establish what could be known of the causes of the blow-out, to examine the legal indemnities between the operating companies (where details were publicly available) and, with them, the apparent chain of legal liability.

Thereafter, an attempt could be made to assess damages scenarios and the ability of the operating and owning companies to bear their costs. In some ways, this was the ultimate calculus of adjusted debt, with huge practical and political unknowns, and the tone of discourse emerging from the various state and federal agencies concerned with the spill was an important qualitative guide as to the likely nature of interactions between the companies involved and the authorities.

Tellingly, BP, the major equity owner in the well (and which had recently undergone a major re-branding exercise emphasising its 'green' credentials), began to be referred to, by no less a figure than Barack Obama, as "British Petroleum" – the name it had long-since shed after merging with the US oil giant Amoco in 1998. Clearly, the US government, on the verge of crucial mid-term elections, was not in a mood to go easy on those responsible, minimising the relevance of 'blue-sky' scenario analysis and providing a clear pointer to the downside. Mitigating these factors was the fact that the expertise in this field lay entirely in the private sector, and the US government would be under pressure to square the circle of its ongoing oil dependency and reliance on domestic deepwater wells.

Armed with this clear emphasis on downside damages scenarios (over which litigation remained ongoing in 2013) assessing the Macondo disaster thereafter became a more straightforward exercise in ascertaining the apparent chain of legal liability, given existing precedents from the data so far available, and speculative exercises in analysing potential outcomes, as well as a more basic credit and liquidity analysis of the main corporations involved.

If BP can't afford to deal with this, who can?

Many of the factors in this scenario were unique: the technological sophistication and difficulty of operations below and on the sea bed that have been said to be as challenging as working in outer space; the scale of the disaster and that of the corporations involved.

This, too, coloured the qualitative assessment of the disaster's credit impact. To give a sense of perspective, BP's annual sales line had averaged over $280bn for each of its previous six fiscal years, the sort of figure more usually associated with the GDP of a mid-sized G10 country. BP had generated an average of $28bn of operating cash flow in each of these years. Clearly, this was a corporation that was close to the zenith of creditworthiness under normal operating conditions: AA-rated by the major rating agencies. What scale of liability would seriously threaten its survival?

The company's bonds and listed equities had undergone a major sell-off as news of the spill intensified, and, to be fair, were probably not helped by poorly managed communications from the company and a widespread media perception that senior management was out of touch with the gravity of the situation.

FIGURE 8: BP EQUITY PRICE

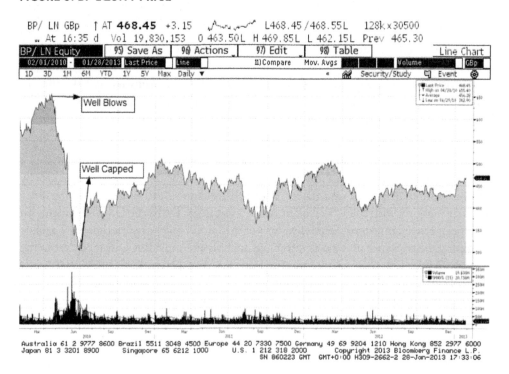

Source: Bloomberg

Deep value or value trap?

As figure 8 shows, BP's stock lost roughly half (43%, to be precise) of its value between March and June 2010, a collapse in market values equivalent to approximately £57bn, or $88bn at the time, which represented 3.1 years of BP's operating cash flow and roughly six years of its free cash flow.

At the same time, five-year CDS protection had ballooned from 43bps to over 600. As a basis of comparison, another company whose CDS was trading around this level at the time was Meritor, a truck parts manufacturer with a market capitalisation of $1.4bn, whose senior unsecured debt was rated Caa1/CC at the time.

BP's senior unsecured bonds had also collapsed in value, with the 3 ⅞% of 2015 trading down from a pre-Macondo level of 105 cents on the dollar to a low point of 82 cents on the dollar, and were offering yields normally associated with credits in the low-single-B or high triple-C ratings categories.

Tempting though the valuations of these securities might have been to investors at their low points, a more thorough analysis of BP's liquidity and financing options was necessary in order to establish whether these were valuable trading opportunities or merely value traps, from which it would be impossible to exit while the company compensated those affected by the disaster and began to interact with the US legal system to establish a final settlement of environmental damages.

FIGURE 9: BP FIVE-YEAR CDS SPREAD PERFORMANCE

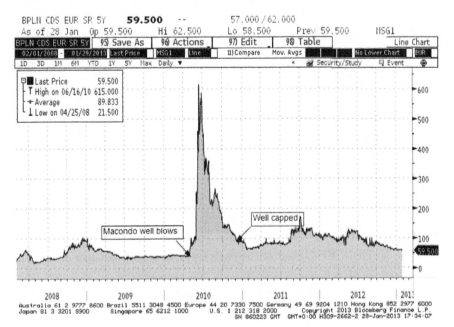

Source: Bloomberg

Scenario analyses

Rather than taking readers through the intricacies of our scenario analyses, we have reduced this to a series of synopses of the major areas that we examined. The five scenarios that we modelled are summarised in table 33, and were assessed over a range of timescales:

TABLE 33: SCENARIO ANALYSIS

Scenario	Clean-up costs ($m)	Punitive damages ($m)	Legal costs ($m)	Total costs ($m)
I.	20,000	10,000	15,000	55,000
II.	25,000	15,000	15,000	55,000
III.	20,000	20,000	20,000	60,000
IV.	30,000	30,000	20,000	80,000
V.	40,000	30,000	20,000	90,000

Source: Company accounts; authors' calculations

Clearly, any of these numbers is material, and would be potentially fatal to all but the financially strongest of corporations. Our analysis sought to test BP's ability to respond to this range of outcomes by accessing its alternative sources of liquidity. Working on the basis that BP would retain a share of the total liability that was proportionate to its own share in the well (i.e. 65%), and that its two equity partners, Anadarko and Mitsui, would probably seek to settle with BP ahead of the final outcome on BP's own liability (which has indeed proven to be the case), we ran the company's hypothetical financials through our model.

In terms of decision-making from a credit standpoint, the scenario analysis was useful insofar as it examined, from the perspective of cash flow, how large the financial penalties would have to get to require BP to make disposals or seek additional funding from the debt or equity markets in order to cope with them. Aside from its scale, many factors militated in favour of BP's being able to access financing in all scenarios. Remember, the assets of international oil companies can be readily valued in a way that is not so straightforward in many other sectors, as there is a ready market in proven reserves that may fit geographically into another company's reserve base in a financially advantageous way.

At the time of the accident, BP looked set to have a year-end cash balance of $19.8bn, un-drawn bank lines of $8.6bn and was generating free cash flow of $13bn a year from operations. Much of this would be more or less immediately available to meet liabilities arising, *and* the company had a huge reserve base of marketable hydrocarbons compared to its likely debt load. These could potentially form the basis of a bank security package or be sold to other oil companies with geographic overlap. For our scenarios above, the projected amount of debt per unit of proven reserves was:

TABLE 34: DEBT PER BARREL OF OIL EQUIVALENT (BOE)

Scenario	TD/Proved reserves 2010E	TD/Proved reserves 2011E	TD/Proved reserves 2012E	TD/Proved reserves 2013E
I.	$1.42	$1.66	$2.06	$0.62
II.	$1.42	$1.94	$2.35	$0.62
III.	$1.42	$1.78	$2.10	$0.65
IV.	$1.42	$2.28	$2.65	$0.64
V.	$1.42	$2.73	$3.19	$0.60

Source: Authors' calculations

It can be seen then that, even under our most drastic scenario, BP's leverage did not look likely to exceed $3.19 per barrel of oil equivalent (BOE). Put another way, BP only needed to make $3.19 per BOE not merely to service, but to liquidate the debts arising from this punitive scenario at the peak of its leverage. The company's leverage and solvency ratios would obviously be meaningfully impacted by the disaster for several years, but, as long as it could maintain market access and shore up its liquidity with some disposals of non-core assets, BP did not look likely to carry more than 1.3 turns of leverage at any point over the forecast period. With oil at close to $100 a barrel, there was ample scope for BP to generate significantly higher returns per BOE than this, and the risk/reward relationship seemed attractive.

There are two issues in this that, while interdependent, can become confused. One, the company's leverage adjusted for the Macondo blow-out and two, its ability to access in a timely manner alternative liquidity to meet any cash demands. Under the scenarios we looked at, while BP's ultimate level of leverage did not seem to be likely to pose a threat to the corporation's long-term health, it was necessary for the company to put in place sufficient additional sources of liquidity to tide it over a period in which potentially huge damages claims could be levelled against it, thereby reassuring the market that it was responding appropriately to the crisis. In the event, BP was able to tap into its non-core asset base for disposals and raise an additional $10bn credit line, which was put in place to increase its total sources of liquidity to approximately $50bn.

Conclusion

Scenario analysis of the potential impact on BP from damages claims helps to illustrate the key factors at play in this scenario:

- the company's undoubted ability to absorb potentially huge liabilities

- the company's actions to shore up its liquidity in the face of these potential liabilities (these actions regained the market's confidence, perhaps more directly than the first factor).

While it would have been a relatively good risk/reward trade from a credit standpoint to invest in BP's credit during the crisis, the position would have remained risky and been unlikely to outperform the market until BP had demonstrated its continued access to the markets for additional liquidity. Which leads us on to our next topic …

3. Liquidity analysis

Liquidity analysis is typically undertaken as part of a company's credit assessment, with the goal of gaining perspective on the corporation's ability to self-finance over the course of the coming year (or longer, depending on the time frame of the investment). Key elements of the analysis are to establish to what extent the company is dependent on external sources of funding, be they banks, equity or credit markets, or the receipt of proceeds from a divestment in order to meet its short-term obligations. Once this exercise is completed, it can provide an insight into how pressing the corporation's short-term financing needs really are.

Maintaining a solid liquidity position sets the tone for a company's overall financial policy. It is hard to present any non-financial corporation as financially conservative if its strategy is underpinned by a requirement for constant rolling of short-term financing in order to pursue its strategic objectives, and, indeed, the overuse of market access has become one of the red flags that can be taken as a potential indication of impending trouble. Those who lived through the crises at Enron or Parmalat will recall the frequency and ease with which both of these companies would issue bonds to keep kicking the can down the road. Both companies appeared to have strong liquidity, with high reported cash balances frequently topped up by tapping the bond markets for fresh funds, but ultimately were found wanting.

Few bankers that had exposure to Xerox in 2000 will forget the day that the company drew down its entire $5bn backup line as it faced the prospect of losing access to the commercial paper market after a ratings downgrade to Prime-3 after a relatively rapid deterioration in the company's competitive position and credit ratings. Xerox had historically funded much of its working capital through the commercial paper market and its management became concerned that it may lose market access if its ratings slipped further. In order to avoid this eventuality and the associated disruption to its business that it might entail, they used their available bank credit lines to repay outstanding commercial paper in full in September of that year.

Traditional liquidity analysis has an important role to play in the overall credit assessment of a corporation's creditworthiness. We will work through one such exercise later in this section in order to demonstrate a practical approach to readers. Before we embark on this, however, it is worth highlighting a range of qualitative areas in which significant uncertainties can lie and that are also well worth looking into before taking any comfort from published financial statements.

Key elements of liquidity analysis

Undertaking a traditional liquidity analysis starts from the company's balance sheet and moves on to the cash flow statement. The key focus points from a liquidity perspective are as follows:

- Is the company likely to generate free cash flow over the period in question?

- To what extent are forthcoming calls on cash not covered from free operating cash flow?

- What is the company's accessible cash balance? (see above)

- What debt maturities is it facing over the next 12 months?

- What access does the company have to any un-drawn banking lines as a possible means of providing liquidity?

- Are these lines committed, or do they contain force majeure or BaW[131] language?

- How close are the company's metrics to the covenants on its facilities and does it look likely to breach them? If there is sufficient headroom to give us confidence that the lines will remain available over this time horizon, then these facilities should be factored into our one-year pro-forma cash flow analysis.

- If not, then what other options does it have to raise funding over the short term?

- Does it trade in a readily realisable asset with clear price transparency such as oil or gold?

- Does it retain the option of securitising a receivables portfolio or using factoring?

- Is the company in a position to sell primary equity?

- Could it execute a sale and leaseback on a readily realisable asset?

- Does it retain non-core activities that could be disposed of, or sold and leased back, to bolster liquidity?

In simple equation form, the liquidity analysis for one year can be reduced to:

```
Cash - short-term debt + undrawn facilities + proceeds of asset sales
÷ securitisations + sale of new equity + free cash flow = liquidity
excess/deficit
```

---

131 *Bis auf Weiteres* – a common form of German loan that can be translated as 'until further notice'.

Cash in the bank ...

Over the last few years we have become accustomed to hearing that we should be less concerned about debt service and maturity runways for US corporates because, by any historical comparison, they are flush with cash. Indeed, when analysts cite a company's debt, they more often than not refer to its net debt, i.e. debt less cash (and typically marketable securities which can be easily liquidated at a predictable value) on the balance sheet, since the former appears available to offset the latter. In broad terms, we would concur. At the time of writing, US non-financial corporations are enjoying liquidity ratios (liquid assets ÷ short-term liabilities) of around 50% – a level last seen in the early 1960s.[132] However, we would nonetheless argue that looking at net debt might be an oversimplification.

First, cash on the balance sheet is a snapshot of the cash and securities available at the close of a given business day. An employee's bank account looks flush with cash briefly after the monthly salary goes in, but, within a couple of days, following the depredations of HMRC and the ever-rising costs of day-to-day living, it looks a whole lot more anaemic. In a similar manner, a company's end-of-period cash balance might be flush with customer payments, yet will be depleted within a few days once it has made new payments to suppliers. Many companies experience significant seasonality in their cash balances. For instance, a US gas distributor will typically draw down heavily on its cash (and short-term lines of credit) as it buys gas in the run-up to winter but will benefit from significant inflows of cash as customers pay their bills in the first quarter. To net off cash against debt at that point would be to underestimate the company's true debt level, since that cash will be needed to maintain the ongoing operations of the company through the year – it is not really available for debt service.

For international companies, one must also question the extent to which cash can be repatriated. The cash that appears on an international company's balance sheet is the sum of cash balances at its operations across the globe. Conversely, the bulk (although by no means all) of the debt is likely to be issued from a holding company or captive finance entity in one jurisdiction. Yet part of the cash located overseas may be required for the operating needs of the local entities and, therefore, be unavailable for debt service; in some emerging markets, exchange controls may also limit the extent to which locally generated cash can be repatriated to meet holding company or finance company obligations. The tax implications of cash repatriation may also reduce the amount that is actually available.

Liquidity case study I: Goodyear

In Goodyear's Q2 2014 presentation to investors and analysts, the company sets forth a slide calculating its year-end net debt position as follows:[133]

---

132   Federal Reserve Statistical Release (2014). Financial Accounts of the United States. [Online]. Available at: **www.federalreserve.gov/releases/z1/20140605** [Accessed 24 November 2014].

133   Goodyear (2014). Second Quarter 2014 Conference Call. [Online]. Available at: **files.shareholder.com/downloads/AMDA-1IFBEB/3436674067x0x772052/88f7b4de-e47c-465c-a84f-8220a700d50b/140729_GT_Q2_Earnings_Call_Slides_FINAL.pdf** [Accessed 24 November 2014].

TABLE 35: GOODYEAR LIQUIDITY 2014[134]

	($ in millions) 30/06/2014
Long-term debt and capital leases	$6,677
Notes payable and overdrafts	$7
Long-term debt and capital leases due within one year	$78
Total debt	$6,762
Less: cash and equivalents	$1,637
Net debt	$5,125

Let's examine the cash number a little more closely. In earlier presentations, where the company delineates its liquidity profile, it acknowledges that $1bn of the cash and equivalents is "required for operations".[135] Doubtless, if strapped for cash with which to service debt, Goodyear could squeeze this figure but, since, by their own admission it is destined for operations rather than debt service, it would at least be prudent to remove it from the net debt calculation.

In a footnote in the Q2 2014 presentation, management also notes that $291m of the cash position is located in Venezuela and is denominated in bolívares fuertes.[136] Venezuela is a highly inflationary economy with strict exchange controls and a singular approach to economic regulation, in light of which it might again be prudent to assume that this cash is not readily available to meet maturing debt. Excluding those two items increases the net debt position by 25% to $6.42bn.

US-based, internationally diversified companies routinely book profits offshore to avoid having to pay tax on those profits in the US, thereby boosting the all-important EPS headline number. To be fair, if we accept that the single goal of a corporate management is to increase the residual cash flow available for shareholders, such an action is logical. If we look at it from the perspective of option-based remuneration for a corporation's executives, it's even more compelling. Consider the theoretical example in table 37.

In the example, we have imagined two theoretical competitors in the same industry trading at the same price–earnings (P/E) multiples. The management of Improbable Corporation chooses to book all earnings in the US and pay the relevant tax rate. Its competitor, Dodgetax, Inc., instead books some profits offshore such that it can reduce its federal tax rate by 2%. This certainly lifts the stock price by a modestly beneficial 3%. However, a significantly greater benefit accrues to Dodgetax's CFO, who has been granted as part of

---

134 Goodyear (2014). Second Quarter 2014 Conference Call [Online]. Available at: **files.shareholder.com/ downloads/AMDA-1IFBEB/3962823872x0x772052/88f7b4de-e47c-465c-a84f-8220a700d50b/140729_ GT_Q2_Earnings_Call_Slides_FINAL.pdf** [Accessed 24 November 2014].

135 Goodyear (2012). Fourth Quarter 2011 Conference Call. [Online]. Available at: **files.shareholder.com/ downloads/AMDA-1IFBEB/3579877367x0x626456/e7c2c3f6-41eb-47ea-a26f-8c81af63e4fd/4qtr11_ slides.pdf** [Accessed 24 November 2014].

136 See note 125.

her remuneration 100,000 options to buy Dodgetax stock at $2 a share and who now sees their embedded value increase by 8%.

TABLE 37: TAX-EFFICIENT CAPITAL STRUCTURES

	Improbable Corporation	Dodgetax, Inc.
Pre-tax icome	$500,000	$500,000
Tax rate	35%	33%
Net income	$325,000	$335,000
Shares outstanding	1,000,000	1,000,000
EPS	$0.33	$0.34
P/E multiple	10	10
Share price	$3.25	$3.35
Embedded value of CFO's 100,000 share options @ $2 per share	$125,000	$135,000

Source: Authors' illustration

Let's now assume that both companies are sitting on $200m in debt and $100m in cash, 30% of which sits overseas. Should we accept the claim probably asserted by both in their quarterly earnings presentations that they have net debt of $100m? Having paid the full 35% in tax, Improbable is indifferent as to whether it keeps its cash abroad or repatriates it to the US (assuming no other constraints). Not so Dodgetax, which, unless it has foreign tax credits with which to shelter its income, would have to pay the full tax rate on anything it repatriated (with a slightly negative impact for shareholders and, more than likely, a material downside for the CFO's remuneration package).

In short, Dodgetax is disincentivised from repatriating cash and, even if we choose not to impute a higher level of net debt than that prevailing at Improbable, we should be mindful of the constraints on Dodgetax when comparing the two companies' ability to meet forthcoming debt maturities. While it can be argued that Dodgetax would, in extremis, be able to access its foreign funds, it is nonetheless worth noting that there may be unforeseen impediments to their speedy repatriation when needed and that they should therefore be considered an inferior source of liquidity to the cash held by Improbable.

How committed are committed facilities?

A key plank of any company's liquidity arrangements is its committed bank facilities. Many companies enjoy access to uncommitted facilities or money at call. However, since a bank can pull these lines at the first sign of trouble (for either the company or the bank), they are rather like an umbrella that does not open in the rain. We are therefore inclined to exclude them from our calculation of available liquidity.

By contrast, we ascribe significant value to committed bank facilities. For larger, more creditworthy companies that enjoy access to the public debt markets, these might take the form of back-up lines for commercial paper (CP), such that, should the company not be able to roll its CP, it may borrow from the bank (or, more probably, group of banks). Alternatively, smaller companies might require access to committed facilities to ensure the ongoing financing of their operations. In order to ensure that the bank remains willing to lend the money, the borrower typically pays a commitment fee to the bank.

Shy of commitment

However, there are conditions under which the bank's commitment to lend money can be withdrawn. Most commitment agreements contain covenants, which set forth conditions to which the borrower must adhere in order for the bank to honour its commitment to lend money.

Some of these are simple, common-sense 'housekeeping' matters – producing timely financial statements; keeping plant in good working order and ensuring the provision of adequate insurance, etc. Others limit management's scope to undertake corporate actions that could be injurious to the interests of the lender – sales or acquisitions of assets; granting security to new lenders which would superordinate their claim on the assets of the company in the event of bankruptcy to that of the extant lenders, the so-called 'negative pledge'. Others, still, impose financial conditions that the company must meet – typically maintaining the level of debt to pre-tax earnings (usually designated as EBITDA) below a certain ratio and pre-tax earnings to fixed charges (interest and rents) above a certain level.

With such 'financial' covenants, the lender tries to ensure that the corporate borrower's management operates the company in a prudent manner to ensure there is a sufficient cushion to service the debt should ambient economic or industry conditions deteriorate or should an idiosyncratic mishap befall the company. Usually – and this is key when assessing a company's access to alternative liquidity – if a company triggers a covenant (exceeds its agreed ratio of debt to earnings or undershoots its agreed fixed charge coverage ratio, say) the lender has the right, if the breach of covenant remains uncured after a certain pre-agreed period, to 'call' the loan; to demand immediate repayment of outstanding amounts and decline any further extension of credit.

In such an event not merely would alternative liquidity be less than originally envisaged by the amount of the commitment, but the company could be faced with a liquidity crisis as a result of its having immediately to repay any outstandings. Where would it source those funds? Moreover, the terms and conditions of bonds often contain so-called 'cross-default' provisions, such that an event of default in one credit agreement (an unremedied covenant breach) precipitates a default in the bonds. Thus, not merely is the company's liquidity much diminished but the bondholder might find themselves with a defaulted credit as a result of the company's failure to keep to terms agreed in another credit agreement.

Covenants often waived

Fortunately, covenant breaches rarely precipitate such a draconian response from banks. After all, it is not usually the bank's intention to pursue a scorched-earth policy that would leave the bank itself with a non-performing loan against which it would have to reserve and pursue a claim through the legal system.

If the company's business is salvageable, it is absolutely in the lender's interest to reach an accommodation with the borrower. Often, this will take the form of a 'waiver' and a renegotiation of covenants, with the bank cutting the company a little more slack over the short term – possibly increasing the leverage test or decreasing the fixed charge test but usually ratcheting them back to a more conservative level over a period of time, thereby imposing external fiscal discipline on the company's management.

However, rarely does a bank not seek to improve its position, lest the new arrangement not work out and the company eventually default on its obligation. This often takes the form of the bank agreeing to waive and ease covenants in exchange for gaining a charge over the company's assets. Then, if the company subsequently fails and the bank is obliged to sue in bankruptcy to recover its loan, it will enjoy a privileged position relative to that of other creditors. If you are one of the other creditors, this is one of those good news/bad news stories. From a liquidity perspective, you clearly benefit from the bank not pulling its line, since the company's access to cash and near-term survival is thereby assured. However, if over the longer term the firm subsequently finds its way into bankruptcy, your recovery will be diminished by the fact that the bank has a superior claim over the firm's assets.

US autos' divergent response to funding crisis

In late 2006, Ford and GM began to realise that the writing was on the wall unless they could dramatically restructure their operations and raise some cash to support them through the challenging period ahead. Ford closed on larger and more extensive secured bank facilities than GM, including an $11.5bn revolver and a $7bn term loan against which it pledged substantially all the personal property of Ford and its guarantors (including the iconic 'Blue Oval'), pledges on the capital stock of first-tier subsidiaries and various domestic manufacturing sites. So extensive was the security that Standard & Poor's (S&P) assessed recovery at 96% in a simulated default scenario.[137]

---

137 S&P (2006). 'Recovery Report: Ford Motor Co.'s Proposed $15bn Senior Secured Credit Facilities'. [Online]. Available at: **www.globalcreditportal.com/ratingsdirect/showArticlePage.**

The new loans left the remaining senior unsecureds profoundly subordinated but provided Ford with enough cash to see it through its restructuring and a sharp downturn in US car demand, while enabling it to maintain investment in new vehicle development. Ford made it through this period and has emerged as a leaner operation with an extensive portfolio of global architectures and operating margins that would not be out of place at a manufacturer of premium/luxury vehicles. GM, which was less aggressive in its debt-raising efforts, filed for protection under Chapter 11 on 1 June 2009.

MAC clauses

Try as a bank might to envisage all the scenarios that could impair its chances of being repaid in a timely manner, there are inevitably developments for which it cannot plan: the sudden discovery that a material used in a company's products has injured and/or killed people exposed to it and the company is hit with multi-billion class action lawsuits; the failure of a make-or-break new product; fraud; etc.

In order to protect itself from such developments, a bank might try to insert a catch-all clause into its loan agreement, known as a 'material adverse change clause' (MAC clause or MAC language), which affords it the right to call the loan and decline extensions of further credit.

Again, this is of immediate consequence to other lenders, since the company's access to alternative liquidity will be constrained when most needed and cross-default provisions could also be triggered. MAC clauses are not without problems for the banks that try to implement them, not least because they are subjective in nature and in need of interpretation. Without the establishment of prior guidelines, who is to say whether an adverse change is 'material'?

As such, these clauses might be paper tigers but other creditors should at least be aware of their existence and factor them into their analysis of a company's liquidity. For instance, under English law, it has historically been difficult to successfully call a MAC event of default. The courts have generally required an insolvent borrower, or an event that has made insolvency look highly likely, before they allow the lender to accelerate facilities on the basis of a material adverse change. Famously, during WPP's takeover of the Tempus Group in 2001, even the events of 11 September were not considered a MAC.[138]

Other sources of liquidity

Apart from cash and committed lines, where else can a company source cash if it finds itself strapped? Even if banks have become a little leery of lending to a corporate entity, they might well find assets within the company against which they are willing to lend on a secured basis or which they are willing to securitise. A manufacturing company might at

do?rand=hJR4JB00QX&articleId=548220&from=CR [Accessed 24 November 2014].

138   The Takeover Panel (2001): 'Offer by WPP Group PLC for Tempus Group PLC'. [Online]. Available at: **www.thetakeoverpanel.org.uk/wp-content/uploads/2008/12/2001-15.pdf**. [Accessed 26 November 2014].

any time have 30–45 days worth of sales tied up in its accounts receivable (sales made to third parties for which invoices have been issued but cash not yet received). If the customer is a sound, high quality credit, a bank or other investors could be persuaded to purchase these receivables from the company at a discount, providing the company with a source of short-term financing, which, as long as it keeps making sales, is reliable alternative liquidity. Companies might well keep this option open in addition to a committed bank line because it could provide a cheaper source of financing.

Commitments made for this type of lending arrangement are typically quite short-dated – 365 days – and are therefore a less reliable source of alternative liquidity than a committed bank line of longer duration. However, an investor might derive greater comfort with a company's ability to roll receivables financing if the customer that provides it relies heavily on the goods the creditor supplies and cannot easily find another source and if the credit quality of the customer is sound. As indicated earlier, high-yield US truck parts supplier, Meritor, maintained off-balance-sheet receivables financing arrangements worth $400m at the end of the last fiscal year[139] (compared to $499m available under its committed credit facility), some of which related to the sale of receivables from the investment-grade rated global lorry manufacturer, Volvo. We believe the latter to be Meritor's largest single customer and, it could be argued, would be unlikely to switch suppliers quickly if Meritor performed to standard. As a result, one might assume that this financing arrangement was quite stable in nature.

Corporate managements can also economise and divert cash from other discretionary uses, which an investor can analyse. How much of a company's capital expenditure is essential rather than discretionary? If cash is tight, capital expenditure related to growth and discretionary projects can be suspended, freeing up cash for debt service; indeed, some essential capital expenditure can be deferred, too, although the maintenance of such action will ultimately jeopardise the company's longer-term survival.

Suspend the dividend

In companies that elect to pay dividends to shareholders, management can also reduce or suspend them or pay them in kind (a so-called scrip dividend) in order to preserve cash. However, credit investors must always bear in mind that it is management's job as agents of the company's shareholders to maximise their returns after contractual obligations have been met. Thus, since dividend reduction/suspension is not usually a popular move with shareholders (especially if they have come to regard the company in question as an 'income' rather than a 'growth' stock), it will not be undertaken lightly.

That said, in the period following the Lehman débâcle and, in the more recent eurozone crisis, we have seen companies as diverse as the American lightbulb-to-leasing Leviathan,

---

139   Meritor (2014). 'Form 10-K for the year ending September 28, 2014'. [Online]. Available at: **investors. meritor.com/phoenix.zhtml?c=122961&p=irol-sec&secCat01.1_rs=1&secCat01.1_rc=10&control_ searchbox=&control_selectgroup=1** [Accessed 24 November 2014].

General Electric,[140] and Italian mega-utility, Enel,[141] cut dividends to ensure an adequate cushion of debt-protection.

Pledge assets

Managements can also take individual assets and either sell them or find innovative ways to extract additional liquidity from them. Real estate is often among the first assets to be targeted because under normal circumstances most companies do not need to own property to function (it can be rented). In addition, it is not uncommon for large corporations that have fallen from grace to be sitting on 'trophy' real estate assets purchased during their salad days (think of the Pan-Am building that straddles Park Avenue in New York like a colossus and, since the airline's demise, briefly became a trophy asset for insurer, MetLife, which sold it in 2005).

Companies often extract liquidity from such assets through a 'sale-leaseback', whereby they sell the building to a third party for an upfront cash payment and then lease it back from them. While this is a credible way of drumming up cash at short notice, remember our earlier observations about operating leases. Inasmuch as the lease forces the company to make regular payments to continue to enjoy the use of the building, it has debt-like characteristics and should be included in an adjusted assessment of total debt.

Alternatively, a company could seek to raise a loan through a mortgage on the property to realise additional liquidity. This could be an attractive option for a company that has a number of large real estate assets with individually identifiable cash flows, such as hotels. Spanish hotelier, Meliá Hotels International, is a highly leveraged company that regularly sails close to the edge of its debt covenants. However, its significant portfolio of unencumbered properties has enabled it to renew financing arrangements through mortgage debt.[142] Its property assets were recently valued at a 61% premium to their book value.[143]

Sell the family silver

In extremis, companies that have multiple operations can sell some of the assets or businesses they own. Such a transaction might have the double benefit not merely of realising liquidity but of reducing the company's debt burden by selling the business with its debt. The overall impact on debt-protection measurements will depend on the earnings and cash flow generation derived from the divested entity.

140   Glader, P., Laise, E and Browning, E.S. (2009). 'GE Joins Parade of Deep Dividend Cuts'. [Online]. Available at: **online.wsj.com/articles/SB123575953983996113** [Accessed 24 November 2014].

141   Moloney, M. and Emsden, C. (2012). 'Enel Cuts Dividend, Investment Plans'. [Online]. Available at: **online.wsj.com/articles/SB10001424052970204781804577269513448361608** [Accessed 24 November 2014].

142   Meliá Hotels International (2013). 'Meliá First-Half 2013 Results'. [Online]. Available at: **www. meliahotelsinternational.com/sites/default/files/informes-financieros/Speech%20Transcription%20 sin%20Q%26A.pdf** [Accessed 24 November 2014].

143   Meliá Hotels International (2012). 'Everything is possible. Valuation of company assets. March 2012'. [Online]. Available at: **www.meliahotelsinternational.com/sites/default/files/informes-financieros/ Valuation%20of%20Company%20Assets%20March%202012.pdf** [Accessed 24 November 2014].

Ascribing values to businesses is a book in its own right but, to the extent that the earnings of the business to be divested are known, investors can apply an earnings multiple from comparable publicly traded businesses and produce a rough estimate of the proceeds that could be realised from an asset sale. To be on the safe side, they should assume a haircut for the fact that it is a fire-sale (if would-be buyers know the company is strapped for cash, they have little incentive to pay top dollar). Moreover, if a company is really staring insolvency in the face, it might find no takers at all. Would-be buyers might feel they could wait and pick up the business more cheaply from bankruptcy.

In addition, in some jurisdictions, if the sale of an important business fails to staunch the sellers' problems and the seller subsequently files for bankruptcy, its shareholders and creditors might try to claim that the sale was a 'fraudulent conveyance'. This could discourage potential buyers from acting before bankruptcy is declared.

It is impossible within the remit of this book to furnish an exhaustive analysis of how an investor should assess sources of alternative liquidity, especially if a company is in distress. What we have tried to provide is a few pointers both to the pitfalls of traditional 'safe' sources of cash and to value which might be concealed within a company. Beyond that, it is really down to digging down into each individual case.

Liquidity case study II: Clear Channel Communications

Radio broadcasting and outdoor advertising giant Clear Channel Communications (CCU) provides us with a good reference point for liquidity analysis as it is one of the most highly levered of the large LBOs that have (at least so far) survived the financial crisis and retained a degree of market access. By any definition, CCU has a large, highly levered and complex capital structure with significant layering of seniority between pre-and post-LBO lenders and a wide range of covenant structures and financing carve-outs that all have to be taken into account in any serious analysis.

Despite the poor timing of the buyout, which was announced more or less at the extremes of the credit bubble and completed as the first signs of distress started to appear at Bear Stearns and Lehman Brothers, the post-LBO capital structure was put into place in 2008 and has, at least so far, proved to have sufficient flexibility to enable the company and its PE sponsors to weather an extremely turbulent period in both financial and operational terms since the buyout.

When CCU emerged from behind the curtains of the LBO in early 2008, its new balance sheet was a thing of wonder – a veritable poster child for the excesses that had led the world financial system to the brink of collapse. The company was carrying $15.7bn of senior secured debt, and a further $3.1bn of senior unsecured debt, all financed by an entity that, in the previous fiscal year, had generated $2.3bn of EBITDA and $1bn of free cash flow on a pre-LBO debt burden of $6.5bn.

It now faced the prospect of paying roughly $1.4bn of interest alone on the new capital structure every year, not to mention that it was facing sporadic bond maturities from the pre-LBO days and had a steepening amortisation schedule from the new capital structure with major refinancing hurdles in 2013 and 2014. Moody's had moved its senior unsecured rating down from a low investment grade of Baa3 to a deep junk Caa1 (it moved it down further to Ca, indicative of a somewhat hand-to-mouth existence at one stage, though ratings continue to fluctuate).

In short, many observers took the view that CCU had all the characteristics of an impending liquidity (and indeed solvency) crisis, even without the additional complications of an operational environment that seemed on the verge of becoming extremely challenging.

Group revenues, which had already contracted by 3.4% year-on-year in 2008, suddenly sank by a further 16.3% in 2009 and cash flow generation fell by 19% and 3% in these years, respectively, despite heroic cost-cutting efforts from the company's new owners. As figure 10 demonstrates, the CDS market priced the company for more or less imminent bankruptcy. Yet CCU is still with us today, with its star radio broadcasters such as Rush Limbaugh continuing to outrage right- (or rather, moderate-) thinking people across the USA. How, you may well ask, has it survived?

FIGURE 10: CLEAR CHANNEL COMMUNICATIONS - FIVE-YEAR CDS SPREAD

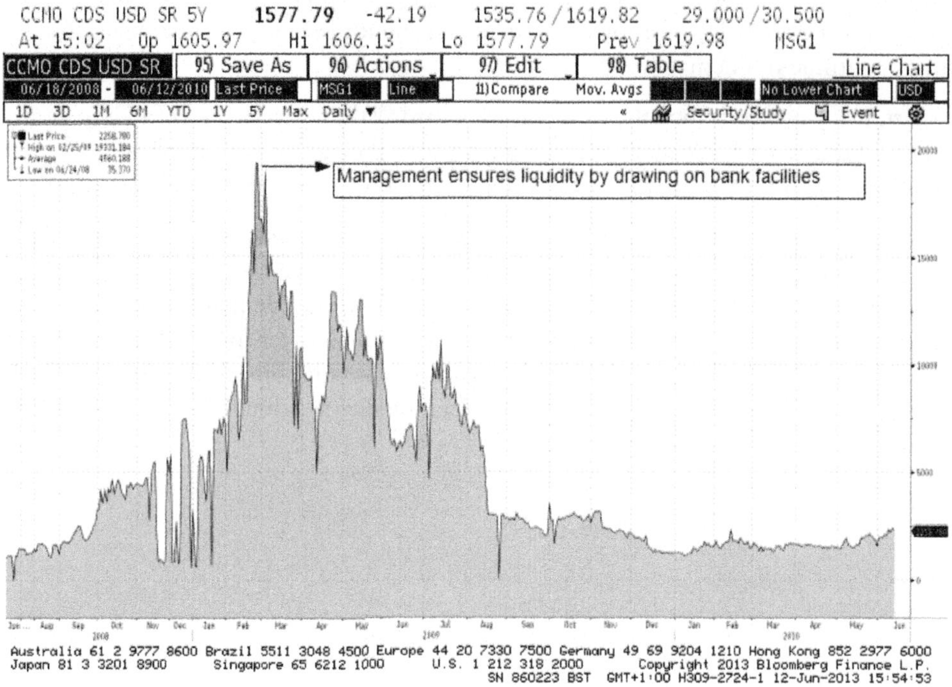

Source: Bloomberg

Equity optionality – the distressed lender's friend

After protracted wrangling, the deal closed on 31 July 2008, a month and a half before Lehman Brothers filed for bankruptcy. On the face of it, CCU's sponsors were facing a potential financial disaster. The PE groups involved had just spent $25.5bn of (mostly borrowed) money on a highly cyclical, ex-growth business that was now entering the most dramatic economic downturn of the previous 80 years. The $25.5bn represented an entry multiple of 11x the company's 2007 EBITDA. If the sponsors were to make any money for themselves and their investors on the deal, they would have to either pay down the LBO debt from CCU's own cash flow over time and then re-list it on the stock market, or contrive to sell the company for a higher multiple than they bought it for.

In short, CCU's outlook was bleak. This very bleakness, however, meant that the sponsors were under great pressure to try to do whatever they could to keep the company as a going concern, buying time and minimising reputational and financial damage to themselves.

Let us examine this period systematically in terms of CCU's liquidity and look at the options that the company decided to exercise in the course of its difficult first years as a privately held entity.

Firstly, how much cash was on CCU's balance sheet at this time?

TABLE 38: CLEAR CHANNEL COMMUNICATIONS - CASH BALANCES

US$ million	3/31/08	6/30/08	9/30/08	12/31/08
Cash and equivalents	433	668	244	1,500

Source: Company accounts

Secondly, what financial debt maturities was the company facing?

TABLE 39: CLEAR CHANNEL COMMUNICATIONS - DEBT MATURITIES

US$ million	3/31/08	6/30/08	9/30/08	12/31/08
Debt maturities	0	0	364	60

Source: Company accounts

From this, we can see that, even if the company were operating on a cash-flow neutral basis, the maturities it was facing in the third quarter of 2008 had severely reduced its cash balance to pay for its ongoing operations. We can also see that the fourth quarter cash balance had suddenly risen to $1.5bn. Did CCU perform an operational miracle in the last quarter of 2008?

Hardly. To explain what happened here, we need to move to the third element of our liquidity analysis: CCU's remaining un-drawn bank facilities. Despite its already massive debt burden, CCU's buyers had wisely negotiated further delayed draw facilities of $2bn, which carried a secured leverage covenant of 9.5×. Now, in the third quarter of 2008, at the senior secured level, CCU was a mere 9× levered, and, despite the operational distress the company was suffering that year, revenues in this industry are seasonally strongest in the fourth quarter of the calendar year. This meant that leverage was likely to decline by year-end, despite a higher absolute level of debt. Therefore CCU's bankers, who were already on the hook for $13.5bn in September 2008, were obliged to extend a further $1.5bn of credit to the company, taking total leverage (that is, including unsecured bonds) to a staggering 10.7×.

TABLE 40: CLEAR CHANNEL COMMUNICATIONS – DEBT AND LEVERAGE 2008-2009

US$m	3/31/08	6/30/08	9/30/08	12/31/08	3/31/09	6/30/09	9/30/09	12/31/09
Secured bank debt	13,470	13,453	13,593	15,093	15,291	15,955	16,053	16,014
Guaranteed and secured debt	15,780	15,763	15,903	17,403	17,601	18,265	18363	18,324
Total debt	20,805	20,788	20,642	22,082	22,278	22,441	22,538	22,497
Sr. sec. debt/ LTM EBITDA	5.8×	5.4×	9.0×	8.7×	7.9×	8.3×	9.0×	8.7×
Bank covenant	9.5×	9.5×	9.5×	9.5×	9.5×	9.5×	9.5×	9.5×
Pass/fail	Pass	Pass	Pass	Pass	Pass	Pass	Pass	Pass
Total debt/ EBITDA	9.0×	8.5×	8.7×	10.7×	11.7×	11.8×	12.1×	11.6×

Source: Authors' calculations

It can be seen from the above that the company remained within its covenants for the period. Did it have any material non-core assets for de-levering? Some, perhaps, key amongst which was a majority stake in Clear Channel Outdoor (CCO), its listed billboard advertising subsidiary, which proved very useful to the parent company from a liquidity standpoint. CCO was able to raise debt in its own name in 2009 and then make an inter-company loan to CCU.

How about free cash flow generation over the period? Here, again, the PE sponsors were facing apparently insurmountable odds. Let us take a closer look at free cash-flow generation over this time.

TABLE 41: CLEAR CHANNEL COMMUNICATIONS - FREE CASH FLOW SUMMARY 2008-2009

US$m	3/31/08	6/30/08	9/30/08	12/31/08	3/31/09	6/30/09	9/30/09	12/31/09
EBITDA (adjusted)	407	800	509	348	241	373	373	408
Interest expense	-408	-348	-330	-332	-315	-306	-298	-298
Taxes	-67	-125	52	59	-27	-135	-77	26
Working capital	71	-108	93	0	0	0	0	0
Capex (maintenance)	-43	-38	-29	-45	-45	-45	-45	-45
Capex (expansion)	-50	-80	-49	-50	-50	-50	-50	-50
Free cash flow	-47	134	321	-19	-196	-163	-97	41

Source: Authors' calculations

By starving the company of investment and cutting operating costs from $4.4bn a year in 2007 to $2.7bn in 2009, the owners were able to limit the annual peak–trough fall in EBITDA to 21%, keeping the show on the road with the aid of additional borrowings and an inter-company loan from CCO.

In summary, CCU's liquidity proved sufficient to meet all loan maturities and interest payments over the peak of the credit crunch and beyond. Although this is an extreme case, it shows that, for a highly levered company, an intense focus on liquidity can keep a firm within its covenants and retain its solvency through all but the most challenging economic times, thereby rendering its short-dated debt issues potentially interesting investments.

6

How Non-Credit Factors Drive Credit

ONE KEY FACTOR IN MAKING MONEY FROM CREDIT OFTEN RESIDES IN SPOTTING transitions in credit risk early on. Unfortunately, such transition risk is not always first signalled by credit market variables. Investors must be ready to read tea-leaves from other cups, since markets for other parts of a company's capital structure may signal change first.

A rigorous quantitative credit analysis of a credit is a vital part of the overall assessment of its attractiveness as a potential investment, but there are other, non-credit-specific elements that enable the investor to position the credit in a broader context, and look at other potential sources of threat to the bondholder's interests.

Four principal areas are well worth investigation to shed light on the context in which each credit is operating:

1. Equity performance

For those companies that have a listed equity, the performance of the stock is an obvious indicator of corporate good- or ill-health, and should reflect recent news-flow on the company. The relative performance of the company's stock should be compared against a general index, or, more meaningfully, against a sector peer group. Furthermore, many of the quantitative credit assessment tools that are available from online providers such as Bond Score or Moody's KMV factor equity volatility into their models as a determinant of credit trajectory.

2. Equity valuation relative to industry peers

We look at a range of traditional equity valuation measures. Price/earnings, enterprise value/EBITDA, dividend and free cash-flow yield vs. sector peers. If the market is valuing a company significantly below its peer group, it can indicate that idiosyncratic factors are at play that are worthy of further investigation. If, on the other hand, the company is trading significantly above the valuation of its peers, this may be a reflection of the market's expectations of M&A activity, involving the company in question as a target.

3. Viability as an LBO

Those who can remember the credit markets before the financial crisis struck may still struggle to recall that, in the heady days of 2006 and early 2007, a good portion of the analytical effort going into the credit markets was dedicated to divining whether or not solid, investment-grade corporates were in danger of undergoing an LBO, funded by a combination of what was then a seemingly-inexhaustible supply of credit and the bulging purses of the PE houses.

Venerable corporations of all sizes went under the market's microscope as potential LBOs, and countless millions were invested in establishing short positions in the credits of those companies that seemed the most likely candidates. In hindsight, and indeed, even at the time, some of the market's supposed LBO targets were absurd. Vodafone, with a £100bn market capitalisation, Home Depot, which in 2006 had an enterprise value of $90bn, and the Hershey Company, defended by a controlling trust with super-voting stock, were among the names that were the focus of speculative LBO-related activity in the credit markets. That said, a staid, regulated electric utility, TXU, became the world's largest-ever LBO while, as we have seen, a specialist lender/servicer of government-subsidised student credits, SLM, was only just saved by the bell.

Although the vast majority of these LBOs never existed beyond the models of analysts, the risk to credit holders in the event of an LBO taking place is real enough, so it is always worth undertaking a preliminary analysis of the viability of any credit being considered for your portfolio as an LBO candidate. Those that seem most viable should then be more rigorously modelled.

One of the few discernible benefits of living in the gloomy days of deleveraging bank balance sheets and constrained liquidity is that LBOs have, so far, not been a first-order risk for credit investors. Although equity market valuations are generally a deterrent to LBO activity, the PE houses are once more replete with investor funds and market conditions are again moving in their favour. In fact, although some of the loose credit conditions that fostered the LBO boom of the mid-2000s have vanished since the credit crunch, the very financial conditions that have prevailed since that crunch – principally loose monetary policy characterised by quantitative easing – have allowed many of the most aggressively financed of the deals of this era to survive well beyond the timespan that would ordinarily have been expected of them. 'Zombie' credits, whose demise would have been assured under normal financial conditions, are still walking the earth. These conditions cannot endure indefinitely and the day of reckoning will come. Indeed, as we write, high levels of corporate liquidity and a renewed market appetite for high-yield corporate bonds have fostered a steady increase in the levels of leverage being employed in LBOs. The average leverage in LBOs moved from 3.7× in 2009 to 5.4× in 2013,[144] though leverage has generally been more judiciously applied than in the credit bubble years. One senses, however, that it is only a matter of time before the cycle turns again and we see the next round of mega-deals totter out, laden with PIK-toggle note structures that have already reached issuance levels matching those before the financial crisis. Fortunately, on this occasion, the regulators have been more proactive in limiting reckless lending, with both the Fed and OCC leaning heavily on banks to keep leverage and maturities on a manageable basis.

---

144 *The Financial Times* (2013). 'Boom-era credit deals raise fears of overheating.' [Online]. Available at: **www.ft.com/cms/s/0/f151df3a-3a6f-11e3-9243-00144feab7de.html#axzz3SZ1JqdJZ**. [Accessed 24 November 2014].

4. Quick and dirty LBO analysis

Many of the inputs needed to perform an initial LBO analysis on a credit are readily available. The vital ones are as follows:

- **Enterprise value[145] of the target.** This is the starting point for any analysis. Depending on market conditions, this can be the single most important limiting factor. Assume that stockholders will require a premium to this number in order to be persuaded to part with their shares. How big a premium is subjective, but recently-completed transactions provide a useful benchmark. It is also important to assess the current leverage of the target. Is the company in question already carrying a substantial debt burden? If so, how viable would it be in the context of an additional debt load from an LBO?

- **Potential for subordination.** Does the existing (pre-LBO) debt carry any change-of-control language which would require it to be refinanced as a high-yield deal? Putting it crudely, the larger the financing needs of the post-LBO entity, the less likely the deal is to get done.

- **Theoretical rating of the LBO and legacy debt.** How would the post-deal company be rated at the senior unsecured level? The senior unsecured ratings would be subject to significant notching downwards, depending on the amount of secured debt ahead of the high-yield bonds in the putative capital structure. In turn, the rating would materially influence the cost of debt.

- **Potential profitability of the LBO.** Private equity sponsors are really only paid to make money. The less likely a deal can be made to work on paper, the less likely it is to get done. In assessing the risk of an LBO happening, this area is open to manipulation (especially by sell-side analysts with an agenda), and there is no substitute for doing your own analysis. Common approaches used in research documents to enhance the internal rate of return (IRR) of rumoured deals are to assign unrealistic values to non-core businesses that are to be disposed of, to reduce the pro-forma cost of debt at the post-LBO business and to grant an overly optimistic exit multiple to the eventual re-sale of the company. It is well worth dissecting each of these before jumping to conclusions.

- **M&A trends within the Sector.** Do the valuations at which a potential target for an LBO is being discussed reflect those of recent transactions within the relevant industrial sector? A quick read-through of news reports on recent M&A activity in the sector can shed light on the probability of an approach being made. If the market valuation of the company in question is significantly higher than those of recent transactions, then there is a significant obstacle in the way of potential buyers. In order for a highly-valued deal to make economic sense, there would have to be material synergy opportunities or undervalued non-core assets ready for disposal.

---

145 Enterprise value = market capitalisation + net debt.

LBO case study I: VNU/Nielsen

Having outlined the major areas of focus in the analysis of a potential LBO, it is worth running through an actual example of a credit that was LBO'd in highly uncertain circumstances and that has been through the de-levering process and subsequently returned to a public listing. In the course of this transition from public to private hands and back to public, its stock moved from an Amsterdam to a New York listing.

In 2005, VNU was already beginning to attract the attentions of activist shareholder groups after its abortive merger with IMS Health, which was vetoed in a shareholder revolt and left the management team looking vulnerable. While the company was headquartered and listed in the Netherlands, the bulk of its business was done in the USA. Shareholders complained that VNU could never achieve a valuation multiple that was appropriate to its attractive mix of businesses, focused on media and marketing information analysis, in a relatively narrow domestic market such as Amsterdam, and that management, whose members were preponderantly Dutch nationals, were missing out on an opportunity to drive shareholder value by retaining the domestic market as the company's principal listing.

The company's principal businesses offered market share data as well as insights into distribution, pricing and promotional activities in retailing, media, telecom and entertainment markets. Most of these businesses had long-term contracts and were in the number one or two position in their markets, making them hard for clients to substitute. A solid business profile with strong earnings visibility is just the kind of business that can successfully service and pay down a significant debt load.

1. Enterprise value of the target

VNU's pre-LBO debt burden was €2.3bn, approximately 3.9× its fiscal-year 2005 EBITDA. Net of the company's cash balance of €861m (which is the figure we should use to calculate enterprise value or EV), this amounted to 2.3× the previous year's EBITDA, which had earned it high BBB ratings over the previous four years. So, prior to any LBO-based activity, VNU had an 'undisturbed' EV of €8.6bn at year-end 2005 (Market cap of €7.1 plus net debt of €1.5bn). The EV/LTM (last 12 months) EBITDA ratio was 14.6×.

Starting from this last statistic, it can be seen that there was a considerable barrier to getting this deal done just in the form of the company's pre-LBO valuation. Coming up with a premium to entice shareholders to part with their stock might mean pushing the valuation beyond the level at which the PE sponsors could actually make money. Many thought that a deal could not be done. When an offer did materialise from a PE consortium, the offer of €29.50 per share was only at a modest premium to the previous trading price of the share (around 7%) – under normal circumstances, hardly a knockout blow. However, despite a brief campaign to militate for a higher offer price, most shareholders eventually did capitulate, when confronted with the prisoner's dilemma that, after all of the recent turmoil at the company, the market price of the share was likely to collapse if the deal did not go through.

2. Potential for subordination

If an investor is caught off guard by an LBO (i.e. they still have credit exposure), then, rather than panicking out of a position, we would counsel doing further analysis to attempt to determine the LBO's chances of success and what the likelihood may be of getting paid out even in a legacy position. One key factor that has to be taken into account here is the concept of subordination, which poses a threat in three possible ways – contractual, structural and temporal subordination all pose risks to a bondholder's chances of getting his or her money.

VNU's existing bonds contained fairly conventional investment-grade covenants and investor protection language, most of which, in practice, can be side-stepped by adroit PE firms by keeping existing bonds outstanding and funding the LBO through a separate vehicle. Figure 11 contains the eventual corporate financing structure of the new, post-LBO Nielsen entity, as set out in the prospectus for the high-yield bonds that were used to finance the LBO. The term 'structural subordination' could have been invented with it in mind.

The key first impression striking the viewer of the above diagram is perhaps the contrast between how close the new financing entities (Nielsen Finance LLC and Nielsen Finance Co.) are to the operating assets of the company and how far, through layers of subsidiary entities there is between these operating assets and the original investment-grade bonds (issued by VNU towards the top of the picture). This image neatly summarises the subordination of the original bonds.

The bonds of the old VNU amount to approximately €720m. After the LBO, they are structurally and contractually subordinated to the new $5,168m of senior secured bank loans, they are structurally subordinated to the $835m senior notes offered in the prospectus and they are contractually senior, though structurally subordinated, to the yet-to-be-specified amount of senior subordinated discount notes.

FIGURE 11: VNU CORPORATE STRUCTURE

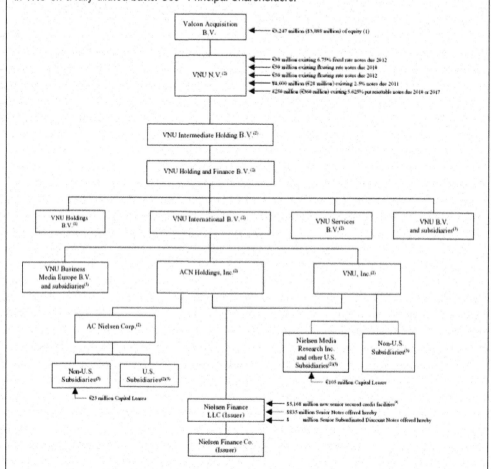

Corporate Structure

As set forth in the diagram below, following consummation of the Transactions, all of our issued and outstanding capital stock will be held by Valcon, and investment funds associated with or designated by the Sponsors, together with the Co-Investors, will, indirectly through their ownership interest in the parent companies of Valcon, own 100% of the issued and outstanding share capital in VNU on a fully diluted basis. See "Principal Shareholders."

(1) Includes cash equity contributed or assumed to be contributed to Valcon through its parent companies by investment funds associated with or designated by the Sponsors and the Co-Investors. As of July 5, 2006, €3,094 million (based on actual contributions of $3,575 million and €109 million) of cash equity had been contributed by investment funds associated with or designated by the Sponsors.

(2) Each of VNU, VNU Intermediate Holding B.V., VNU Holding and Finance B.V., VNU Holdings B.V., VNU International B.V., VNU Services B.V., ACN Holdings, Inc., VNU, Inc. and the wholly owned subsidiaries thereof, including the wholly owned U.S. subsidiaries of ACN Holdings, Inc. and VNU, Inc., in each case that guarantee the new senior secured credit facilities are expected to guarantee the notes. Neither VNU nor VNU Intermediate Holding B.V. will be subject to any of

Source: Offering prospectus

Is time on your side?

Still, there was hope for the former VNU investment grade believers, at least those who had patience and loose ratings criteria for their portfolio constituents. Despite the multiple layers of contractual and structural subordination between them and VNU's cash flows, despite their ratings' having slipped deep into junk territory, reflecting a high probability of default, despite all – most of them were temporally senior to the LBO financing. That is to say that, although in a bankruptcy they would be at the back of the queue for any payout, in a going concern situation, many of them had relatively short-term maturities. Assuming VNU stayed in business, they would be repaid before almost any of the new debt (barring a few amortisation payments on the bank deal).

It may have taken a strong stomach for bondholders to stay with their holdings, and indeed, many were forced to sell their positions at a loss because of ratings constraints on their portfolios, but ultimately these bonds were repaid at par. VNU's strong business profile and the sponsors' active management of the franchise combined to repay debt and emerge a more efficient company than in its pre-LBO guise.

Indeed, this story has a happy ending – since 2011, the former VNU is now listed on the NYSE as Nielsen Holdings, under the ticker NLSN.

3. Theoretical rating of the LBO

An EV of €8.9bn constitutes a large LBO, though the VNU deal was to be dwarfed by the deals that were later completed in the course of 2007–8 at the height of the credit bubble. In practical terms, a larger EV requires a higher proportion of bank financing, since typically only a relatively modest proportion of the deal's debt could realistically be funded in the less liquid high-yield bond market. A high proportion of bank financing typically is only available on a secured basis, which immediately contractually subordinates other debt.

VNU's initial pro-forma leverage was very high, at around 9× LTM EBITDA, while approximately 67% of the LBO's total debt was secured. This debt was rated high single B by the agencies, and its size and the security held by the banks led to senior unsecured debt being rated at high CCC, which is arguably the lowest rating at which new bond financing can realistically be raised.

4. Potential profitability of the deal

Potential profitability should be the next area for analysis, a kind of sanity check on the viability of the supposed deal. Armed with a pro-forma rating for the company's debt instruments, it becomes possible to model its finances with a reasonable degree of certainty as to the likely cost of financing at the various levels. In the event, while the LBO had to offer generous coupons of 9%, 10% and 12.5% on its unsecured and subordinated bonds in order to get them sold, its banks offered it significantly enhanced terms of LIBOR plus 3% on the term loans and revolving credit facility. This is one of the key variables in forecasting the potential IRRs of LBOs. Low IRRs offer poor risk/reward opportunities and reputational risk to PE firms.

TABLE 42: PRO-FORMA FINANCING COST OF THE VNU LBO CAPITAL STRUCTURE

Debt instrument	Coupon	Annual interest cost
New bank facilities		
Revolving credit	LIBOR + 3%	$44m
Term loans	LIBOR + 3%	$410m
New bonds		
$650m senior notes	10%	$65m
$150m senior notes	9%	$13.5m
$590m sub. notes	12.5%	$73.5m (max)
Pre-LBO bonds	5.9% (weighted avg)	$93m
Total (pro-forma)		$699m

Source: Authors' calculations

It is safe to assume that the PE sponsors are at least as aware of the need to make a positive IRR on their investment as bondholders. The sponsors of the VNU LBO saw scope to achieve this even having paid what was then the highest EV/EBITDA multiple in the European media sector. What levers were there for them to pull to enhance their returns?

By performing a simple IRR calculation on the proposed transaction, under a range of scenarios, it is possible to understand what steps might hypothetically be required to achieve the kind of IRR targets (in the low-mid teens) that PE investors seek from a deal. If it didn't make sense financially, it would pose a far greater risk to debt-holders as the sponsors would be more aggressive in pursuing their returns.

TABLE 43: SIMPLE IRR CALCULATION FOR VNU LBO

1. Enterprise value at purchase	$10.3bn
2. Entry multiple of EBITDA	15.6× (2005A) 15.3× 2006E
3. Interest cost (annual Y1)	$ 699m
4. Non-core disposals	$1.5bn
5. Estimated holding period (years)	6
6. Y1 EBITDA ($)	$700
7. Annual EBITDA growth %	15%
8. Free cash flow to de-lever (cumulative over six years)	$1.5bn
9. Exit multiple of EBITDA	12.7× (LTM at time of listing)
10. EV at exit	$17.129bn
11. IRR (estimate	13% (excl. dividends)

Source: Authors' calculations

The table helps to highlight the key areas for exploration. These are how the quant factors stacked up for VNU. In the notes below, the terms negative and positive refer to factors affecting the viability of the LBO:

1. Entry enterprise value – big, meaning existing bonds will be deeply subordinated. **Negative**.

2. Entry multiple of EBITDA – to get a positive IRR, you need either to increase the multiple on exit, grow EBITDA or, ideally, do both. **Neutral** – the sponsors paid a high price for a high quality acyclical business with prospects.

3. Estimated interest cost – big annual payments relative to EBITDA will drag down IRR. **Negative** – barely covered in the first year. The pressure is on to make inroads into the debt.

4. Potential non-core disposals – **Positive** – there are sizeable assets that could be sold on without damaging the core franchises.

5. Estimated Holding Period – **Neutral** as entirely subjective

And ...

7. EBITDA growth needs to be strong to achieve target IRRs – **Neutral**

8. Cumulative free cash flow. **Positive** – if the growth forecasts are plausible

9. Exit Multiple. **Positive** – can be lower than entry multiple if growth can be achieved. In fact, as 9 and 7 are dependent variables, it is clear that there is some flexibility in the structure.

Bottom line - a viable LBO

So, three positives, three neutrals and two negatives. On balance, the deal can be seen to make sense, though it clearly entails a good deal of risk. Although the initial financing structure of the LBO is aggressive, there are grounds for believing that its objectives are achievable and that, as a senior unsecured bondholder with few rights, you are not facing an imminent liquidity or solvency crisis.

In fact, most LBOs build in a window over an initial period of one to three years where the capital structure and covenant terms are relatively undemanding. Owning short-dated bonds in these deals, even if they lack covenant protection, can be a profitable trading strategy.

Our simple IRR calculation derives free cash flow over a given time frame by deducting interest cost and maintenance capex from the forecast EBITDA of the LBO target at a given rate of growth. A 13% IRR is acceptable, and, although initial leverage was high, there was scope for material debt paydown over a medium-term holding period.

In fact, over the six years that followed the buyout, a rationalisation of the firm's cost base and distribution methods enhanced VNU's margins, meaning that a strong compound annual growth rate (CAGR) of EBITDA was achieved. Given the company's stable revenue profile and leading market positions, there was scope for the PE sponsors to improve the underlying profitability of the business without destabilising its core.

As it turned out, their ability to do so confounded the sceptics. They were able to add nearly ten percentage points to the EBITDA margin and roughly double the operating margin between 2006 and 2010. With the EBITDA margin rising so strongly, the leverage assumed in the LBO went from being extreme to becoming more easily manageable, and was further enhanced by free cash flow and non-core disposals to further erode the initial debt burden.

M&A trends within the sector

A quick reality check on the levels at which recent transactions have been completed within the target's industrial sector can often shed light on whether or not it is actually worth going through the process of performing a thorough-going LBO analysis on a company. Although PE firms have been known to outbid potential industrial buyers in their pursuit of an attractive target, in practice this rarely happens. Unless an LBO firm already has a significant number of portfolio companies within the relevant sector, then it is unlikely to be able to match the synergies that would be available to an industrial buyer of the same company. For this reason alone, the valuation levels at which deals in the sector have been completed is a helpful rule of thumb in assessing whether or not an LBO is likely to be feasible.

Before taking this logic too far, we should issue a word of warning. Since PE buyers are not constrained by the same criteria as listed industrial companies, some deals are viable for them that would potentially be dilutive to the earnings of an industrial. For instance, if a company pays a higher valuation for a target than its own market valuation, then the deal will push up the acquirer's cost of capital and potentially be value-destructive unless it can achieve significant operational and/or purchasing synergies. For a PE firm, the goal of achieving an acceptable IRR for the risk involved can be assessed more idiosyncratically.

LBO analysis can highlight other areas of credit risk

This is a rich and complex topic, replete with areas in which subjective value calls must be made with the backing of imperfect data. One reason that we have laboured the detail in assessing LBO risk is that many of the same analytical processes should be undertaken in any credit assessment. If a company's equity is severely underperforming the sector peer group, this can in itself be an indicator of poor corporate and credit health.

Similarly, if there is a significant mismatch between the market's valuation of a company's equity and the underlying value of its assets and cash flows, then this is likely to attract the attention of both PE and industry buyers. Likewise, a large cash balance, though clearly a positive from a liquidity perspective, can be indicative of a lack of opportunity in the industry, leading companies to take credit-unfriendly action such as share buybacks, diversifying M&A and recapitalisations.

LBOs ≠ defaults, but no room for complacency

Georgia Pacific - Koch and bull

It is important to recognise that not all LBOs have disastrous implications for credit investors. In another case, a senior unsecured bondholder in Georgia Pacific in 2005 was holding a mid-BB piece of paper which seemed to be en route to an investment-grade rating over the course of the next 12 months when the company was effectively LBO'd by a subsidiary of Koch Industries through a special purpose vehicle, sending GP's rating down to single-B. However, by September 2011, with most of the LBO financing repaid from the company's free cash flow, GP's senior unsecured rating had finally risen to investment grade.

Nonetheless, plenty of LBOs truly do pose significant default risk to bondholders, with significant impairments taking place at, among others, Tribune, Seat Pagine Gialle, Schefenacker (now Visiocorp). Recovery rates can be as low as 1.5% of the initial principal lent. Indeed, Moody's reports that many "Bubble-Era" LBOs have performed poorly:

"Moody's studied 40 LBOs rated by the agency during 2006–2008 including casino owner Harrah's Inc., (now known as Caesar's Entertainment Inc.), energy conglomerate Energy Future Holdings Corp. (formerly TXU) [see the case study later in this chapter] and automaker Chrysler LLC. While some companies have seen (ratings) improvement, including discount retailer Dollar General now rated at Ba2, from B3 at the LBO close, only four have obtained a higher rating than during their buyouts without a default." [146]

According to the piece, 15/40 are rated lower than at the point they were LBO'd, 3/40 have filed for bankruptcy and 4/40 have been upgraded. 9/40 have seen their ratings downgraded to the Caa category.

TABLE 44: SELECTED DEFAULTED LBOS 2008-2011 AND SENIOR UNSECURED RECOVERY RATES

Defaulted credit	Credit event	Default date	Recovery rate
Tribune	Bankruptcy	Dec 2008	1.5%
Lyondell	Bankruptcy	Jan 2009	15.5%
Idearc	Bankruptcy	April 2009	1.75%
RH Donnelley	Bankruptcy	May 2009	4.875%
Seat Pagine Gialle	Failure to pay	Dec 2011	10.0%

Source: Markit

Lest we be accused of dismissing the risks to bondholders of many LBO structures, it is well worth examining in more detail one instance in which the outcome for credit has been anything but positive: Energy Future Holdings (formerly TXU).

LBO case study II: TXU

In 2005, TXU was an investment-grade (at the operating subsidiary level) utility, boasting 18,000MW of generating capacity, principally in nuclear and coal/lignite fired plant, owned by a subsidiary called TXU Energy. 8,000MW of the generating capacity is located in Texas,[147] which, subsequent to 1999 legislation, is an unregulated wholesale market managed by the Electric Reliability Council of Texas (ERCOT). At the time, ERCOT had very limited interconnection to the rest of the US transmission system, effectively rendering

---

146 Moody's (2011): 'Lackluster Performance for Bubble-Era Leveraged Buyouts'. [Online]. Available at: **www.moodys.com/research/Moodys-Lackluster-Performance-for-Bubble-Era-Leveraged-Buyouts--PR_232792** [Accessed 24 November 2014].
147 Moody's (2005). 'Analysis: TXU Corp'. [Online]. Available at: **www.moodys.com/ researchdocumentcontentpage.aspx?docid=PBC_94348** [Accessed 24 November 2014].

Texas a 'transmission island' (industry participants and analysts would make jokes about when 'ERCOT would join the Union') and protecting generation within Texas from external competition.

In addition, TXU's thermal assets had a substantial fuel-cost advantage over natural gas-fired plant, which set the market clearing price for power in the ERCOT region. Consequently, when natural gas prices increased, spark spreads (price of electricity - (cost of fuel × heat rate)) also rose, boosting gross margins and allowing the TXU Energy assets to churn off cash. Over 2005, natural gas prices had reached stratospheric levels and, even if they were to moderate, were nonetheless expected to remain elevated.

FIGURE 12: HENRY HUB PRICE ($/MMBTU)

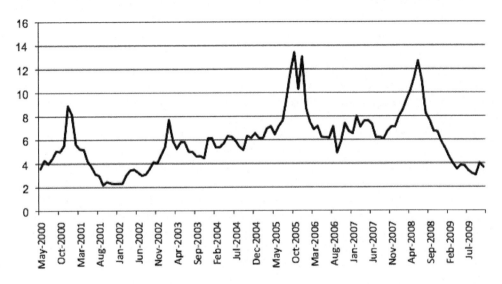

Source: Bloomberg

"[W]e anticipate an environment of sustained high natural gas prices over the intermediate term"[148] wrote Moody's in their analysis of TXU Corp in September 2005 (also, to be fair, noting "uncertainty regarding [the] resiliency of [the] business plan under declining gas price environment"[149], leading them to believe that TXU's ERCOT-based generation would "produce substantial margins and cash flow".[150]

To complete our scene-setting, the reader should remember that these were the years of easy liquidity. Although US intermediate-term rates crept up through 2006–2007, they were still low in the context of recent history. Moreover, credit spreads for high yield credits collapsed over this period, with the median spread of an intermediate-term corporate bond

---

148 Moody's (2005).
149 Moody's (2005).
150 Moody's (2005).

for a B1-rated company shrinking by over 35% from January 1994 to January 2007.[151] So famished were investors for yield that they would abandon traditional covenant protections for a few extra basis points and accept structures which enabled the issuer to pay coupons with more debt that would simply roll up at maturity (so-called payment-in-kind or 'PIK Toggle' bonds). These factors, which, as we have said, are beginning once more to prevail in market conditions, made leverage – and leveraged enhancements to shareholder value – very attractive.

FIGURE 13: US TEN-YEAR TREASURY RATE

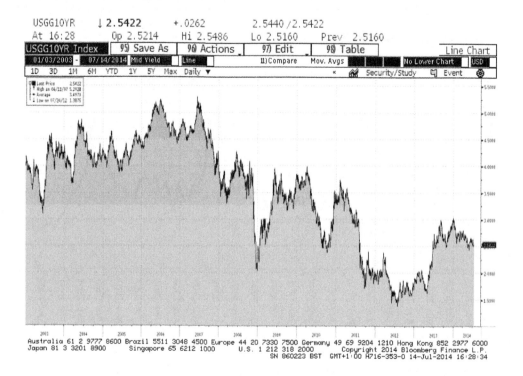

Source: Bloomberg

The growth of the CLO market provided an easy conduit, whereby banks could move loans extended for corporate releveraging initiatives straight to investors. Not surprisingly, the volume of LBOs between 2004 and 2007 was, at $535bn, tenfold that of the period from 1996 to 2003 and more than double that of the last major LBO boom in 1986–1989 (in 2007 dollars).[152]

151 Moody's (2014). 'Moody's Credit Trends' [Online]. Available at: **credittrends.moodys.com/pro/ chartroom_chart.asp?status=1&cid=77** [Accessed 24 November 2014]

152 Shivdasani, A. and Wang, Y. (2011). 'Did Structured Credit Fuel the LBO Boom?. *The Journal of Finance*, 66(4) [Online]. Available at: **onlinelibrary.wiley.com/doi/10.1111/j.1540-6261.2011.01667.x/ abstract** [Accessed 24 November 2014]. *Journal of Finance*, Forthcoming.

TXU: A ground-breaking deal

Many investors doubted that a utility could be LBO'd, let alone a utility of TXU's size. The buy-in of regulators at both the federal and state level would be required, not to mention that of the Nuclear Regulatory Commission, which would have to be convinced that a new, highly leveraged TXU could safely operate nuclear plants. Politicians and consumer advocates would have to be persuaded that additional interest charges would not be paid from higher rates or at the expense of service quality and environmentalists had to be appeased. Also, a deal to LBO TXU, at $45bn, would be the biggest the market had ever attempted.

Such was the conviction that the obstacles to an LBO for TXU would prove insurmountable that even after management received the bid from Kohlberg Kravis Roberts & Co (KKR) and Texas Pacific Group (TPG) and Moody's had warned of potential multi-notch downgrades, Moody's Credit Strategy Group stated that " … past experience indicates that there could be value in selling CDS protection (i.e. going long TXU risk) at these levels … "[153] which reached 214bps (for five-year protection) on 7 March 2007.

But the deal, which was indeed the biggest LBO in history, did go ahead and TXU was taken private. When the deal was approved by shareholders on 7 September 2007, five-year CDS had reached 507bps[154] – almost 100% wider than when Moody's first mooted the possibility of long risk. Existing bondholders suffered multiple downgrades (from Ba1/ BBB- at the senior unsecured level for TXU to B3/B-) reflecting not merely a huge increase in leverage and financial risk (with total debt/trailing 12-month EBITDA increasing from 2.27× pre-buyout to 7.5×) but also significant structural subordination as much of the new debt enjoyed security in TXU's assets, which was not extended to the existing bonds.

Moreover, the assumptions about gas prices, which at the time of writing are only $3.75/ MMBtu,[155] were seriously flawed. Energy Future Holdings (EFH), TXU's successor company, found itself facing significant refinancing cliffs from 2014–2017 and on 29 April 2014 filed for protection under Chapter 11.

A bullet that could have been dodged

Could investors have avoided this outcome? We think so. The CEO at the time of the LBO, C. John Wilder, had joined TXU as president and CEO in February 2004, having previously been CFO of Entergy. His tenure at Entergy was marked by a phenomenal equity performance, which saw the company's stock outperform the S&P 500 by 106% and the S&P utility sub-index by 171%.[156] In the words of *Bloomberg Businessweek* he "transformed it [Entergy] from a bottom-quartile regulated monopoly to a competitive, high-performance industrial enterprise."[157] Here was an executive who looked after

153 Moody's Credit Strategy Group (2007). 'TXU: Too Big for an LBO?' [Online]. Available at: **www. moodys.com/researchdocumentcontentpage.aspx?docid=PBC_102466** [Accessed 24 November 2014].
154 Bloomberg.
155 15 August 2014.
156 Bloomberg; author's calculations.
157 *Bloomberg Businessweek* (2014). 'Executive Profile: Charles John Wilder'. [Online]

shareholder returns first and foremost and clearly was not bound by a traditional view of a utility. S&P picked up on this in 2005, noting that:

> "since John Wilder became CEO of TXU in February of 2004, he and his management team have projected a dynamic image and strive to be regarded as a premier energy company that will run more like an efficient industrial company rather than a regulated utility."[158]

Initially it appeared that the new CEO's ambition was to grow the company by expanding into coal-fired generation outside Texas. While that, in and of itself, was not a source of concern – it seemed like a natural extension of the company's wholesale generating activities – the willingness to finance the expansion with additional debt, was. Again, S&P:

> "From a financial management perspective, the company's willingness to issue additional long-term debt in 2004 against an increasing cash flow that is tied to volatile commodity cycles is considered unfavorable to credit quality."[159]

So, a confluence of factors should have been flashing a few amber lights to credit investors: a new management, with a strong equity focus; a willingness to add leverage despite the commodity-dependent nature of TXU's cash flows. When Wilder, in 2005, combined his presidential and chief executive office with that of the chairman of the board on the resignation of former CEO, Erle Nye, the light should have switched from amber to red, since this signalled that the board was more likely to acquiesce in Wilder's shareholder-focused initiatives.

Credit investors might well have been lulled into a false sense of security by management's claim at its presentation to the 2006 Edison Electric Institute (EEI) financial conference that it would not undertake initiatives that would materially weaken the company's capital structure.[160] However, had they also kept an eye on TXU's stock performance, they would have noticed that over the period March 2006 to February 2007, at the end of which the LBO deal was first rumoured, that the MSCI USA IMI Utilities Index increased by almost 19%, while TXU lagged at only 7.5%; bearing in mind the equity-focused track record of new management, they might well have felt a need for greater caution.

In any event, KKR and TPG launched their bid at the end of February 2007 and it was approved by shareholders the following September. The rest, as they say, is history. So, too,

---

Available at: **investing.businessweek.com/research/stocks/private/person. asp?personId=269800&privcapId=54869159&previousCapId=190268&previousTitle=TORO%20CO** [Accessed 24 November 2014].

158   S&P (2006). 'Summary: TXU Corp'. [Online]. Available at: **www.globalcreditportal.com/ ratingsdirect/showArticlePage.do?rand=4FzHnFnfQy&sid=487043&sind=A&object_id=42617&rev_id=72&from=SR** [Accessed 24 November 2014].

159   *See note 145.*

160   Indeed, on slide 3 of their presentation to the 2006 EEI financial conference (7 November 2006), management listed long-term objective number five as "…ensuring the financial risk profile is commensurate with the business risk profile" while, on slide 35, earmarking $1.5bn–$2bn of estimated 2007–2011 cash flow for de-levering. See TXU (2006). EEI Conference Presentation. [Online]. Available at: **library.corporate-ir.net/library/10/102/102498/items/220201/txu_110906.pdf** [Accessed 24 November 2014].

is TXU. One footnote: had credit investors also sifted through the arcana of executive compensation detail in the 10-K, they would have found that Wilder's interests were firmly allied to those of shareholders rather than stakeholders. The *Chicago Tribune* estimated that he walked away from the deal with approximately $288m.[161] We level no criticism at him for this. During his tenure at TXU, he presided over a fivefold-plus increase in the company's stock price and equity investors should thank him. However, credit investors were left holding not so much the baby as the still-born, given the amount of debt with which the company was now saddled. With some of the qualitative analysis outlined above, they might well have seen it coming.

Conclusion

This and the preceding chapters have all addressed ways of interpreting a combination of published financial data and scrutiny of the actions and statements of management teams through a combination of rigorous numerical analysis in addition to awareness of the importance of corporate governance and interlinked social networks to which these individuals belong. The final chapter of this book will add another perspective to the analytical process – how market considerations drive credit.

---

161 *Chicago Tribune* (2007). 'TXU Holders OK $32bn Sale' [Online]. Available at: **articles.chicagotribune. com/2007-09-08/business/0709070614_1_txu-corp-leveraged-buyout-glass-lewis** [Accessed 24 November 2014].

7

How Market Considerations Affect Credit

1. Why sound fundamental analysis may not make you a penny

GIVEN THE MANY AREAS WE HAVE COVERED SO FAR IN THIS BOOK, IT MAY BE TEMPTING to believe that the investor is by now ready to enter the market and actually start making money. Well, perhaps, but in our experience awareness of the topics covered in previous chapters has often not proved sufficient in itself to operate successfully in the credit markets.

The problem lies not merely in identifying mispriced instruments in which to take a long or short position, but in identifying a counterparty willing and able to trade that position with you.

Credit dealers are different

The role of the dealer in credit markets is simply not as clearly mandated as that of their counterparts in the world of equities. Equity traders are also known as market makers. They make a bid-offer price in a certain volume of a particular stock in which they are then obliged to trade (until such time as they change their price and/or volume). This information is publicly disclosed and becomes a matter of historical record. In the credit market, however, where most activity is institutional (i.e. one professional investor dealing with another) the equivalent market makers give prices that are only indicative in nature and can prove illusory when put to the test (i.e. when an order is actually placed, potential investors are often told that the price has moved).

The Trade Reporting and Compliance Engine (TRACE) systems, and other price disclosure records such as Markit, allow a degree of historical perspective on volumes and prices once they are actually traded, but in order to get to this point there is often a process of negotiation between buyer and seller that has no equivalent in the equity market. In these markets, the days of programme-trading for a wide range of credit instruments still seem some time away (although certain areas such as credit indices do have the facility for electronic execution and can be exchange-traded, they are the exception rather than the rule) and the more esoteric the instrument concerned, the more manual and bespoke is the transaction.

FIGURE 14: TRACE PRICING RECAP FOR A CORPORATE BOND

<HELP> for explanation, <MENU> for similar functions.

MS 6 05/13/14 Corp			94) Export to Excel		99) Feedback			TRACE Trade History	
Cusip 61747YCF					95) Buy		96) Sell	97) Settings	
View Sprd to Bench		Range 10/11/12	- 02/08/13			Trade Size >=250M			
Spread to Benchmark			Total		Dealer to Client Volume(M)				D→D
High	Low	Last	Vol(M)	Trds	Dlr Buy	Dlr Sell	Net		Vol(M)
175.2	63.1	102.3	270,065	213	95,445	106,059	-10,61	1	68,561

98) Charts

		Spread to Benchmark					Dealer to Client Volume(M)				D→D
	Date	High	Low	Last	Vol(M)	Trds	Dlr Buy	Dlr Sell	Net		Vol(M)
1)	02/07/13	102.3	85.7	102.3	10,062	6	5,400	1,000	4,400	-.44	3,662
2)	02/06/13	103.7	103.7	103.7	1,800	3	1,200	600	600	-.06	0
3)	02/05/13	128.7	114.9	128.7	1,750	2	1,000	750	250	-.05	0
4)	02/01/13	112.1	74.9	112.1	2,425	3	1,425	1,000	425	-.05	0
5)	01/31/13	100.3	63.1	89.6	5,000	6	0	1,500	-1,500	.15	3,500
6)	01/29/13	104.8	98.7	98.7	3,000	3	1,000	1,000	0	.05	1,000
7)	01/28/13	125.7	125.7	125.7	400	1	400	0	400	-.05	0
8)	01/25/13	124.9	95.1	114.6	6,820	8	2,910	3,160	-250	.05	750
9)	01/24/13	140.4	112.5	112.5	3,240	4	600	0	600	-.06	2,640
10)	01/23/13	120.8	114.4	114.4	2,609	3	1,320	900	420	-.05	389
11)	01/18/13	119.8	114.8	119.4	14,297	3	9,297	5,000	4,297	-.43	0
12)	01/17/13	139.3	114.9	114.9	10,500	3	500	10,000	-9,500	.95	0
13)	01/16/13	133.9	125.3	126.7	3,500	3	1,500	1,000	500	-.05	1,000
14)	01/15/13	127.8	122.4	122.4	1,600	5	350	300	50	-.05	950

Source: Bloomberg

FIGURE 15: TRACE RECAP OF INDIVIDUAL TRADES IN THIS SECURITY

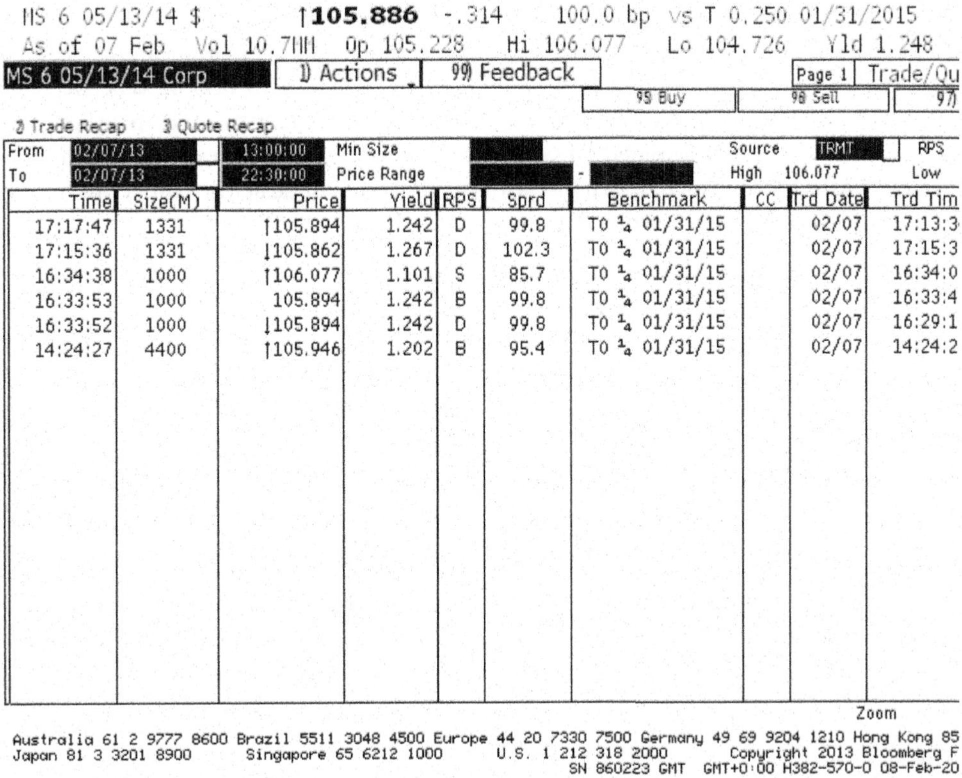

```
MS 6 05/13/14 $        ↑105.886  -.314    100.0 bp  vs T 0.250 01/31/2015
As of 07 Feb   Vol 10.7MM   Op 105.228   Hi 106.077   Lo 104.726   Yld 1.248
MS 6 05/13/14 Corp         1) Actions    99) Feedback              Page 1  Trade/Qu
                                                   95 Buy          98 Sell        97
  2 Trade Recap    3 Quote Recap
From  02/07/13        13:00:00   Min Size                    Source   TRMT      RPS
To    02/07/13        22:30:00   Price Range          -               High 106.077   Low
```

Time	Size(M)	Price	Yield	RPS	Sprd	Benchmark	CC	Trd Date	Trd Tim
17:17:47	1331	↑105.894	1.242	D	99.8	T0 ¼ 01/31/15		02/07	17:13:3
17:15:36	1331	↓105.862	1.267	D	102.3	T0 ¼ 01/31/15		02/07	17:15:3
16:34:38	1000	↑106.077	1.101	S	85.7	T0 ¼ 01/31/15		02/07	16:34:0
16:33:53	1000	105.894	1.242	B	99.8	T0 ¼ 01/31/15		02/07	16:33:4
16:33:52	1000	↓105.894	1.242	D	99.8	T0 ¼ 01/31/15		02/07	16:29:1
14:24:27	4400	↑105.946	1.202	B	95.4	T0 ¼ 01/31/15		02/07	14:24:2

```
                                                                          Zoom
Australia 61 2 9777 8600 Brazil 5511 3048 4500 Europe 44 20 7330 7500 Germany 49 69 9204 1210 Hong Kong 85
Japan 81 3 3201 8900      Singapore 65 6212 1000      U.S. 1 212 318 2000      Copyright 2013 Bloomberg F
                                                      SN 860223 GMT  GMT+0:00 H382-570-0 08-Feb-20
```

Source: Bloomberg

Credit markets are large but illiquid

As in any over-the-counter market, prices will move against the buyer or seller when trying to deal in a particularly small or large volume of an instrument. The first is justified by the dealer as a function of its inconvenience, the second as a potential distortion of the available volume of a finite number of instruments. This latter point is crucial in understanding the dynamics of credit trading. Whereas, in equities, there is usually only a single class or perhaps two classes of share traded, a single large corporation may have hundreds of separate bond issues, each of which will be more or less widely held by investing institutions and be subject to its own technical peculiarities of supply and demand. Some bond issues simply do not trade, as they are owned entirely by buy-and-hold investors. Dealer inventory of particular issues is not to be taken for granted.

Attempts to improve liquidity

The buy-side has repeatedly tried to improve liquidity in corporate bonds through a number of initiatives. One potential option is the establishment of a trading platform from which dealers are excluded, and which operates on a peer-to-peer basis between the major institutional investors. Banks have cut their bond inventory by more than 75% since the financial crisis. An estimated 99.5% of US corporate bonds, for example, are held by buy-side institutions, which, in parallel with the reduction of dealer inventory, means that dealing volumes have been radically reduced.[162]

So far, alternative platforms such as MarketAxess's open lists system, have also proved unable to attract significant participation from the buy-side. Mutual distrust between buy-side firms may be partly to blame, but in our view another important factor has been that the buy-side is conflicted by its need to maintain access to the banks' new issue pipeline and its desire to have a functioning, liquid secondary market in corporate bonds. The fate of many of the brokerage firms that set up shop in credit after the financial crisis illustrates the difficulty of breaking the practical and commercial connections between the primary and secondary markets. Many of these new market entrants have found their market opportunity to be far more limited than it first appeared.

Patchy liquidity is mitigated to some degree by the existence of the repurchase agreement (repo) market, through which dealers who are short inventory of a particular bond may be able temporarily to borrow securities for a fee. However, some smaller issues can be wholly owned by a single institution, and indeed might have been created as a result of the specific demand of that institution – so-called 'reverse enquiry'. Other issues, especially in eurozone countries with active retail bond markets – Italy, Benelux, Germany – may be retail-designated and, once sold, never see the light of day in the secondary market again.

Thus, the availability of tradable inventory on the books of a dealer is generally a function of the bank's physically owning the bonds in question as well as its view of whether or not owning the bonds represents good or bad relative value in its own right.

Either situation renders the quest for investable alpha in credit a potentially frustrating one. Despite the gigantic volumes of credit that are traded every day, liquidity, paradoxically, can be a significant obstacle to overcome.

Credit default swaps

The CDS market is in part the result of an attempt to create uniform risk instruments that can isolate corporate, financial or sovereign credit risk. Initially, the CDS market came into being as a means of insuring investors' bond positions against the default of the underlying issuer. Conceptually, the initial idea was to create an instrument which disaggregated credit

---

162   Wigan, D. (2013). 'Buy side looks to cut dealers out of new credit trading platform'. [Online]. Available at: **creditflux.com/Newsletter/2013-12-05/Buy-side-looks-to-cut-dealers-out-of-new-credit-trading-platform** [Accessed 24 November 2014].

and interest rate risk. In doing this, however, the CDS market has created its own technical factors that need to be taken into account (see the market technicals section of this chapter).

Credit default swaps enable investors to protect their investments from default, isolating credit risk from interest rate risk in a way that is impossible with bonds or loans and enabling investors to trade 'pure credit'.

In theory, this market should not suffer from the same kinds of liquidity issues that are faced in the bond and loan markets since the CDS itself is created between two willing counterparties, one insuring the other in exchange for a fee or spread, independently of any participation on the part of the corporation whose risk is being traded. Hence, the volume of CDS outstanding now vastly exceeds the size of the underlying bonds that are theoretically being insured.

In practice, CDS contracts and the risk that they insure rarely net to zero because of the nature of other, related hedging activity that takes place in the market. For example, an investor may buy CDS protection of $10m over a three-year term from a bank counterparty, but the bank in question may in turn hedge its own exposure on this contract by buying only $7 million of the more liquid but longer-dated 5 year CDS contract, thereby creating a difference in the two counterparties' notional exposure, or "jump to default" risk, while being fully hedged on a duration basis. (Note that this duration-based approach to hedging also played a role in exacerbating the market distortions caused by the downgrades to high yield of Ford and GM and their related financing companies in 2005, as discussed later in this chapter). Trades of this nature are entered into hundreds or even thousands of times by market counterparties, creating potentially large "jump to default" positions in the market. Should the underlying credit subsequently get into difficulty and become distressed, banks and other investors with exposure to the name will then attempt to cover their positions by buying short-dated CDS protection, often creating a situation where the CDS curve becomes inverted - i.e. short dated protection becomes more costly to buy than longer-dated maturities of the same name.

This surfeit of CDS relative to underlying bonds of a corporation is what is referred to by the media and politicians as 'naked' CDS positions, rather than presumably more acceptable and fully-clothed CDS positions that relate to an underlying long position in a company's bonds or loans.

From the perspective of these opinion-moulders, there is an injustice in the fact that the market allows 'speculators' to express their view (positive or negative) on the creditworthiness of an issuer without having previously expressed a positive view on its creditworthiness by buying its bonds or loans. The argument is that CDS should be restricted to its original role as a means of hedging investors against default. In truth, most financial markets, even those such as the commodity markets which are conceptually easier to tie to real-life commercial transactions, are subject to similar dynamics, with only tiny fractions of their daily trade volumes representing such 'legitimate' activity and the rest being purely financial in nature.

CDS – remain controversial

To state the position of these commentators more equitably, they view the CDS purely in its insurance role rather than as a vehicle for the expression of credit risk. To be fair, in the sovereign CDS market in particular, the use of these instruments has proved controversial as market participants have, in the case of the eurozone crisis, arguably stoked the fires burning beneath troubled sovereign states by pushing CDS spreads so wide that it has resulted in impaired market access for the sovereign debt of these nations.

Whether this is a true or a false reflection of their underlying credit risk is the source of significant controversy. As Richard Portes has put it, the price leadership of the CDS market "may be the result not of better information, but of the effect of CDS prices on the perceived creditworthiness of the issuer".[163]

The CDS market has also been accused of providing a means whereby banks may be able to bypass their customary due diligence processes in making lending decisions, since it enables them to hedge their credit exposure by buying a CDS on the underlying credit, a factor that may have contributed to the free and easy lending standards of the pre-2008 credit bubble.

A CDS-based product, the synthetic collateralised debt obligation (CDO), has also been criticised for potential moral hazard, stemming from the asymmetry of information between counterparties, notably in the case of Goldman Sachs' now-notorious Abacus CDO, put together at the behest of Paulson & Co. to express a negative view on the US mortgage market. Goldman did not reveal in the marketing of the CDO that Paulson had participated in the selection of the underlying mortgage-backed securities on which the investors concerned were providing protection. Goldman initially argued, somewhat disingenuously, that this was not material as the provider of protection was intrinsically aware of the existence of a counterparty who wished to buy it, but was ultimately found to be at fault, settling with the SEC and paying a $550m fine.[164]

On 25 June 2010, Judge John G. Koeltl of the US District Court for the Southern District of New York issued a 122-page opinion clearing defendants Jon-Paul Rorech, a high-yield bond salesman from Deutsche Bank, and Renato Negrin, a former portfolio manager for Millennium Partners L.P. and one of Mr. Rorech's hedge fund clients, of all wrongdoing in the first-ever insider trading case involving CDS. The court's opinion was the first one to address the jurisdiction of the SEC over CDS and the manner in which high-yield bond deals are marketed and sold throughout the fixed income market. It had been the subject of extensive media coverage in the financial press.[165]

---

163 Portes, Richard (2010), 'Ban Naked CDS'. [Online] Available at: **www.eurointelligence.com/news-details/article/ban-nakedcds.html?cHash=8d1cdb3c68fcffb16fd8c0b1c0ad1of3** [Accessed 15 August 2014].

164 SEC (2010). 'Goldman Sachs to Pay Record $550 Million to Settle SEC Charges Related to Subprime Mortgage CDO'. [Online]. Available at: **www.sec.gov/news/press/2010/2010-123.htm** [Accessed 24 November 2014].

165 On 5 May 2009, the SEC filed charges alleging that Rorech tipped Negrin as to allegedly confidential 'inside' information regarding a proposed restructuring of a high-yield bond offering. Negrin then allegedly traded a CDS based on this information ahead of the restructuring announcement for a profit of approximately $1.2m. The bond deal was brought by VNU, a Dutch media company, and a group of

CDS and market liquidity

Traded volumes in the CDS market are tracked by the Depository Trust and Clearing Corporation (DTCC) in New York. An example of the weekly volume data published on its website follows:

TABLE 45: TOTAL VOLUME FOR CDS CREDIT PRODUCTS

Week of 04/13/12	Seller type							
	Dealer			**Non-dealer/customer**		**Totals**		
	Gross notional ($m equivalent)	Contracts		Gross notional ($m equivalent)	Contracts	Gross notional ($m equivalent)	Contracts	
Buyer type Dealer	10,640,200	1,673,670		2,284,320	257,711	12,924,520	1,931,381	
Buyer type Non-dealer/customer	2,235,750	247,378		22,999	2,460	2,258,749	249,838	
Total	12,875,950	1,921,048		2,307,319	260,171		2,181,219	

Source: DTCC

CDS have enhanced the liquidity of the credit markets

The existence of the CDS markets as a further means of gaining or reducing exposure to credit risk has not definitively changed the variability of liquidity in the credit markets, though it has increased the range of tradable credit instruments and facilitated the expression of long and short views, while disaggregating credit risk from interest rate risk.

The liquidity of individual CDS contracts can also vary significantly. For example, according to the same source,[166] in the week ending 13 April 2012 a total of $94.1bn of single-name CDS was traded in the top 812 issuers. Of this group, only 28 issuers accounted for more than $470m of notional trade in the week (that is, more than $94m per day) and only one of these was a corporate credit (in this case Safeway), while the other 27 were either sovereign issuers, banks or other financial institutions. Index volumes have been robust,

---

financial sponsors, including Blackstone Group., KKR and Thomas H. Lee Partners. Deutsche Bank served as the lead underwriter. Immediately after the deal was announced on 10 July 2006, the terms of the VNU bond offering were widely discussed in the market, particularly among market participants who traded CDS contracts referencing VNU ('VNU CDS').After the VNU bond offering was announced, market participants who traded VNU CDS expressed concern that the new bonds, which were going to be issued from VNU's operating company, would not be deliverable into (or covered by) their VNU CDS contracts and asked that the terms of the bond offering be changed to issue additional deliverable bonds. As is typical in primary high-yield bond offerings, capital markets and sales professionals at Deutsche Bank, including Rorech, actively engaged in an open dialogue with prospective investors to find the best solution. On 24 July 2006, two weeks after the bond deal was launched, Deutsche Bank announced that some of the operating company bonds would be issued from VNU's holding company, because holding company bonds would be deliverable into VNU CDS contracts. By making some of the bonds deliverable, Deutsche Bank and the issuer were able to increase demand for the bond offering among CDS investors. On 25 June 2010, the court held that the SEC's allegations of insider trading were without merit. It rejected every aspect of the SEC's theory of the case, finding that the inside information did not exist at the time of the alleged tip, the information at issue was not confidential or material, Rorech never breached his duty to his employer, and there was no deception or scienter.

166 DTCC (2014). [Online]. Available at: **www.dtcc.com/products/derivserv/data_table_iv.php** [Accessed 24 November 2014].

with cumulative traded volumes of the iTraxx Main index increasing by 14% year-on-year in 2013[167] and volumes of the iTraxx Crossover index increasing by 35% in the same period.[168]

Bond market: illiquidity most challenging problem

Bond mutual funds and ETF holdings of corporate bonds have almost doubled since 2008.[169] These now account for approximately 22% of foreign and corporate bond holdings in the US, compared to 14% in 2009. The funds holding these bonds tend to be retail-facing and therefore less 'sticky' than traditional life, property and casualty and pension fund money.

US dealer inventories in corporate bonds and other non-US treasuries have declined 78% from their 2007 peak. This is, in part, a function of new regulatory initiatives such as the Volcker Rule and the Basel III limitation on proprietary trading desks, which have undermined the economics of market making, while the underlying volume of the US corporate bond market has grown by 42% since 2008.[170]

A widespread concern arising from these initiatives, however well-intentioned they may be, is that, in a systemic bond market sell-off, for example, following an interest rate rise, this illiquidity could turn a correction into a rout. Recent examples of this abound in individual corporate bonds which have been subject to idiosyncratic sell-offs. For example, in June 2014, when Portugal Telecom disclosed that it had exposure to a troubled domestic counterparty, the Z-spread on its 5% bonds of 2019 widened 150bps as investors wishing to close positions struggled to sell, while the corresponding 5-year CDS contract continued to trade on a 5 basis point bid–offer spread and remained liquid. The Fed itself has been contemplating imposing exit fees on bond funds in an attempt to restrain the impact of widespread investor selling on a potentially illiquid market.[171]

2. The role of the credit ratings agencies

The ratings of the major ratings agencies are a widely utilised means of categorising credit risk, which investors are then able to map onto the returns available to them in the market as a means of generating relative value investment ideas. As such, they have provided useful benchmarks for credit investors.

John Moody published the first public bond ratings in 1909, and was followed in 1916 by the Poor's Publishing Company, in 1922 by the Standard Statistics Company and in 1924 by

167 2013 Trading Volumes in European Credit. CDS Indices, Single Name CDS and IG Bonds. Citi Research. 5 December 2013.

168 DTCC(2014) [Online] Available at: **www.dtcc.com/repository-otc-data.aspx**. [Accessed 26 Novermber 2014].

169 Financial Accounts of the United States Federal Reserve, authors' estimates.

170 *The Financial Times* (10 September 2013) 'Markets: The Debt Penalty' [Online]. Available at: **www.ft.com** [Accessed 2 April 2015].

171 *The Financial Times* (16 June 2014) 'Fed Looks at Exit Fees on Bond Funds'. Available at: **www.ft.com** [Accessed 2 April 2015].

the Fitch Publishing Company. All, therefore, were extant before the 1929 Wall Street Crash and the ensuing Depression, but their role was not yet enshrined in financial regulation.

The US regulatory framework that followed the Great Depression in 1936, embedded the concept of the Nationally Recognized Statistical Rating Organizations (NRSROs) at the heart of the credit market as a means of enhancing the measurement of the credit quality of bond investments made by US banks. The Code of Federal Regulations (CFR) states that "an insured state savings association … may not acquire … any corporate debt securities not of investment grade".

As the role and scope of the agencies' activities have expanded to meet the demands of a more geographically diverse capital market, with a growing range of rated instruments, so this role has become increasingly important to, and more deeply embedded in, the credit market's functions. Subsequent regulation has reinforced the importance of the agencies' position, effectively out-sourcing much of the decision-making process for many bond investors. The regulation that sought to reduce portfolio credit risk, through the law of unintended consequences, has in fact amplified the impact of those times when the agencies get it wrong.

Furthermore, in attempting to reform NRSRO regulation in 2010, after the debacle of the structured finance market during the credit crunch, the 2010 Dodd-Frank Act effectively further enhanced the anti-competitive moats behind which the agencies operate, by imposing compliance and documentation requirements that are so onerous that new competitors are effectively barred from the market.

The big three credit ratings agencies (Moody's, S&P and Fitch) are hugely influential in the credit markets (the first two rate approximately 40% of all rated debt each and Fitch about 20%)[172]. Any investor in the asset class therefore needs to have an understanding of their methodologies and their sometimes confusing approach to issues such as ratings subordination in order to take an informed view on potential investments. It behoves the authors of this book to state up front that we are both alumni of one of these agencies and that we consequently have significant first-hand experience of some of the strengths and, perhaps, a few of the weaknesses of their approach to ranking corporations, financial institutions and sovereign states on a relative scale.

Generating alpha from the agencies

Despite their well-documented imperfections, ratings are used by investors, issuers, bankers and governments, increasing the range of credit investment opportunities and offering a ready-to-use and intuitive scale of relative creditworthiness from AAA at the top (Aaa for Moody's) to D at the bottom. The agencies remain useful, in part because most investors do not have the resources to maintain their own research teams. In a disintermediated investment world, the agencies are the ultimate outsourced credit team, widening and deepening the range of investable assets for the credit world.

---

172 Authors' estimates.

In theory, the increase that their research creates in the range of investment opportunities in turn increases the propensity to invest: if risk capital is plentiful, all other things being equal, the cost of capital falls, thereby fostering economic growth and opening the capital markets to hitherto unknown issuers.

Rather than embarking on a crusade over the rights and wrongs of the position of the agencies, it is perhaps best to accept them as imperfect, but useful, facts of life in the credit markets, generally playing a helpful role but occasionally going wrong with catastrophic consequences. It is worth remembering that their access to the management of underlying corporations in whose debt investors are interested is generally far superior to that of the sell-side analyst community, their processes are relatively transparent and their committee-based approach is generally rigorous and consistent across sectors. An investor who is well-acquainted with the agencies' workings is potentially in a position to react to ratings changes before they actually happen – potentially a source of additional alpha for their fund.

Reading the signs

One of the most important skills in gauging the attractiveness of an investment in a credit lies in attempting to assess with some degree of accuracy what the likely reaction of the major ratings agencies may be to events that may alter the perception of a corporation's creditworthiness, either positively or negatively. Have the agencies already 'baked' the transitional trends within a credit into their ratings or can investors take a position ahead of expected reactions from the agencies that are yet to materialise?

Whether and when the agencies will change their ratings can have huge implications for the value of a corporation's debt instruments (see the Lafarge case study later in this chapter). Some changes, particularly for threshold ratings on either side of the key investment-grade/high-yield divide, can lead to multi-point falls and rises in an instrument's price – creating valuable trading opportunities. Many funds are obliged to sell any bonds whose ratings fall below the crucial investment-grade threshold, creating significant price volatility in the run-up to the decision and shortly thereafter. The issue here is that the investor must operate ahead of and not in reaction to the agencies. Spotting transition risk early is how big money is made and lost in credit.

He who pays the piper ...

Let us also state up front that there is one apparent conflict of interest that investors have to accept if they are planning to use ratings as a guide to creditworthiness. Prior to its re-naming at the time of its stock listing, Moody's, for one, went by the name of Moody's Investors Service. Now, the investors in question do pay a subscription fee to all the agencies to obtain access to their statistics and research and to have the benefit of email and telephone contact with their analysts. However, the majority of the agencies' income is actually provided by the very debt issuers on whose creditworthiness they are supposed to express an objective opinion.

In 2011, in the case of Moody's, 58% of its revenues are described as "Transaction Revenues" (i.e. relating to rating activities) with the remainder "Recurring Revenues" which relate more to subscriptions, although it also includes revenues from frequent issuers. Debt issuance accounted for the bulk of revenues in 2011 (to be fair, in 2010, it was 50%). [173]Frequent and large issuers thus pay more in fees than infrequent and smaller issuers.

The agencies have historically managed this apparent conflict with success. If, for example, an issuer receives a lower rating than it is looking for, it is not obliged to publish it, but it still has to pay the agency for it. The agencies have experimented with unsolicited ratings for unrated issuers. Indeed S&P's rating on the USA is itself unsolicited, which is perhaps a good measure of the agency's independence.

In the context of corporates, however, the agencies' rationale for publishing unsolicited ratings was partly in response to investor interest in the credit standing of such issuers, and partly, less altruistically, in an attempt to turn un-rated into rated, and therefore potentially fee-paying, issuers. For the most part, however, this did not prove to be a durable product line in the corporate context.

In the end, a balance has had to be struck between the credibility of the agencies' ratings and the access to management at the rated entities that is an important part of the credibility of their published ratings.

Defining terms

Since 1975, the SEC refers to the agencies as NRSROs, while the Basel Committee on Banking Supervision (BCBS) refers to them as External Credit Assessment Institutions (ECAIs). There are currently ten NRSROs, though the big three continue to dominate the market.

Achieving recognition as one of these accredited organisations is an arduous task, requiring significant proof of due process, documentation and staffing to validate stringent demands on objectivity, independence and transparency, the flip side of which is a significant barrier to entry for would-be NRSROs.

Having achieved these goals, the agencies' ratings are then allowed to be used as a reference point for potential investment decisions. From the agencies' own perspective, they are then allowed to start charging issuers for their ratings, a privilege that Warren Buffett, whose Berkshire Hathaway remains a significant shareholder in Moody's, has referred to as "a bullet-proof franchise". The following table and figure show why:

---

173 Company accounts.

TABLE 46: MOODY'S - OPERATING PERFORMANCE 2007-2011

$m	2011	2010	2009	2008	2007
Revenues	2,280	2,032	1,797	1,755	2,259
EBITDA	967	839	769	820	1,223
Margin (%)	42.4	41.3	42.8	46.8	54.1
Net profit	578	513	407	457	701
Margin (%)	25.3	25.3	22.7	26.1	31.1

Source: Company reports

FIGURE 16: MOODY'S AND MCGRAW-HILL RELATIVE TO S&P 500

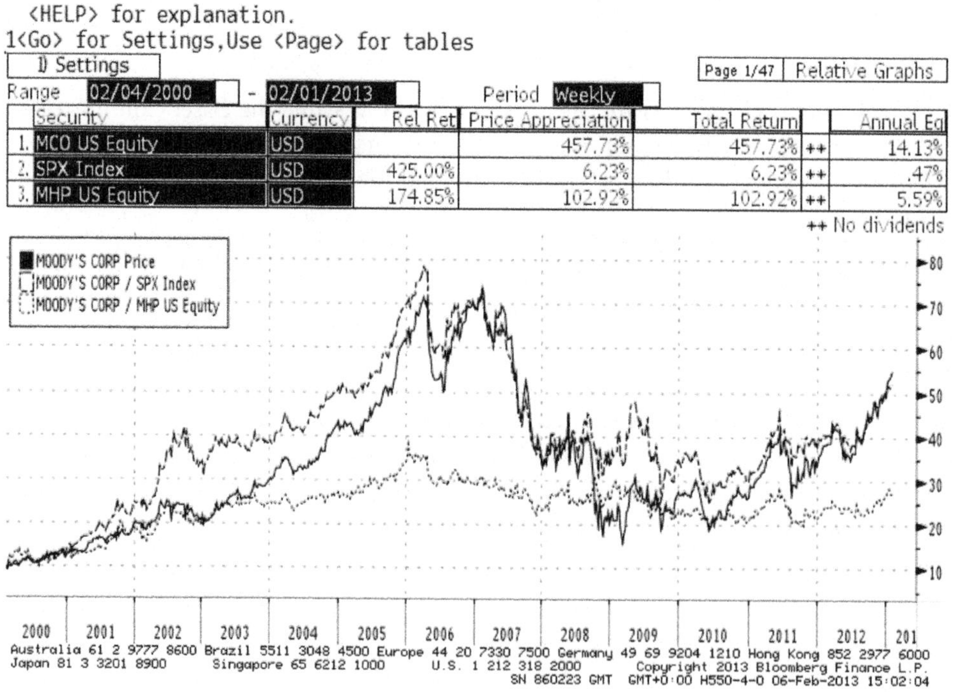

Source: Bloomberg

The ratings agencies are highly profitable businesses that can be seen to have weathered the storm of the credit crunch in some style relative to many of their peers in the financial services industry. Hence they rarely receive positive media coverage, being variously blamed for 'missing' corporate frauds like Enron, despite their privileged access to management and for 'misunderstanding' the relative risk of issuing entities or states.

The value of their ratings has been called into question time and again with almost every financial crisis, and is at present subject to much complaint from the offended leaders of European sovereign states whose credit standing is daily being called into question, as well as significant litigation in the USA. For example, in February 2013, S&P received notice of a $5bn lawsuit from the Department of Justice, relating to its ratings of structured products.

Globalisation: expanding – and diluting? – the brand

Over the course of the last 15 years, not only have ratings moved from a largely US domestic phenomenon to a global one, but the range of asset classes that carry ratings has also proliferated. Moving from a traditional domestic base of ratings on the debt of US corporations, municipal authorities and financial institutions, the agencies have expanded their coverage universe to include sovereign states, non-US local governments, emerging markets corporates and financial institutions and structured finance products. In the process, they have been accused of undermining the value of ratings as a guide to credit quality.

Fragility of the model-based approach to credit – again

In particular, the credit crunch laid bare the weakness of the rationale for ratings that were assigned to a range of structured finance products that quickly moved from being rated AAA or equivalent to being in default once underlying problems in the US mortgage market started to raise their heads. In April 2013, Moody's and S&P settled lawsuits against them by a diverse group of institutional investors for a reported $225m.

The structured products fiasco has had a damaging effect on the agencies' reputation for competence, with classes of securities that had previously been rated AAA or equivalent being downgraded to the verge of default, often over very short time periods. Most notoriously, the Rhinebridge securitisation went from AAA to high-yield ratings within a matter of months.

Moreover, structured products ratings used a model-based rather than analyst-based approach, which helped foster both the proliferation of numerically justified but ultimately unsound ratings and their sudden demise when faced with unforeseen systemic challenges. The model-based approach was attractive to the agencies, we suspect, because it is much cheaper to run than the labour- and judgment-intensive traditional credit analysis which forms the backbone of the agencies' corporate ratings franchise. Coupled with the sheer volume of structured issuance in the first seven years of the 21st Century, it produced a massive fillip to the agencies' operating margins, which, in turn, was the benchmark for rewarding their senior managements.

In terms of workload and due process, the agencies were overwhelmed. Between 2000 and 2007, they gave nearly 45,000 mortgage-backed securities AAA ratings. Under pressure from a Morgan Stanley banker to rate deals using 'grandfathering' techniques, an S&P executive commented as follows: "Lord help our fucking scam … this has to be the stupidest place I have worked at" and "As you know, I had difficulties explaining 'HOW' we got to those numbers since there is no science behind it".

"If we are just going to make it up in order to rate deals, then quants [quantitative analysts] are of precious little value," complained a further senior S&P man. "Let's hope we are all wealthy and retired by the time this house of card[s] falters," wrote another.[174]

Management's motivation a key driver

Here we stray back into territory covered in chapter 1. It is important to recognise that the agencies, as commercial enterprises, are susceptible to the same challenges of corporate governance that feature in our analysis of corporations from a credit standpoint.

The profitability of structured finance ratings was so substantial that the integrity of the agencies' own processes became seriously compromised. Part of the reason for this lay in the fact that there was a meaningful concentration of intermediaries in this area of finance, which significantly increased pressure between the agencies competing for ratings business (i.e. a handful of investment banks were managing all of the pools of assets being securitised, rather than the usual wide range of corporations in a portfolio), which led to accusations that there was scope for notable suasion of the agencies on the part of large structured products managers.

Furthermore, the banks concerned would typically hire several agencies for each deal to avoid the possibility of its being 'notched' (i.e. rated more conservatively) by another agency.

Ultimately, when it came to applying a model-based ratings process to data on subprime mortgages, which was not as robust as the data the agencies had access to on their prime counterparts, they used broadly the same modelling process, despite the lower quality of the data, principally for commercial reasons. Fees for rating mortgage-backed securities doubled for Moody's and S&P between 2002 and 2007, from $3bn to $6bn. This ultimately led to massive investor losses and significant brand damage for the agencies, but had its roots in the agencies' own willingness to sacrifice analytical integrity in order to achieve higher profits. Subsequently, the eurozone crisis has clearly reduced the credibility of sovereign ratings as a guide to a country's creditworthiness (viz. Greece, which has moved from single-A to single-C ratings over the last ten years) while also impacting the validity of the rationale for rating financial institutions and corporations within the eurozone countries.

---

174 Taibi, M. (2013). 'The Last Mystery of the Financial Crisis.' [Online]. Available at: **www.rollingstone. com/politics/news/the-last-mystery-of-the-financial-crisis-20130619** [Accessed 24 November 2014].

Lagging indicators?

Furthermore, ratings are often criticised as lagging indicators of the true creditworthiness of an issuer. This criticism in part ignores the fact that the agencies attempt to rate an issuer 'through-the-cycle', rather than changing the rating to reflect every minor tweak in the underlying entity's credit standing. This, too, comes back to the issue of management motivation. The agencies are accused of being more willing to take a credit rating down more quickly than they will bring it back up because they have a hugely asymmetric risk/reward payoff. Getting a rating right on the upside brings them no reward; however, getting it wrong on the downside carries serious reputational risk.

Hence, they tend to be swift to chide and slow to bless – which is something that investors can arbitrage. However, although ratings are not intended as a guide for trading purposes, an understanding of the ways and means of the agencies can help investors to position their portfolios around ratings-sensitive events to insulate them from the negative effect of downgrades and to profit from the potential for ratings upgrades.

For all the high-profile problems of the agencies, they remain a vital resource for credit investors, especially in the world of corporate finance, where they retain the advantage of their privileged access to senior management and are (at least largely) staffed by seasoned industry specialists who have often followed their industries through several economic cycles.

Case study: Lafarge - madness in the methodology?

Rather than getting overly bogged down in the rights and wrongs of ratings agency activities, which have been discussed at length both by the agencies' own methodology publications and by press and finance industry commentators (and indeed in this book), it may be more enlightening to examine a concrete example of ratings changes in action and of the trading opportunities created by shifts in the agencies' approaches, both in absolute terms and relative to one another.

Firstly, take a look at the following table, which summarises the ratings of French-domiciled cement giant Lafarge over the years 2008–12. In all cases the ratings identified relate to the company's senior unsecured obligations:

TABLE 47: LAFARGE - SENIOR UNSECURED RATINGS 2008-12

Date	Moody's	Outlook/Review	Date	S&P	Outlook/Review	Date	Fitch	Outlook/Review
11/12/08	Baa2	Review for DG	11/12/08	BBB	Stable	12/5/08	BBB	Review for DG
1/16/09	Baa3	Outlook stable	1/21/09	BBB-	Stable	3/27/09	BBB-	Outlook stable
8/3/10	Baa3	Review for DG	2/23/11	BBB-	Review for DG			
8/31/10	Baa3	Outlook negative, ratings affirmed	3/17/11	BB+	Stable			
8/2/11	Baa3	Review for DG	3/13/12	BB+	Outlook negative	11/9/11	BB+	Outlook stable
8/5/11	Ba1	Outlook stable						

Source: Bloomberg

What does this series of actions show us? It is hard to prove causality, but a few features stand out quite clearly from this sequence of changes in the ratings of Lafarge:

- **Moving in a pack.** A multi-notch gap between one agency's ratings and those of the peer group can be a worrying thing. The agencies are managed on a system whereby the analyst who is directly responsible for a credit is managed by a more senior figure with broader industry experience but less depth of knowledge on the individual credit. Ratings changes take place on a committee basis, where the first analyst's in-depth views are subjected to the scrutiny of a panel consisting of several other credit professionals with a range of potentially relevant insights. After a thorough exposé to the committee, a vote is taken. Remember, it is in the agency's interest to err on the side of caution, as rapid transitions in ratings damage their franchise. Thus, they are often accused of moving in formation.

- **Or follow the leader?** After Lafarge's weaker-than-forecast quarterly results for the third quarter of 2008, with consensus estimates for the company being cut back materially, all three agencies took action. In early 2009, they were clustered at BBB- with stable outlooks across the board. Then, in early August 2010, Moody's broke ranks and put the company on review for downgrade – one notch here would mean the company would be non-investment-grade, potentially triggering step-up coupons on some of its bonds and increasing its general cost of funding. By late August, however, Moody's returned to the fold, affirming the low investment-grade ratings and moving Lafarge's outlook to negative. In its press release on the decision, the agency noted the cyclical nature of the weakness in Lafarge's credit metrics, which, it highlighted, were not currently at a level consistent with investment-grade ratings, but were expected to improve over the next two years towards more compatible levels.

- **A race to the bottom**. Then, faced with mounting evidence of weakening operating performance at the company, S&P put the ratings on review in February 2011, and within three weeks had unceremoniously taken Lafarge down to junk status. The other agencies now had to either reconcile themselves to taking a more bullish position on a credit in a capital-intensive industry that was clearly showing signs of strain or fall into line with S&P, which they eventually did with a lag of five and eight months respectively. By September 2011, they were all at high BB ratings and S&P has since emphasised its hawkish stance by moving its outlook to negative.

- **But direction and magnitude well-flagged**. Despite an element of back-tracking on the part of Moody's in particular in this case, the overall direction of the ratings moves was pretty clearly signalled to investors by the agencies over the period in question. With the help of some simple scenario analysis, investors were given substantial guidance as to the scale and direction of the moves. Again, this is typical agency behaviour and allows investors to position around the scenario that they deem most likely to eventuate.

What has happened to Lafarge on a fundamental basis over this period? Its markets have weakened significantly, as have its credit ratios, but the company has taken some effective action to shore up liquidity, extending and enlarging its lines of credit and selling non-core assets to raise cash. Its fall from investment grade grace has not dented its ability to access the market, though it is paying a higher price for new debt (although with absolute yields at low rates, coupon levels are not punitive). For investors with a strong stomach, the volatility in its cost of credit over this time has offered significant trading opportunities.

Let us now try to assess what impact the ratings changes had on Lafarge's credit standing in the market. The simplest measure of this is the company's five-year CDS spread over the period concerned. Although the CDS is not an instrument available to all investors, it is a proxy for perceived default risk, and the five-year contract is the most liquid part of the CDS curve and therefore the most representative.

Figure 17 illustrates the significant volatility that accompanied the ratings actions. The fact that this period was one of unprecedented market volatility certainly exaggerates the impact of the agencies' moves (see the relationship depicted in figure 18 showing the company's five-year spread relative to the index to illustrate this), and it can be seen that, after an initial period of volatility that followed the ratings changes and which may have brought about forced selling of Lafarge's debt by institutional investors constrained by investment-grade ratings, most of the widening in spreads was retraced.

Being correctly positioned relative to the agencies' moves would have enabled an investor with insight into their processes and the drivers of their ratings actions to capture some meaningful alpha over this period.

FIGURE 17: EVOLUTION OF LAFARGE CDS SPREADS AND RATINGS CHANGES

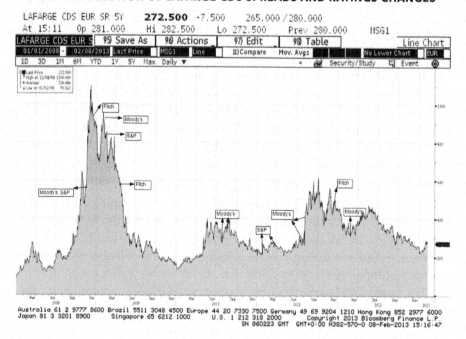

Source: Bloomberg

FIGURE 18: LAFARGE SPREADS RELATIVE TO ITRAXX CROSSOVER INDEX 2008-2013

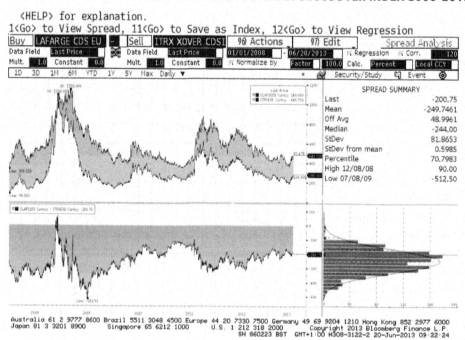

Source: Bloomberg

3. Indexation and absolute return investing

We strongly advocate a preference for absolute return products in the credit sphere above their index-benchmarked rivals. Traditional index-benchmarked funds that aim to outperform a particular market return are usually restricted in terms of where they can invest according to the weighting of particular asset classes, countries or sectors within a reference index, with the majority of the fund's capital held in benchmark or near-benchmark assets.

In order to be able to generate positive returns, irrespective of market conditions, absolute return funds often have broader, more diverse investment guidelines in order to be able to invest in whichever areas of the market the managers believe that the best opportunities currently lie. This includes the option of having zero or even negative (short) positions in asset classes or sectors which are deemed to be unattractive, unlike traditional funds which are obliged to maintain an allocation in such holdings, even if on an underweight basis. (In essence, by choosing an absolute return product the investors are pinning their colours to the skill of the fund manager, whereas an indexed fund will have a greater market bias.)

Absolute return funds, such as PIMCO's Credit Absolute Return Fund, and the same company's Global Investment Grade Credit Fund, to name but two, differ in that the former is able to protect itself from market volatility though the use of derivatives, while the latter is not. Hence, the Credit Absolute Return Fund's Sharpe Ratio[175] is 3.55, while that of its sister fund is 2.4. This is simply one example that serves to support our preference, but it is true to say that absolute return funds usually have more flexible mandates, often with some degree of downside protection, and entail employing a broader range of investment techniques and tools such as the use of derivatives. While the latter has been questioned by some commentators (mainly in the context of traders who have lost money due to excessive derivative position sizes), we would maintain that, conservatively deployed within an appropriate risk-management framework, derivatives can and do enhance returns.

Why is indexation ill-suited to credit?

In equity markets, benchmark indices are typically formed as a function of the market capitalisation and trading liquidity of the underlying corporations. Being an 'index-hugger' is a recognised, if not widely respected, approach to equity portfolio management and relative performance is used as a means of determining managers' remuneration as well as for marketing purposes. A lot of credit funds are managed on a similar basis. However, the practical implications for credit investment are somewhat different. Some of the reasons for this relate to our earlier digressions on market efficiency, and others are purely technical to the workings of the bond, loan and CDS markets.

For an equity fund, the benchmark index is partly a function of market capitalisation (i.e. those companies that the market ascribes a high value to weigh most heavily in the index,

---

175 A measure of excess return per unit of deviation in an investment asset, named after William Forsyth Sharpe.

creating a potentially virtuous circle insofar as 'better' companies receive a higher valuation – although this can create its own difficulties in terms of confirmatory bias).

For credit indices, however, the index weighting of a credit is a function of the amount of debt a company has outstanding. Think about that. A company with more debt is more heavily represented in such an index than one with less debt.

Now, having a lot of debt is not usually taken to be a sign of strong corporate health, though, of course, it is too simplistic to state that a large debt balance is per se a bad thing for, say, a large corporation. In credit, however, it is all about *context* – what is the company's debt in relation to its overall capitalisation, cash generation and cyclicality?

All the same, to base an index on the fact that an issuer has a material dependence on access to the public bond market seems like perverse and circular logic, and can have unforeseen negative consequences. In credit, index-huggers are perforce tracking an index that combines the most heavily indebted corporate names with the most frequent borrowers – i.e. a group of companies that could logically be expected to have a weaker market performance than an average, and perhaps more representative, sample of corporate credits.

GM and Ford 2005

An extreme example of the distortions that indexation can cause came about in 2005, when the ratings of Ford and GM were put on review for downgrade at both Moody's and S&P. Both companies had huge debt balances (together with their financing subsidiaries, each had approximately $175bn of rated debt outstanding at the time)[176]. Both were necessarily frequent borrowers, both accounted for approximately 3% of the index by volume and both were now on the cusp of high yield (to which they were duly downgraded over the course of that summer).

The market panicked at the prospect of such large amounts of debt moving into the less liquid high-yield bond market, with spreads on Ford's five-year CDS moving out from the mid-200bps mark to 850bps in the period January–mid-May 2005.[177] It is fair to say that this effect was exacerbated by a simultaneous crisis in the correlation market.

---

176 Authors' estimates.
177 Bloomberg.

FIGURE 19: FORD FIVE-YEAR CDS SPREAD 2004-6

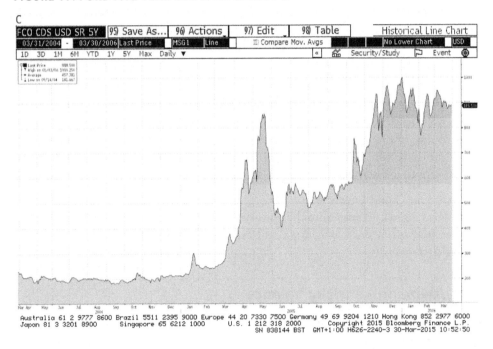

Source: Bloomberg

Further technical distortions of indexation

Further technical effects exacerbated the impact of these ratings moves. For example, the risk limits that most traders operate under preclude their taking a position in any one credit that accounts for more than 1% of their total book assets, but here were two issuers whose combined index weight was closer to 6%. In order to perform in line with the index, traders had to attempt to replicate this exposure without breaching their 1% limit.

Many worked around this difficulty by increasing the duration of their holdings in the two credits, i.e. taking a position in longer-dated bonds, so that they could stay within the 1% limit in terms of notional dollar, euro or sterling exposure but actually increasing their sensitivity to changes in the company's spreads to attempt to approximate its index weight – thereby greatly increasing the volatility of their positions. Clearly, when the downgrades came, these longer-dated positions were significantly more volatile and underperformed the index dramatically.

4. New issues – picking up pennies in front of a steamroller

Some credit funds seek to enhance returns by playing an active part in the primary market for new issues of corporate bonds, lured to it in part by their need to gain exposure to potential new index participants but also by the perception that any new issue carries with it the possibility of a significant mispricing which those who have been fortunate enough to receive an allocation of the new bond will stand to profit by. (It is also the case that new issues, at least for a short while after they come to market, are generally supported by the lead manager during their first few days out of the stalls to make the issue go well, appeal to investors and keep issuers happy.)

In reality, this can be a far higher-risk strategy than it may appear. In general, the lead manager in the new issue market exists in order to minimise any such arbitrage opportunity. The lead sounds out the market's level of interest in a new bond, helping to identify areas on the yield curve which may elicit greater interest from buyers or where an attractive source of term funds is available at a given time.

Given that many bond buyers are of a buy-and-hold nature, additional pressure to get involved in a new issue comes from the sense that the opportunity to buy a particular deal may never arise again, since, once the deal breaks, a significant proportion of the bonds will be held to maturity.

Supply/demand - a tricky balance

The new issue process, in our view, is far from ideal from a buyer's perspective.

Firstly, the lead sounds out interest for an issue of a particular size, maturity and approximate coupon level from market participants. The lead then builds a book based on these expressions of interest. (One problem arising from this is that, often, funds will exaggerate the scale of their interest in the expectation that, because a deal may be 'hot', demand will outstrip supply and eventual allocations will be scaled back.)

At this point, if the deal is significantly over-subscribed, it can be enlarged or its coupon can be reduced, either of which poses a potential threat to the post-issue performance of the bonds.

Finally, allocations are revealed by the lead to each client individually and the bond begins to trade in the grey market (ahead of settlement and allocation to client accounts). If the deal is indeed 'hot', then the lead is under material pressure to allocate bonds to his most reliable, and largest, clients first, paring back the remaining allocations to second- and third-tier clients once the demands of the top clients have been satisfied and then breaking the bad news to the latter, thereby neatly conveying to them the fact of their low-rent status and often provoking indignation from clients who perceive themselves as having been unfairly treated.

The lead listens to these complaints with apparent sympathy, secure in the knowledge that anyone who wants to buy bonds from their pipeline of new issues will be obliged to come back to them. One high-risk trading strategy, known as 'flipping', is attractive to speculative players as it enables traders to potentially sell on at a profit bonds for which they have not yet had to pay, thereby tying up no capital. But it is very risky, as we demonstrate in the next section.

Aston Martin 9.25% bonds – a cautionary tale for flippers

If overall demand for the new issue is weaker than expected, even worse news has to be given to these same clients. That is, that they got all the bonds that they asked for. The subtext to this translates to: "We know you exaggerated the scale of your demand in order to improve your chances of getting a reasonable allocation, but then we doubled the size of the deal and reduced its coupon by 1% due to the initial strength of demand. Then a lot of people pulled their orders, leaving you and a handful of other players with outsize positions in this new issue."

If the bond trades up, it is likely that there will be 'flipping' by some market participants before settlement date. The danger, though, is that general market conditions deteriorate as the deal is being launched and demand collapses, leading the new issue to under rather than outperform in the first few days of trading. This, broadly speaking, is what happened to an issue of bonds from Aston Martin in June 2011.

Any flipper who had hoped for a quick profit would initially have faced a 5% deterioration in the value of their bonds after the deal broke and subsequently seen this accelerate to over one third of face value in the first six months of the deal's life, as disappointing results from the company combined with a generalised weakening of market sentiment as the crisis in the Eurozone brought about a generalised collapse in demand for risk assets.

FIGURE 20: ASTON MARTIN 9.25% BOND PERFORMANCE AFTER ISSUE

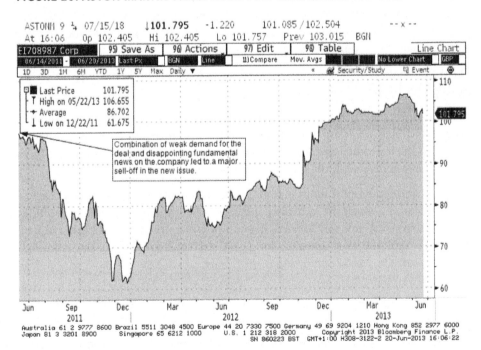

Source: Bloomberg

5. Turning analysis into alpha

1. Credit instruments – what options are available to investors?

Having discussed at some length some of the technical aspects of the credit market, we now address the issue of the instruments available to investors to gain exposure to corporate credit, and outline some of the vehicles through which credit investors attempt to turn analysis into alpha. The principal vehicles at the disposal of the credit investor are:

- Investment-grade and high-yield corporate bonds – many issues, though by no means all, trade in minimum unit sizes that exceed most individual investors' portfolio constraints. Case-by-case research is necessary to determine suitability.[178]

- Investment-grade and high-yield corporate loans – institutional investors only. However, funds that invest in these strategies are available to the individual investor.

- CDS contracts – institutional investors only. Funds that invest in these strategies are available to the individual investor.

- Credit indices, such as those maintained by iTraxx in Europe and CDX in the US – institutional investors only. Funds that invest in these strategies are available to the individual investor.

- ETFs that attempt to replicate the performance of these indices trade in unit sizes that are accessible to individual investors. These have the advantage of typically having very low expense ratios for the investor, along with good daily liquidity, but they are not actively managed by a portfolio management team.

- ETFs that attempt to replicate the returns of an underlying bond or loan portfolio are also accessible by individual investors.

- Structured credit: CDOs, CSOs and CLOs. Direct investment is limited to institutional investors and high-net-worth individuals. Funds that invest in these strategies are available to the individual investor. Further innovations in this field may make these products more accessible to the individual investor over time.

- Traditional corporate bond funds – high-yield and investment-grade. These are the principal means by which the individual investor currently gains exposure to credit, as they enable the small investor to participate in instruments that would otherwise be inaccessible. Typically, they operate a long-only strategy and generate alpha through bond selection.

---

178 Note that few funds offer a combination of investment-grade and high-yield portfolios, maintaining the long-standing separation of the two investment categories. While statistically important in terms of defining the parameters of a fund's default risk, it is also to some extent a shibboleth. In our view, the black-and-white approach to this divide creates inefficiencies due to forced selling and the inability of the funds to invest in 'rising star' or 'crossover' credits.

- Hedge funds: usually, credit hedge funds require a degree of expertise from individual investors, as well as a willingness to forego some of the statutory protections afforded to the smaller investor by regulation. Certain of the UCITS-compliant hedge fund strategies are available to individuals with smaller entry tickets. The world of credit hedge funds covers a wide gamut of strategies – long only, leveraged long-only, long/short, market neutral, long/short with a long bias to name but a few. Although originally targeted only at high-net-worth individuals, hedge funds are increasingly included in diversified investment portfolios and constitute a growing portion of pension fund assets globally.

2. Relative value – a fundamental credit concept

The concept of relative value is perhaps the key driver of credit trading decisions. Most portfolio managers are obliged to remain invested in their asset class, but are of course looking to optimise available returns within the constraints of their asset class, so they need to find a suitable substitute for any asset they are looking to replace.

For example, if Corporation A has a five-year bond with a 5% coupon outstanding and carries the same degree of credit risk as Corporation B, whose five-year bond has a 4.75% coupon, then – assuming both bonds trade at the same price – Corporation A's bond is relatively attractive (all other things being equal).

Sadly, in practice, the decision is never so straightforward – that is where the subtleties of credit analysis come into play. Bonds from the same issuer have can differing seniority of claims, different call dates, carry marginally different maturities and durations, have provisions for coupon step-ups and step-downs on ratings triggers, carry springing liens once specific leverage or coverage thresholds are breached, all of which affect their attractiveness as credit investments on both an absolute and a relative basis.

In practice, a portfolio manager or individual investor has to base the relative value case for an investment decision on a multiplicity of these complex variables. For example, corporations that have similar credit ratings are not necessarily perceived by the market as having the same level of credit risk, and comparing the relative value of corporate credit across issuers and across sectors poses significant challenges. Is the same yield to maturity appropriate for similarly levered (or, indeed, rated) companies in sectors as economically disparate as integrated oil and retailing, for example?

Let's begin by restricting the question to just one sector, the better to illustrate the problem. In this case, we have chosen the US retail sector, a highly cyclical sector with a wide range of credit quality.

FIGURE 21: FIVE-YEAR CDS SPREADS/SENIOR UNSECURED MOODY'S RATING 24/6/2013

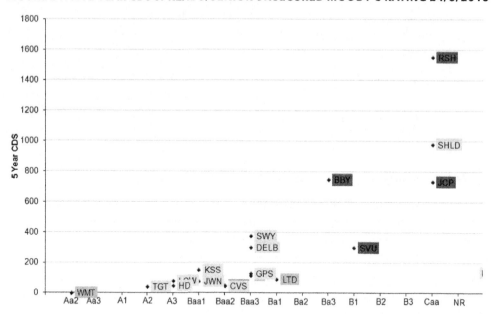

Source: Markit, Capital IQ, authors' calculations

Ratings relationships quite well-established

For the bulk of the constituents of this universe, there is a pretty clear relationship between the company's credit rating and the level at which its five-year CDS contracts (usually the most liquid) trade – though the relationship clearly does not hold for all companies. These outliers could be presenting opportunities to earn excess returns relative to their credit risk. On the other hand, they could merely be accurately reflecting the market's view of the likelihood of their credit standing deteriorating. Only analysis of the individual company can shed light on which is closer to presenting a truthful picture of the company's risk.

Adjusted leverage also well-established – but there are pricing anomalies

What happens when we look at these market spreads against another measure of credit risk for the same universe of companies – adjusted debt/EBITDAR – or, conversely, when we look at the level of CDS spread on the basis of each 'turn' of adjusted leverage?

Adjusted leverage is particularly relevant in the retail sector as many companies carry little balance sheet debt but have significant levels of operating leases. Does this shed a different light on their relative value?

The widest names in the list tend to be those with the highest levels of leverage, especially adjusted leverage, and the lowest ratings. However, two of the companies that present among the highest levels of spread per turn of adjusted leverage are RadioShack (RSH) and Best Buy (BBY). These are two businesses that, broadly speaking, are in the same narrow branch of the retail industry – consumer electronics – but which present very different credit profiles from a fundamental point of view. BBY has been considered the US industry leader, while RSH, an older franchise, has been perceived as struggling to retain its market position. BBY has a split investment-grade/high-yield rating, depending on the agency, while RSH is at the lower end of the high-yield spectrum.

TABLE 48: RELATIVE VALUE IN THE US RETAIL SECTOR

Issuer	Ticker	Moody's rating	CDS	Gross leverage Total debt / EBITDA 2014E	Adjusted leverage Adj. debt / EBITDAR 2014E	5 Year CDS
SUPERVALU INC.	SVU	B1	300	3.9x	5.5x	300
Macy's, Inc.	M	Baa3	114	1.8x	2.1x	114
Best Buy Co., Inc.	BBY	Baa2	749	0.8x	0.8x	749
SEARS ROEBUCK ACCEPTANCE CORP.	SHLD	Caa1	982	15.1x	10.6x	982
Limited Brands, Inc.	LTD	Ba1	90	2.1x	3.2x	90
Lowe's Companies, Inc.	LOW	A3	80	1.6x	2.0x	80
J. C. Penney Company, Inc.	JCP	Caa1	736	(8.8x)	14.9x	736
RadioShack Corporation	RSH	Caa2	1555	23.7x	12.1x	1555
Kohl's Corporation	KSS	Baa1	150	1.7x	2.6x	150
The Home Depot, Inc.	HD	A3	48	1.2x	1.6x	48
Nordstrom, Inc.	JWN	Baa1	75	1.7x	2.1x	75
Wal-Mart Stores, Inc.	WMT	Aa2	41	1.5x	1.7x	41
Safeway Inc.	SWY	Baa3	377	2.9x	4.3x	377
AutoZone, Inc.	AZO	Baa2	49	2.0x	2.6x	49
THE KROGER CO.	KR	Baa2	136	1.8x	3.0x	136
CVS Caremark Corporation	CVS	Baa2	44	1.0x	2.3x	44
Target Corporation	TGT	A2	41	1.9x	1.9x	41
Delhaize America, LLC	DELB	Baa3	300	2.2x	3.4x	300
The Gap, Inc.	GPS	Baa3	126	0.5x	2.8x	126

Source: Capital IQ, authors' calculations

FIGURE 22: RELATIVE VALUE IN THE US RETAIL SECTOR JUNE 2013 (SPREAD VS. CONSENSUS LEVERAGE)

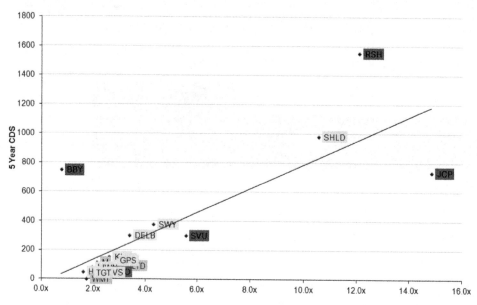

Source: Bloomberg, Capital IQ, Markit, authors' calculations

Financial flexibility varies widely

Digging a little further into the two companies' credit profiles, it can be seen that, while the industry as a whole has been suffering intense price competition and the effects of substitution from online suppliers of consumer electronics products, these two companies have been coping with this pressure to differing degrees, and with differing strategies to address their respective market segments.

They also present very widely differing profiles in terms of their liquidity, as well as having differing degrees of financial flexibility insofar as potential asset sales are concerned.

TABLE 49: BBY + RSH MARGIN AND SALES PERFORMANCE FY 2007-12

Gross margin	2012	2011	2010	2009	2008	2007
BBY	24.83%	25.23%	24.47%	24.43%	23.85%	24.40%
RSH	n/a	41.36%	44.86%	45.9%	45.51%	47.65%
Operating margin						
BBY	4.63%	5.07%	4.60%	4.47%	5.40%	5.56%
RSH	n/a	3.61%	8.3%	8.67%	7.69%	9.05%
Sales Growth						
BBY	1.93%	0.11%	10.39%	12.47%	11.38%	16.49%
RSH	n/a	2.63%	-0.24%	1.22%	-0.64%	-11.01%
FCF ($m)						
BBY	2,299	209	1,357	351	1,024	855
RSH	85.4	48.4	133.5	157.7	300.9	189.9

Source: Authors' calculations

From the above, we can see that there has been slower growth and more significant margin pressure at RSH than at BBY over this period. Free cash-flow generation too, though somewhat patchy, has been more consistently strong at BBY.

It can be seen from figure 23 that, on the mean, RSH has traded over this period at approximately 2.132× BBY's spread over the period in question. On the day the chart was drawn up, this had narrowed to 2.087×, i.e. RSH was trading slightly "tight" to its mean, but within the normal range over the period January–May 2012. It can also be seen that spreads on BBY (the lower line in the upper box) have widened markedly (by 52%) since the end of March, while those of RSH have widened (by 24%) over the same period, albeit from a wider starting point.

On a relative basis, then, RSH has underperformed BBY since April, though the actual widening of 232bps for BBY and 276bps is more comparable in scale.

FIGURE 23: RELATIVE TRADING RELATIONSHIP JANUARY 2011 TO MAY 2012

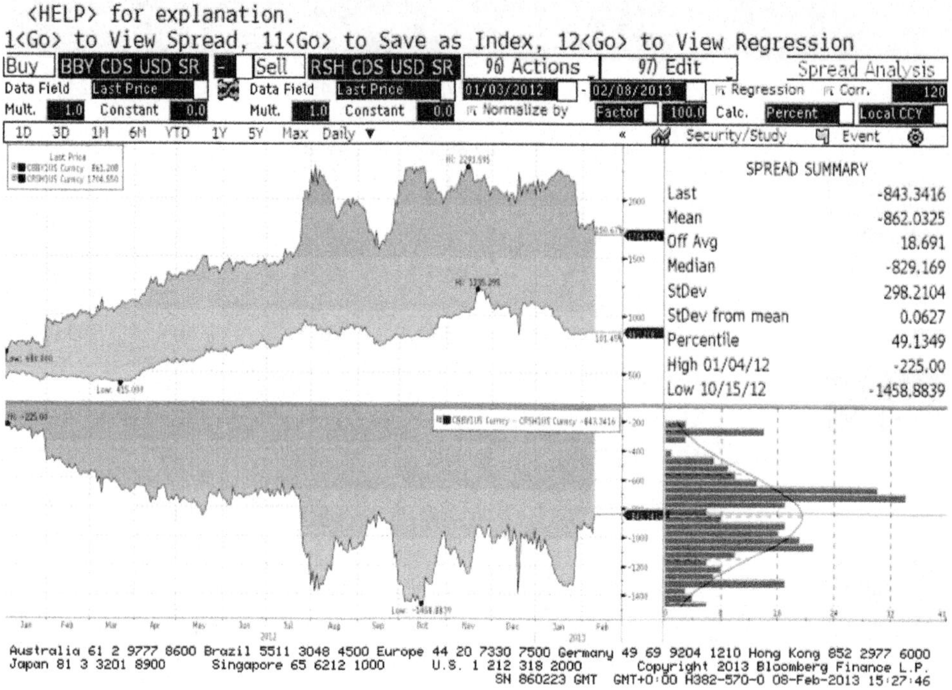

Source: Bloomberg

Technical considerations

In the mind of the credit trader (insofar as this is knowable) the performance outlined here tends to generate another concern, not so much about the companies' fundamental attributes as to the technical impact on other dealers' positions that such substantial moves are likely to have created.

Those who were short one or both credits through CDS are in a position to lock in a significant trading profit, but only if they can actually get the trade done. Others will be looking to cover some of their losses on any tightening that happens on the back of such profit-taking, or to allow these technical pressures to create a 'short squeeze' in which a lack of trading liquidity brings spreads tighter. All the same, at some not-too-distant point, risk managers will instruct dealers to restrict their losses and a clearing price will emerge. Similar considerations apply even more to bonds, given the limits on access to the underlying instruments.[179]

---

179 See chapters 6 and 7.

Trading relationship

Before we jump to too many conclusions about what the future may hold for these two companies, another perspective has to be taken into account prior to investment. Despite the fact that we assess credit investments from the basis of fundamental analysis, it is hard to argue that this is the only factor that influences their performance. In our view, it is also vital to examine the degree to which the market itself has, rightly or wrongly (given the information and other technical factors in play) already begun to discount these inputs and reflect all known data in its evaluation of their risk.

One way of doing this is to look at the relationship between the ways the two companies' CDS spreads trade. This is informative because it isolates the companies' credit risk from interest-rate risk. It takes us away from fundamental comparisons between the two companies and instead focuses on the actual trading dynamics of the two instruments and the market's perception of the two as 'pure' credits.

Market performance can, however, also be affected by technical factors such as:

- Loan hedging: banks buying CDS protection to hedge loan exposure will push spreads wider.

- Inclusion of the entity in indices: generally increases liquidity of the single-name CDS.

- Inclusion of the single-name CDS in structured credit products: tends to tighten spreads on single-name CDS.

- Issuance of bonds or loans: generally, new supply will widen spreads on existing instruments.

- Large exposure on the long or short side from the 'street'. Can create technical short or long squeezes. Contracts with a large short base, for example, will usually fail to widen when they might be expected to.

- Orphaning: CDS contracts can tighten dramatically if a company redeems the bonds that are deliverable, creating a so-called 'dead box'.

- A range of other non-fundamental criteria, some of which we illustrate in the following sections, and which can materially affect the performance of credit instruments.

FIGURE 24: BOLLINGER BANDS – BEST BUY FIVE-YEAR CDS

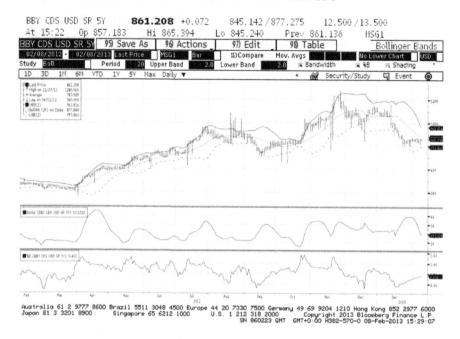

Source: Bloomberg

FIGURE 25: BOLLINGER BANDS – RSH FIVE-YEAR CDS

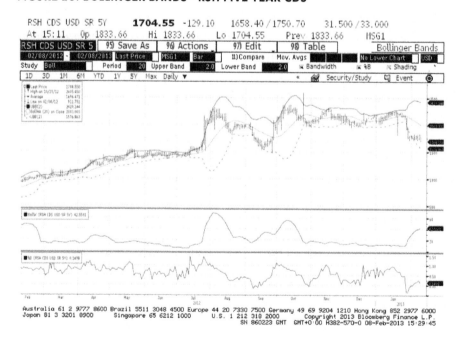

Source: Bloomberg

Historical context

Some traders are further influenced by technical factors such as where spreads are currently trading relative to their historical patterns. In this example, we have shown the performance of RSH and BBY relative to their Bollinger Bands.[180] Looking at the two companies in this context, BBY can be seen to be trading wide of the mean and RSH somewhat tight – in this situation, a technically driven trader would be minded to put on a position whereby they would take a long position in BBY against a short position in RSH, hoping to capture any relative movement in spreads while remaining broadly hedged through these offsetting positions. However, in general, most market practitioners apply a strategy that reflects a mixture of fundamental and technical considerations in their trading.

Predicting the default horizon

Of course, what none of the technical data can convey is that perhaps the most important relative value investment judgments are qualitative in nature, and hinge on the manager's degree of certainty that an investment fulfils the principal criterion for credit: the ability and willingness to repay the principal of the loan within its expected maturity horizon.

For the investment manager, getting comfort on this one issue area is paramount. It is perhaps more important to get a solid view of when a credit may face default than whether this is likely to happen. This judgment can only be arrived at by a combination of fundamental credit and liquidity analysis, an awareness of anticipated liquidity events within the investment horizon, an insight into management's priorities and a number of other factors such as the current operational trajectory of the business, its access to bank and capital market financing, the support of shareholders and idiosyncratic features of the company's capital structure, such as contractual, temporal and structural seniority.

In extremis, for example, the short-dated bonds of a severely weakened credit can offer an investment opportunity so long as the investor can be reasonably confident of the bond being repaid. Characteristics that can offer some comfort that bonds will be repaid include factors such as a generally strong liquidity profile in a credit profile that is deteriorating overall and temporal seniority relative to structurally or contractually senior instruments. This is another instance that is perhaps best illustrated with a real-world example.

Case study – Aiful

One example of this was given by the Japanese consumer finance company, Aiful, whose 4.45% bonds maturing on 2 February 2010 fell sharply after the company declared what is euphemistically known in Japan as an alternative dispute resolution process (ADR) in

---

180 A popular technical analysis tool, invented by technical trader John Bollinger in the 1980s, the Bollinger Band is a band plotted two standard deviations away from the simple moving average of the price or spread of an asset. In our examples, this band is plotted over a 20-day moving average spanning the last year's trading, though different periods are thought to provide more or less predictive insights into the performance of different asset classes. When markets increase in volatility, the bands widen and as they decrease in volatility, they contract. The closer prices move to the upper band the more 'overbought' the market is and vice versa.

September 2009, relating to a bank debt restructuring which eventually led it to trigger its CDS contracts on 15 February 2010.

While the ADR process was considered sufficient to constitute what is known under CDS contracts as a restructuring event, it did not amount to a default on Aiful's 4.45% bonds. These had traded off to a level of 55 cents on the dollar in the immediate aftermath of the ADR announcement, yet were eventually repaid at par, together with their final coupon, less than five months later – a potential 90% return for any investor who had bought at 55 cents, while those who had taken a long position through five-year CDS recovered only approximately 33 cents of every dollar they had invested.

Some investors who bought the bonds post ADR were betting on the unwillingness of a Japanese company to default on debt owed to foreign investors given a presumed cultural aversion to loss of face. Such things cannot be modelled. Making trades of this nature is clearly a high-risk proposition, and could never constitute a major proportion of a portfolio strategy except in the case of a distressed or stressed credit portfolio mandate.

Nonetheless, the Aiful example neatly illustrates that the portfolio manager's decision has to be based on a careful evaluation of the risk-weighted return available on a relative value basis.

Concluding Thoughts

ACROSS OUR 50-PLUS COMBINED YEARS IN THE MARKETS WE HAVE SEEN THE EFFECTS of market deregulation and privatisation on corporate credits; the opening and flowering (and in a few cases, deflowering) of the emerging markets; three major global recessions; serious governance scandals in the early part of the millennium, which robbed the public of what little faith it had in the paladins of the corporate world; massive liquidity-fuelled bubbles in dotcom, housing, debt and equity markets; the excrescence and collapse of the structured credit market; the largest LBO boom in history; the near-collapse of the global banking sector; the near-demise of one of the world's largest single-currency zones; and a recovery in asset markets driven almost entirely by unprecedented central bank liquidity, which, at the time of writing, threatens perhaps to undermine the very transmission mechanisms that ensure the efficient use of debt and equity capital in capitalist economies. In the words of the Grateful Dead, "what a long, strange trip it's been".

However, if we can take one leitmotif from that journey – as far as it refers to corporate credit analysis and investment – it is one that was quite literally set in stone above the entrance to Moody's old headquarters on 99 Church Street in New York and read: "Credit: Man's Confidence in Man".

Belief, which lies at the etymological root of the very term credit, is also at the heart of the decision-making process in investment and is not, in our experience, something that can or should be attained by numerical modelling alone. Human factors still account for the decisive parts of this process. Thus, the analysis of corporate numbers is more valuable as an investment tool when it takes into account the quality and substance of corporate governance within the corporations in question and, more importantly still, the quality of their management. We hope, above all, to have brought the human role in understanding credit to the front and centre, where experience tells us it belongs.

At a rather less grandiose level, we also hope to have made investors aware of some of the myriad ways in which quantitative data can be presented by corporations and how best to interpret it to get at the heart of what is actually going on with the corporation in question. Finally, we hope to have given the investor a few insights into the technical workings of the credit market that, while far from exhaustive, should at least leave him in no doubt that credit is a very different beast from equity, requiring a different approach and different tools. We will close by saying that the market remains in constant evolution and that these skills and approaches will need regular updating.

Index

A

B

V

W

X

CPSIA information can be obtained
at www.ICGtesting.com
Printed in the USA
BVOW09*1419300317

479361BV00006B/8/P